MW01193483

Shufflebrain

SHUFFLEBRAIN

PAUL PIETSCH

HOUGHTON MIFFLIN COMPANY BOSTON
1981

To Mothermouse and her brood

Library of Congress Cataloging in Publication Data

Pietsch, Paul, date
Shufflebrain.

Bibliography: p.
Includes index.
1. Memory. 2. Brain — Localization of functions.
3. Memory — Philosophy. 4. Holography in medicine.
I. Title.
QP406.P53   153.1   80-21726
ISBN 0-395-29480-0

Printed in the United States of America

V 10 9 8 7 6 5 4 3 2 1

Line drawings by Diane Jung.

Acknowledgments

I WISH to thank Linda Keenan and Shari Lentz for typing the manuscript, Carolyn Balog for proofreading, and Jacque Kubley for photography. Diane Jung drew the figures.

I also pay tribute to *Harper's* for having the courage to publish parts of this story, and thank particularly Nelson W. Aldrich, Jr., formerly of that magazine, for his superb editing. I am also indebted to editors Larry Burns and Tony Jones for their continued interest in my work and for the opportunity to communicate some of my findings. I have been encouraged in various ways by Bob Cromie of Universal Science News, Dr. Samuel L. Hart of Fairleigh Dickinson University, Dr. Maynard B. Chenoweth of Midland, Michigan, and Dr. Gordon G. Heath, presently the dean of the School of Optometry, Indiana University. I wish to praise the crew of CBS's "60 Minutes," especially the producer, Igor Oganesoff, for an excellent program based on the work in my laboratory.

During those perilous last moments when the book was still somewhere between thesis and antithesis, like an aerialist between trapezes, and not yet a synthesis, my agent Harriet Wasserman, with a note here, a mot there, became my angel.

I will always be grateful to Tony Stern, who introduced me to my editor, Jonathan Galassi. The opportunity to observe Jon's rich literary insight at work became a reward unto itself.

With some stains I use for nerve fibers, one has the option, as a final step, to tone the tissues in gold, thereby adding an extra-sharp quality to the details. If copy editing does a similar thing to a manuscript, then I would substitute something more precious than gold to describe Clay Morgan's contributions to this book.

Preface

UNTIL RATHER RECENTLY, a natural scientist could offer the public little more insight into the fundamental principles of the mind than could an ancient Greek philosopher or a present-day guru. For there had been a total absence of even the prospects of a general theory of biological memory. This situation has changed. For within comparatively recent years just such a theory has come along. And this theory is the subject of *Shufflebrain*.

I did not originate the theory. But I have been investigating, perfecting, and using it for well into a second decade. The theory has power. It has range and generality. It is consistent with every relevant fact I know about memory in living organisms. It relates mind-brain to nonliving systems, and thereby suggests that the mind is not a supernatural entity but a part of Nature. The theory reconciles diverse bodies of previously equivocal evidence. And, without fail, it has predicted the results of all my experiments, some of which I still find hard to comprehend.

Yet the theory could be false, in the logician's sense of the word. And nowhere will I try to tell the reader that the theory is true. A scientific theory is a system of thought, a rational explanation of facts or events, and not really an assertion of truth. Strictly speaking, true scientific theories do not exist. Does a

given theory work? Is it logical? Does it generate new understanding? Can it allow the human mind to fathom what has
always seemed beyond the depths of reason? Does it allow the
intellect and imagination to place the phrase "what if" at the
front of new and novel questions about Nature? These are the
important questions to ask about any scientific theory. And
when the answers turn out to be yes, the theory's existence —
its *Existenz* — rather than its proofs turns out to be what
counts; and the existence of the theory may alter the future
course of thought and change the destiny of civilization. The
subject of this book has very suggestive historical markings. My
hunch — and I carefully label it as hunch — is that the existence of a general theory of biological memory means that we,
all of us, have entered into the early, uncertain cycles of the age
when science began to penetrate the core of the subjective cosmos.

    Shufflebrain is not written for a readership of technical spe-
cialists. It is for a general audience, for the cornfield philosophers of the world, the cab driver who packs works of Carl
Sandburg along with the salami sandwich and the banana, the
librarian who arrives extra-early each morning to sample the infinity of treasures among the stacks; for the student who studies
because of the hunger to know, and the teacher who teaches for
the same reason; for the journalist whose curiosity becomes
sharpened instead of dulled by the daily brush against new
events and novel ideas; for the life scout who camps on a ridge
overlooking a great meandering river and uses the day's last
good light for reading; for the lovers of thought — the true
keepers of civilization — whoever they are.

    But in spite of its informal style, this book is not a popular-
ization of a technical topic. It is a definitive statement of the
subject, not a surrogate or a shadowy hint of it. My intent is to
involve the reader intimately in the inner workings of the whole
story. And when I resort to the generic *we,* I mean the reader

and me, together, not a group of experts in armchairs dispensing wisdom.

I am not trying to snub or circumvent the scholar by using the writing style I have chosen. But I could not bring the elements of the story together in the impersonal, detached lingo of the bench scientist or formal philosopher. I really did not fully understand the dynamics of the message until I had finished. Without my realizing it, much of the actual investigation of the subject went on as I wrote the book. The subject was too global for the assumptions of any particular discipline. The story demanded a synoptic statement. I found that only by using everyday language could I faithfully represent the meaning in the subject. I had to call heavily upon the ideas of science and philosophy, of course. But without general language, given all its imperfections, *Shufflebrain* would not exist.

Paul Pietsch
Bloomington, Indiana

One touch of nature makes the whole world kin

Shakespeare, *Troilus and Cressida*

Contents

Shufflebrain

1

Quest of Hologramic Memory

I AM AN ANATOMIST. I say that with pride and satisfaction, even now. And during much of my career, I was certain beyond a conscious doubt that the truth about life would reduce directly and explicitly to the architecture of the things that do the living. I had complete faith, too, that my science would one day write the most important scientific story of all: how a brain gives existence to a mind. But I was wrong. And my very own research, which I call *shufflebrain,* forced me to junk the axioms of my youth and begin my intellectual life all over again.

My research supports, vindicates, and extends a theory of biological memory, of neural information generally, whether ordained by instinct or acquired through experience — a general theory of the very nature of mind. "Hologramic theory," I shall call it in this book. As its name implies, hologramic theory relates mind to the principle involved in the hologram. Its conclusions, predictions, and assertions represent the antithesis of what I once believed.

Holograms encode messages carried by waves, waves of any sort, in theory. And holograms of all types share in common the fact that they encode information about a property of waves known as *phase.* I will defer definition of wave phase until later in the book. But phase is a relative property, without definite size or absolute mass; it is elusive and seemed virtually unknowable until the development of holography, the branch of optics concerned directly with holograms. To reconstruct phase, which a hologram permits, is to regenerate a wave's relative shape and thus re-create any message or image the original wave communicated to the recording and storage medium. Thus the basic assertion in hologramic[1] theory, and the thesis I develop in this book, is that the brain stores the mind as codes of wave phase.

Where did hologramic theory begin? Its origins are complex, and this question should be answered by a professional historian; but the connection between holograms and the brain caught hold in biology and psychology in the late 1960s. Then a neurophysiologist named Karl Pribram,[2] who was writing and lecturing eloquently and insightfully on the subject, proposed the hologram as a model to explain the results not only of his many intensive years investigating the living monkey brain, but also to account for many paradoxes about memory that had persisted unabated since antiquity.

Memory often survives massive brain damage, even the removal of an entire cerebral hemisphere. In the 1920s the celebrated psychologist Karl Lashley, with whom Pribram once

---

[1] A former editor at *Harper's,* Larry Burns, supplied the term *hologramic* in 1975 when I complained that *holographic* disturbed me on two counts. First, a holograph is a handwritten document, such as a will, and the word evokes the wrong imagery for a discussion of memory. Second, holographers use *holographic* in a highly technical sense, and I believe they should be allowed to continue to do so without becoming involved in whatever bitter controversy a serious theory of neural storage may yet provoke. If I had created hologramic theory, I would have opted for a quieter term, such as *phaseogram*. While I couldn't keep on using *holographic*, I didn't feel that my rhetorical license allowed me to drop the Greek prefix *holos*.

[2] In most instances when I refer to someone by name, the reader will find a reference to the person's work in the bibliography.

worked, demonstrated that the engram, or memory trace, cannot be isolated in any specific compartment of a rat's brain. Certain optical holograms invented in the early 1960s, the most common today, exhibit just what Lashley had alleged of memory: a piece cut from such a hologram — any piece — will reconstruct the entire image. For, as unlikely as this may seem, the message exists, whole, at every point in the medium.[3]

My own research has not always focused directly on memory. Regeneration of tissues and organs held my fascination for many years, and I am still pursuing certain questions about the molecular aspects of the regrowth of muscle tissue. But even as a sophomore in college I had the persistent hunch that all recurrent biological events, developmental or neural, might be explained by one unified theory. I spent some years in the pursuit of a structural explanation of how new muscles and skeletons regenerate in the limb of the salamander. My investigations began to suggest that the cells responsible for each new tissue acted as independent mathematical sets. Using transplantations and various other means, I tried to model transformations of independent sets. This approach was very productive.[4] In the mid-1960s, while searching for a system that would allow me to extend my theory from regeneration to memory, I decided to perform experiments with the brain. Hologramic theory had just begun to emerge as I was gearing up.[5] Its predictions were diametric to those of my theory; and its implications were at odds with virtually everything else I believed. Hol-

---

[3] *Holos* in hologram does not refer to this distributive property — every point containing a coded version of the entire message — but to the preservation of all the information necessary to reproduce the precise form of the original waves. For those familiar with holography who may wonder what happened to amplitude, see Alexander Metherell's discussion of phase-only holograms (Metherell, 1969a). I will come back to amplitude in chapter 3.

[4] See Pietsch, 1962.

[5] See van Heerden, 1963; Julesz and Pennington, 1965.

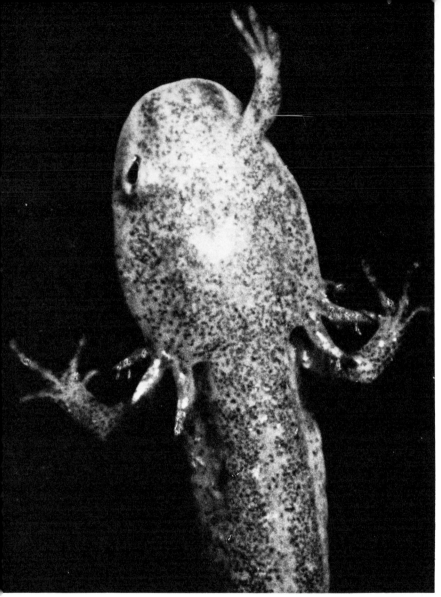

No other creature rivals the salamander larva as donor and host of transplanted organs and tissues.

Photo by David Ort

ogramic theory predicted that memory cannot be explained by the structure of the brain.

"What kind of a nitwit would seriously believe a thing like that?" I asked a senior colleague. Don't we use legs to stand on, teeth to chew with, bronchioles to breathe through? Sperms swim with their tails. Hairs curl or don't curl depending on the detailed structure of their proteins. Even genes work because of molecular anatomy. Why should the storing of mind be different?

Hologramic theory not only stirred my prejudice, it also seemed highly vulnerable to the very experiments I was planning: shuffling neuroanatomy, reorganizing the brain, scrambling the sets and subsets that I theorized were the carriers of neural programs. I fully expected to retire hologramic theory to the boneyard of meaningless ideas. I'd begun licking my canine

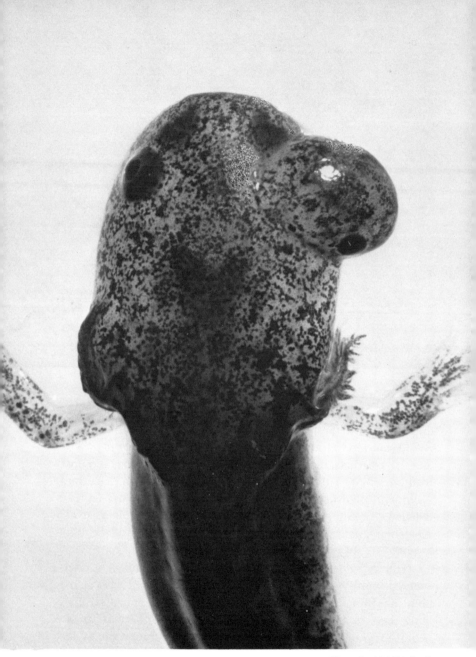

Photo by Mel Diedrick

teeth like a mink who has cornered a chicken. I even began considering which scientific meetings would be best for the announcement of my theory. I should have awaited Nature's answers. For hologramic theory was to survive every trial, and my own theory went down to utter defeat.

Will my experiments prove hologramic theory to the careful reader? Maybe, in the casual or even legal sense of establishing truth. Possibly, according to the pragmatist's test: for hologramic theory works. But as the logician tests truth, my answer is, I hope not.

No experiment can deliver the whole truth about a theory. Take Einstein's special theory of relativity, for instance — the most powerful and durable theory in all the natural sciences, and the source of the famous equation $e = mc^2$. Unless Einstein was totally wrong, there is no actual c^2 — the *square* of the speed of light. He assumed that the speed of light is the maximum velocity any mass-energy can attain. Obviously, no experiment will ever detect what is greater than an attainable maximum.

Theories deal with generic features of a subject, with explanations of groups of facts or classes of events as a whole. They serve our understanding precisely because they exist in the ideal, operate in the abstract, and lend themselves to perfectibility. For many of Nature's secrets lie beyond experience. Experiments yield controlled experiences. By their very character, experiments must focus on particular observations. They furnish concrete examples of a subject in the reality we know best. But experiments cannot penetrate to the ideal core of a theory, and they cannot take us to the repository of the theory's meaning.

Experiments may let us examine a theory's consequences and test its predictions. They may produce the results a theory forecasts, and by so doing establish widespread belief in the theory. And that's fine, as long as we don't forget the distinction between belief in the truth and the truth itself. Failure to make this seemingly obvious differentiation is a serious philosophical malady within many sciences today.

Setting philosophy aside, I am still unwilling to declare hologramic theory *true*. Do I believe the theory? Yes, of course, or I wouldn't be writing a book about it. But belief has an irrational component built in. As a logic professor of mine used to insist, "the routes to certitude and certainty pass through different territories." The reader is entitled to find his or her own certitude. Science does not elevate its practitioners above mortality and fallibility, not even in judging the implications of scientific data. Only the writer with this thought in the prow of the mind may guide a reader to a brand-new universe of understanding; and only as another mortal can I make shufflebrain a window on the hologramic mind.

Shufflebrain gives us sufficient reason to develop hologramic theory into a carefully reasoned system of propositions. After we deal with the theory in the abstract — where we can take it apart, where we can "see" the hologramic mind, where we can construct rational explanations of what we find in our world — then shufflebrain experiments will justify our putting hologramic theory to work.

And what uses it has! The theory explains observations about the brain that once defied explanation; it reconciles contradictory evidence that today alienates different groups of scientists into rigid, hostile, xenophobic camps; it gives the brain's architecture new significance; it sharpens the anatomist's mission. Hologramic theory, when fully developed, liberates us from the tyranny of reductionism and the pitfalls of trivialization. But the theory connects mind to the same Nature science has been studying all along. We take no magic carpet on our journey through this book.

Hologramic theory permits us to tour the vast ranges and reaches where minds abide; but this book only begins the tour.

Above all, hologramic theory provides a system in which human reason and imagination, coalesced, may comprehend and appreciate themselves. If, in some transcending design, the theory is false, it will still be of human value. It is as such that I offer it to the reader.

The following chapter primarily deals with the mind-brain conundrum, or what the situation is like without a general theory. I found that if I chose examples carefully, I could, in passing, present background about the brain that could be used later in the book. Selecting from the vast possibilities in the literature, I tried to pick examples that are interesting in their own right.

Chapter 3 surveys the hologram and its underlying principles. My intention is to provide the reader with enough theoretical background to deal with chapters 4 through 6. There is a vast literature on holography, much of it not directly related to our discussion and not included in this book. The reader whose interests in this subject develop along the way will find various works listed in the bibliography; and most libraries contain excellent popular books on holography.

Why would any serious thinker even consider the hologram as a potential model of the brain? I try to answer this question in chapter 4 with examples of how holograms mimic brain and mind functions. These examples illustrate how the hologram can be used in a casual way to conceptualize a surprising list of previously imponderable considerations about ourselves.

Chapters 5 and 6 describe my experiments on the brain. Having explored the possibilities of the hologram, and the theory, in earlier chapters, we now need experimental evidence to justify further work on hologramic theory itself.

Chapter 7 is an introduction to the wave as a theoretical entity. In this chapter, we begin the process of determining the underlying propositions and principles we will need to formulate hologramic theory. In chapter 8, we put our new rules and our recently acquired background knowledge to work, and, by inductive reasoning, we assemble hologramic theory, at least in rudimentary form. Having produced a theory, we then employ the much simpler process of deduction to explain the results of shufflebrain experiments, and to take a "look" at the hypothetical hologramic mind. But in its simple form, hologramic theory is too reductionistic for our quest. In chapter 9, therefore, we reformulate hologramic theory in the most general terms available. The result is a theoretical entity I call the "hologramic continuum." But hologramic theory, even in its general form, does not solve all existing problems in science. It will not, for instance, cure warts. The theory restricts itself, as we will be able to deduce in chapter 9; but there's an ironic consequence awaiting us there.

Whereas chapters 7 through 9 focus on mind, chapter 10 returns to living organisms. Up to this point, we have been asking, What is mind? In chapter 10, we pose the question, What is brain? The answers may surprise the reader. Chapter 10 also looks at a few interesting facts about the brain and behavior.

Chapter 11 provides a glimpse at the meaning of intelligence, from the vantage of hologramic theory. Can we describe and define intelligence in a hologramic mind?

During the late 1960s, when my work on shufflebrain was beginning, I worked with a brilliant physiological psychologist and remarkable person. His name is Carl Schneider. Our joint investigations were very rewarding, and Carl and I also became friends. But on the question of Lashley's work, Carl and I had deep philosophical differences at the time. To preserve our collaboration, I did not involve Carl in shufflebrain experiments. Yet, unwittingly, our joint projects were producing the very evidence that would, years later, place hologramic theory in a wider context. And that wider context is the purpose of chapter 12, the conclusion of the book.

I think one of the first phrases a novice scientist or philosopher must learn is, "What do you mean by . . ." Some scholars never quite outgrow the definitions game. Few of us need to be reminded of the ambiguities built into language. But protracted definitions rarely correct the problem, often render a serious work solemn, and frequently preempt splendid general words for narrow and polemical purposes. When our discussion requires careful definitions, we will build up to them rather than proceed from them. Otherwise, the lexicographer has already done a much better job than an anatomist can hope to accomplish. Generally, I defer to him or her.

But two terms do warrant special note here: *theory* and *memory*. Solely to minimize confusion, I will employ *theory* in the sense of *explanation*.

The usages of *memory* differ in empirical versus rational schools of philosophy and psychology. Empiricists, the intellectual heirs of John Locke, who believe that experience is the source of all knowledge, define memory in terms of learning. Rationalists, the followers of René Descartes, who believe in innate ideas and hold that reason is the source of knowledge, do not accept experience, and thus learning, as the principal source of the brain's stores of information. Well into this book, I develop the point that *how* the brain acquires information is of little significance in hologramic theory. Meanwhile, believing that empiricists and rationalists both have their rights, I use the term *memory* in reference to all the brain's stored information, whether learned, innate, or installed by some still unknown means. I use the term interchangeably with *stored mind*. In fact, if you look in a dictionary you'll find *memory* given as one definition of *mind*.

2

The Mind–Brain Conundrum

WE HAVE a genuine dilemma on our hands, the logician tells us, when we can assert the truth of two mutually incompatible propositions or statements. By this standard, science could have been in a perilous philosophical position, had any of its critics seized upon memory research. On the one hand, specific functions, and presumably memory, seemed to be localized in particular parts of the brain. On the other, memory defied careful attempts to isolate or fraction it with a scalpel. Two equally convincing and opposite conclusions had emerged from the clinics and laboratories. Because these conclusions represented the entire memory-brain universe of discourse, their simultaneous validity created a conundrum.

I don't mean to suggest that scientists sat around in smoking parlors, speakeasies, or faculty clubs lamenting (or trying to solve) the dilemma that memory posed. Judging from my own former frame of mind, I doubt that anyone was fully aware of the philosophical problem. If scientists assumed any position at all, it was at either of two poles, structuralists at the one, holists at the other, atomization and localization the summum bonum of the former, distributiveness and equipotentiality that of the latter.

Holism, as a generic doctrine, asserts that a universe as a whole cannot be reduced to the sum of its parts; try to dissect the parts and, as with the value of π, $^{22}/_7$ or $3.14 \cdot \cdot \cdot$, you don't come out with discrete numbers or elements but with a fraction. Holism entered the study of brain in the 1820s, following the experiments and speculations of Pierre Flourens.[1]

A structuralism, idealistic or materialistic, can be identified by the idea that wholes are indeed the sums of discrete parts — atoms. Thus the neural structuralist would insist that memories reduce to individual units or bits — like 22 rather than $^{22}/_7$. And to a structuralist a memory would be a structure of such discrete elements. Add materialism to the theory and you'd want to store those elements, each in its own structure in the brain.

To the holist, mind depends on the brain as a whole; the mental cosmos cannot be mapped like the surface of the earth or broken into subunits, this bit going here, that bit over there. Historically, holists have based their beliefs on the survival of cognition and the retention of memory after massive injury to the brain. Structuralists conceded that the brain's programs are not easily found; but holists consistently failed to link their theories to physical reality. To me, structuralist that I was, holism looked at best like metaphysics, and at worst like magic.

Let me say a few words about the genesis of my former faith in structuralism, and about anatomy as it is practiced today. Anatomy of course includes what rests on the dissecting table, but the scope of the science goes far beyond this. Anatomy is an attempt to explain living events by observing, analyzing, and, if necessary, conceptualizing the body's components, whether the object of study happens to be a genital organ or the genes within its cells, whether the search calls for a sophisticated Japanese electron microscope or the stout crucible steel blade of a Swedish butcher knife. Anatomy rests upon a belief shared by many in our culture, in and out of science. Robert Traver's

---

[1] See Clarke and Dewhurst, 1972.

Anatomy of a Murder and Ashley Montagu's *Anatomy of Swearing* express metaphorically what many in our day embrace epistemologically: in order to find out how something *really* works, take it apart. What could seem more reasonable?

As a student entering science in the 1950s, during some of the most exciting moments in intellectual history, I could see no basic philosophical difference between what anatomists were seeking to discover and what other scientists, with different titles, were actually finding out about the cell and the molecular side of life. In the 1950s and 1960s, scientists in large numbers and from diverse fields had begun accepting the anatomist's already ancient credo: physiological functions explicitly and specifically reduce to the interplay between discrete structural entities. Structure was suddenly being used to account for events that only a generation before seemed beyond reason: how genes maintain a molecular record of heredity; how muscles contract, cells divide, the sperm penetrates the egg; how a cell's membrane actively picks and chooses from the body's milieu what shall and shall not pass across its boundary; how an irritated nerve cell generates and propagates a neural signal and then transmits the message to the next cell in the network; how cells fuel and refuel their insatiable demands for energy. Those investigators who abided by the structural faith were coming up with answers any child of our thing-bound culture could easily comprehend — and they were winning the Nobel Prizes in the process. The intellectual environment in which I grew up vindicated every fundamentalism of my chosen field, virtually everywhere anyone chose to look. Everywhere except the brain.

Judging from artifacts, club-wielding cave men seemed to know that something essential to behavior existed inside the skull of a foe or quarry. Physicians of ancient Egypt correlated malfunctioning minds with diseased brains. Gladiators wore helmets, and those who lost them sometimes contributed personally to the early anecdotal wisdom about the brain's biology. Phrenologists, seeking to map the facets of the human personality over the surface of the cerebrum, laid the very foundations for modern neuroanatomy. High-velocity rifle bullets, which could inflict discrete wounds, afforded mid-nineteenth-century battlefield surgeons with insights into the brain that they and others pursued at the laboratory bench. And the study of the nervous system in our own times can be traced directly to the science and surgery of Victorian and Edwardian Europe.

Today there are entire libraries, university departments, and learned societies devoted exclusively to storing, disseminating, and promoting the wisdom of the "neurosciences." So vast is knowledge about the nervous system that the study of human neuroanatomy alone requires a separate course. Facts abound on the brain's chemical composition, anatomical organization, and electrophysiological activities. The main routes for incoming sensory messages, for example, have been plotted and replotted — the signals enabling us to see a sunrise, hear a sparrow, smell a rose, taste a drop of honey, feel the sting of a wasp, appreciate the texture of another human hand. The images of these words, for instance, land on the retinas of the reader's eyes and trigger well-worked-out photochemical reactions, which, in turn, detonate electrical signals within the receptor cells — the rods and cones. The retina itself begins sorting, integrating, and encoding the signals into messages, which it transmits through highly specific routes via the optic nerves and optic tracts to relays in the core of the brain. From the relays, the message moves to specific cells in what are called the occipital lobes of the cerebrum, and there establishes point-for-point communication between loci out in the visual fields, and particular input stations in the brain.

Much is known, too, of outflow pathways used in carrying direct orders to the effectors of our overt behavior — the muscles and glands that enable us to walk, talk, laugh, blush, cry,

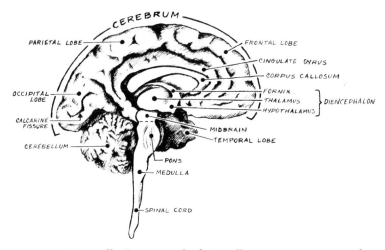

CEREBRUM

PARIETAL LOBE

FRONTAL LOBE

CINGULATE GYRUS

CORPUS CALLOSUM

FORNIX

THALAMUS

HYPOTHALAMUS

DIENCEPHALON

OCCIPITAL LOBE

CALCARINE FISSURE

CEREBELLUM

MIDBRAIN

TEMPORAL LOBE

PONS

MEDULLA

SPINAL CORD

sweat, or give milk. In spite of admittedly vast gaps among the facts, enough is known today to fill in the blanks with plausible hypotheses about circuits used in language, emotions, arousal, and sleep — hypotheses for many of our actions and even a few of our feelings and thoughts. Damage to a known pathway yields reasonably predictable changes or deficits in behavior, perception, or cognition. Neurological diagnoses would be impossible, otherwise. For example, a person with partial blindness involving the upper, outer sector of the visual field, with accompanying hallucinations about odors and with a history of sudden outbursts of violence, quite likely has a diseased temporal lobe of the cerebrum — the forward part of the temporal lobe on the side opposite the blindness, in fact. Or a person who suffers a stroke, cannot speak but understands language, and is paralyzed on the right side of the body almost assuredly has suffered damage at the rear of the cerebrum's frontal lobe — the lower portion of the left frontal lobe, to be precise.

◇　　　◇　　　◇

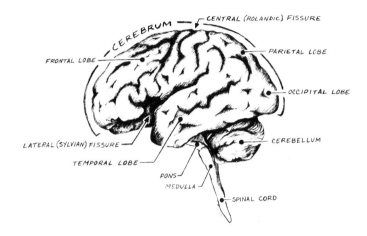

Up to a point, in other words, the brain fits neatly and simply into the anatomical scheme of things. But throughout history, the battle-ax, shrapnel, tumors, infections, even the deliberate stroke of the surgeon's knife, have paralyzed, blinded, deafened, muted, and numbed human beings, via the brain, without necessarily destroying cognition, erasing memory, or fractioning the mind. It wasn't that anatomists couldn't link specific functions to particular parts of the brain. Far from it. But when we reached for the dénouement, for an explanation of the most pivotal features of the brain, the structural argument teetered under the weight of contradictory evidence.

Consider a paradox about vision known as *macular sparing*. No part of the human brain has been worked on more exhaustively and extensively than the visual system. Nor, seemingly, could any structural realist ask for a more explicit relationship between form and function than one finds there. Every locus in our fields of view corresponds virtually point-for-point with microscopic routes through our visual pathways. As you can dem-

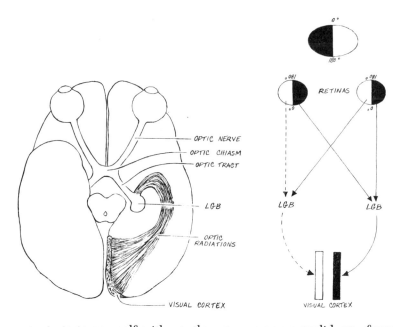

onstrate to yourself with gentle pressure on an eyelid, you form an image of right and left fields on both retinas. (The nose blocks the periphery of the eye's opposite field.) For optical reasons, however, the images of the field do a 180-degree rotation in projecting onto the two retinas. Thus the left field registers on the left eye's inner half and the right eye's outer half; vice versa for the right field. The fibers from the retina, which form the optic nerve, strictly obey the following rule: those from the inner half of the retina cross to the opposite side of the brain; those from the outer half do not. Thus all information about the visual fields splits precisely down the middle and flashes to the opposite side of the brain. Corresponding fibers from the two eyes join each other in the centers of our heads (at a structure known as the optic chiasm) and form what are called optic tracts — the right tract carrying messages about left field exclusively, and the left tract carrying information about right field. If an optic tract is totally destroyed we become blind to the entire opposite visual field.

Optic tracts end where they make connections with a highly organized collection of cells known as the LGB (lateral geniculate body). The LGB has the job of communicating visual signals to the visual cortex of the occipital lobe. Now there is every anatomical reason to predict that destruction of one occipital lobe will split a visual field map into seen and blank halves, as sometimes occurs. Usually, though, a person with a lesion beyond the LGB will lose the peripheral parts of the opposite field but retain a whole, unsplit view of the central field. The macula, a yellowish spot on the center of the retina, receives the projection from the central field. Thus the term *macular sparing* means that an otherwise split visual field remains unsplit on *both* sides of the central zone, which is precisely as it should *not* be.

If the visual pathways were haphazardly arranged, with fibers coursing everywhere, macular sparing would be understandable. But clinical records, autopsy reports, the results of

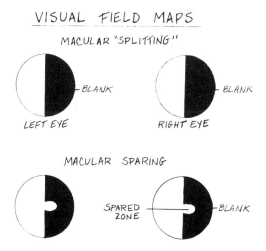

VISUAL FIELD MAPS

MACULAR "SPLITTING"

BLANK — LEFT EYE

BLANK — RIGHT EYE

MACULAR SPARING

SPARED ZONE — BLANK

direct stimulation of conscious human brains during surgery, and probings into ape and monkey brains with minute electrodes — all means of gathering evidence — consistently show that the visual system is minutely precise in organization. For a while, some authors explained away macular sparing by assuming that central retinal fibers violate the crossing rule. But in 1934, a famous ophthalmologist, Stephen Polyak, studied the chimpanzee's visual pathways and found that central fibers *do* obey crossing rules, just like fibers of the rest of the retina: nasals cross, temporals don't! And repeated searches of human pathways has led to an identical conclusion — namely that crossing doesn't explain macular sparing.[2]

Until 1940, one could assume either or both of two additional hypotheses to explain macular sparing: that of partial survival of the visual pathways, and/or that of careless examination of the visual fields. But in that year Ward Halstead and his colleagues published data in the *Archives of Ophthalmology* that eliminated these simple hypotheses as well.

Halstead's group reported the case history of a twenty-five-year-old filing clerk who arrived at a clinic in Chicago in the autumn of 1937 with a massive tumor in her left occipital lobe. Summarizing what the surgeons had to cut out to save the woman's life, Halstead et al. wrote, "The ablation had removed completely the left striate [visual] cortex and areas 18 and 19 of the occipital lobe posterior to the parieto-occipital fissure." Translated, this means that the young woman lost her entire left optic lobe — the entire half of her brain onto which the right visual field projects and in which information is processed into higher-order percepts. Visual field maps showed that the operation caused blindness in the young woman's right visual

---

[2] Some cats and tigers show an exception to the crossing rule; but such animals are also cross-eyed, their perception evidently seeking to correct the flaw in their anatomy.

field (*homonymous hemianopsia,* as it is called), but with macular sparing.

If macular sparing always occurred after occipital-lobe damage, one might explain the phenomenon by assuming that the macular-projection area of one LGB somehow sends fibers to both occipital lobes. But the Halstead article nullified this explanation, too, with an almost identical case history of a twenty-two-year-old stenographer. A patient in the same hospital, she also had a massive tumor, but in her right occipital lobe. After surgery, visual-field mapping showed that she was totally blind to the left field of view — *without macular sparing!*

In other words, not only did Halstead's group document macular sparing as a genuine anatomical paradox; they even showed that one cannot apply simple, linear cause-and-effect reasoning to it: in the case of the two young women, the same antecedents had produced decidedly different consequences.

In no way does macular sparing detract from the orderliness of the visual system. Indeed, this was part of the mystery. Specific places on the retina excite particular cells in both the LGB and the visual cortex. When stimulated, the macular zone on the retina does excite specific cells of the occipital cortex — in the rear tip of the lobe, to be exact — on the side opposite the half visual field. But the phenomenon of macular sparing (and thousands of people have exhibited the sign) shows that there is not an exclusive center in the brain for seeing the central field. If the message can make it into the LGB, it *may* make it to the mind.

But what about the mind after the loss of a visual lobe of the brain? Halstead's group had something to say about this, too. The twenty-two-year-old secretary had scored 133 points on an

IQ test before surgery. A month after the operation, she again scored 133. And five weeks after the operation she left the hospital and returned to her job. About the filing clerk, whose IQ also remained unchanged, Halstead et al. wrote, "Immediately on awakening from the anesthetic the patient talked coherently and read without hesitation. At no time was there any evidence of aphasia [speech loss] or alexia [reading deficits]."

Thus, in spite of the loss of half the visual areas of their cerebrums, despite a halved, or nearly halved, view of the external world, both young women retained *whole* visual cognition and *whole* visual memories. They are far from unique. Three floors below where I sit, there is an eye clinic whose filing cabinets contain thousands of visual-field maps and case upon case documenting the survival of a complete mind on the receiving end of severely damaged visual pathways.

The structuralists attempted to dodge Halstead's evidence by insisting that visual cognition and memory must lie outside the occipital lobe — somewhere!

Nor is vision the sole brain function whose story begins true to an anatomist's expectations only to end in uncertainty. Take language. Certain speech and reading deficits correlate with damage to particular areas of the brain (and provide important diagnostic signs). Broca's motor-speech aphasia most often results from blockage or hemorrhage of the arteries supplying the rear of the frontal lobe, and occurs on the left cerebral hemisphere about 80 to 85 percent of the time. In Broca's aphasia a person understands language, communicates nonverbally, and writes, if not also paralyzed, but cannot articulate or speak fluently. (A sudden drop in fluency may in fact signal an impending stroke.) In contrast, another speech aphasia is associated with damage to the temporal lobe. Known as Wernicke's aphasia, this malady is characterized not by apparent loss of fluency but by absence of meaning in what the person says. The words don't add up to informative sentences, or the person may have problems naming familiar objects, and call a cup an ashtray, for instance, or be unable to name a loved one.

Broca's and Wernicke's speech areas intercommunicate via a thick arching bundle (called the arcuate bundle). When damage to this pathway disconnects the two speech areas, language fluency and comprehension are not affected; however, the sufferer cannot repeat newly presented phrases.

Alexia, the inability to read, and its partial form, dyslexia, may suggest a tumor or arteriosclerosis in an area directly in front of the occipital lobe. Or, if a person begins to have problems writing down what he or she hears, a lesion may be developing in a span of brain between the occipital lobe and Wernicke's area.

In other words, anatomy functions in language as it does in vision. And those who tend to our health ought to be well informed about what a particular malfunction may portend. But aphasias do not supply evidence for a theory of mind. Damage to a specific cerebral area does not always produce the anticipated deficit. Individuals vary. Many malfunctions correlate with no detectable anatomical lesion (this is often true in dyslexia). And whereas massive cerebral damage (for instance, surgical removal of an entire cerebral hemisphere) may have only marginal effects on one person, a pin prick in the same area may destroy another's personality. Scientific law, qua law, cannot be founded on maybes. Yet in every bona fide case the structuralist has been able to make for the anatomy of memory, the holist has managed to find maybes. One of the best illustrations of this occurs in what is called "split-brain" research.

The two cerebral hemispheres intercommunicate via a massive formation of nerve fibers called the corpus callosum. A splitting

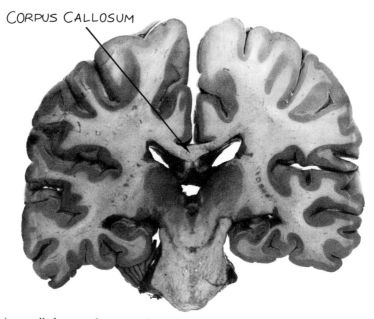

CORPUS CALLOSUM

A so-called coronal section through a human brain, showing the corpus callosum bridging the interval between the two cerebral hemispheres. The headband on a pair of earmuffs would demarcate the location from which this slice was taken. The section in the photograph was stained with mythelene blue and then embedded in plexiglass; the sweatlike beads are artifactual air bubbles trapped in the plastic. The convoluted gray-appearing mantle on the exterior of the hemispheres is the cerebral cortex. The corpus callosum directly intercommunicates the cortex on the two hemispheres. (Photo by Jacque Kubley)

headache marks roughly where the corpus callosum crosses the midline (although pain signals travel along nerves in blood vessels and connective tissue-wrappings of the brain). A feature of mammals, the corpus callosum develops in our embryonic brain as we start acquiring mammalian form; on occasion, however, a person is born without one.

In spite of its relatively large mass — four inches long, two inches wide, and as thick as the sole of a shoe — the corpus callosum received surprisingly little attention until the 1950s. But in the 1960s it made the newspapers. When surgeons split the corpus callosum, they produced two independent mentalities within one human body.

Surgeons had cut into the corpus callosum many years earlier, in an attempt to treat epilepsy. In fact, brain surgery developed in the 1880s after Sir Victor Horsley found that cutting into the brains of laboratory animals could terminate seizures. Until the drug dilantin came along in the 1930s, surgery, when it worked at all, was the only effective therapy for epilepsy. In epilepsy, convulsions occur when electrical discharges sweep the surface of the brain. A diseased locus may initiate the discharges, and removal of the zone may reduce or even eliminate seizures. Often just an incision works, possibly by setting up countercurrents and short-circuiting the discharge. At any rate, splitting the entire corpus callosum seemed too drastic a measure. What would two half-minds be like?

In the 1950s, Ronald Meyers, a student of Roger Sperry's at California Institute of Technology, showed that cats can lead a fairly normal life even after total disconnection of their cerebral hemispheres. Sperry and his associates soon extended their investigations to include the monkey. The ensuing success prompted two California neurosurgeons, Joseph Bogen and P. J. Vogel, to try the split-brain operation on human beings.

Bogen and Vogel's first patient was an epileptic middle-aged World War II veteran. When he awoke from surgery, he couldn't talk. No doubt to the relief of everyone concerned, his speech did return the next day. His seizures could be controlled. And to outward appearances, he and others who have undergone the operation are "just folks," as Michael Gazzaniga, another former student of Sperry's, said during a lecture.

But the split-brain operation has profound effects, although it took careful observation to detect them. Recall that an object in the left visual field signals the right hemisphere, and vice versa. Taking advantage of this, and presenting visual cues in one field at a time, Gazzaniga discovered that most people who had undergone split-brain operations could read, write, and do arithmetic normally, but only with their left cerebral hemispheres. When tested in their right hemispheres, they seemed illiterate, unable to write, and incapable of adding simple sums. Addressing a symposium a few years ago, Gazzaniga described a typical experiment. He held up the word HEART, in such a way that H and E, presented in the left visual field, signaled the nonreading right hemisphere, while the rest of the word cued the left hemisphere. "What did you see?" Gazzaniga asked. His subject responded, "I saw ART." The right hemisphere seemed blind to words. But was the right hemisphere really blind? Worse, did it simply lack intelligence? Or even a human mind?

Gazzaniga soon found that the right side of the cerebrum functioned admirably in nonverbal situations. For instance, when shown a picture of a cup, in such a way that it cued the right hemisphere, the person could reach behind a screen, feel among a collection of objects, and find a cup. In fact, the right hemisphere could manifest profound intelligence and sardonic wit. When presented with a picture of a smoldering cigarette, one subject, instead of matching it with a cigarette, brought forth an ashtray.

Not only is the right side capable of humor, but various studies indicate that people tend to use this hemisphere to comprehend geometric form, textures, and music. It's as though, in most of us, the dominant left side does the mundane jobs of reading, writing, and arithmetic, leaving the right hemisphere free to create and appreciate art.

Lateralization, as hemispheric differentiation is called, need not be investigated with the knife.[3] The psychologist Victor Milstein showed me a visual-field rig that he and his colleagues

---

[3] See Kimura, 1973; also see Galaburda et al., 1978.

use in screening for brain damage. In fact, some of the best evidence of musical tendencies in the right hemisphere came from a test used by Bogen's group prior to actual surgery. Called the amobarbital test, it was perfected by Bogen in collaboration with another member of Sperry's group, Harold Gordon. Amobarbital is an anesthetic. The test involves injecting anesthetic into either the left or the right common carotid artery in the neck, thus anesthetizing one hemisphere at a time. (Actually, blood from a carotid artery on one side will reach the other side of the brain, through a channel called the circle of Willis. But the volume of blood crossing over is small in relation to what flows to the same side.) Gordon compared audio tapes of Bogen's patients singing before and after either the right or left hemisphere had been put to sleep. With the left hemisphere unconscious and the right one awake, most people sang well. But, with exceptions, the subjects sang flat and off-key when the right hemisphere was unconscious.

Laboratory animals display interesting behavior after split-brain surgery. Two disconnected hemispheres may learn to respond to what would otherwise be conflicting stimuli. The animals can even learn at a faster pace. (There are, after all, two intelligences instead of one.) Also one side of the brain may be taught to avoid a stimulus the other side responds to favorably. A split-brain monkey, for instance, may lovingly fondle a toy doll with its right hand and angrily beat it with the left hand. (Arms are voluntarily controlled by opposite hemispheres.) Sperry has even reported that persons with split brains sometimes maintain two entirely different attitudes toward the very same object — simultaneously.

At first glance, and when the results were new, split-brain research looked like a powerful case for a structural theory of mind-brain. Language memory, for example, seemed to be housed in the dominant hemisphere (along with handedness). Music memories seemed to be stored over on the nondominant side. But as more facts emerged, and as all the evidence was carefully weighed, what seemed like such a clearcut case became fuzzy again.

Some people, remember, are born without a corpus callosum. Sperry's group studied one such young woman extensively.[4] Unlike persons who have undergone split-brain surgery, those born without a corpus callosum don't show lateralization: both hemispheres reveal similar linguistic ability. Children who have had split-brain operations show much less lateralization than adults. A few years ago, after I'd written a couple of feature articles on hemispheric differences, a student who'd read one of them came to see me, puzzled. If the left side of the brain stores language, he asked, how do people taking an amobarbital test know the lyrics of a song when only the right hemisphere sings?

It was a perceptive question. Clearly, no natural law confines language to one and only one side of the brain. Otherwise no one with complete separation of the cerebral hemispheres could handle language on the right side; and children would show the same degree of lateralization as adults. Nor would Bogen and Gordon have found individual variations in music or language during the amobarbital test.

Gazzaniga has conducted a great deal of research on children. Before the age of two or three, they exhibit little if any lateralization. Hemispheric differences develop with maturity. We're not born with lateralized brains. How do most of us end up that way?

Circuitries in the visual system can be altered by the early visual environment.[5] There's direct evidence about this for laboratory animals, and a good circumstantial case has been made

---

[4] See Saul and Sperry, 1968.
[5] See Blakemore and Cooper, 1970.

for humans. Environment has a much more profound effect on even relatively uncomplicated reflexes than anyone had ever suspected. Maybe culture and learning play critical roles in lateralizing. Maybe as we mature, we learn, unconsciously, to inhibit the flow of information into one side of the brain or the other. Maybe we train ourselves to repress memories of language in the right hemisphere. Maybe the formation of language and the routines in arithmetic proceed more efficiently when carried out asymmetrically — unless we're singing.

Inability of a right hemisphere to read doesn't necessarily preclude memory there, though. Maybe the right hemisphere has amnesia. Or, relying on the left side to handle language, the right hemisphere simply may not remember how it's done. We *do* repress and *don't* remember all sorts of things, all the time. I can't recall my third-grade teacher's name, although I'll bet I could under hypnosis. With regard to repression, consider something like functional amblyopia, for instance — blindness in an eye after double vision, even when there are no structural defects in the eye. It is as though the mind prefers *not* to see what's confusing or painful — as double vision can be. But with correction of the double view, that same blind eye sometimes regains 20/20 vision.

Thus we really can't turn the results of split-brain research into a conclusive argument in favor of a structural theory of mind. We don't know whether split brains show us the repository or the conduits of memory. We don't know if what's coming out flows directly from the source or from the plumbing.

But the split brain raises still another question: What does the operation *not* do? Why didn't the knife create half-minded individuals? Why were both personalities "just folks," as Gazzaniga said? Why two *whole* personalities? Isn't personality part of the mind? Why doesn't personality follow the structural symmetry of the brain? If we split this page in two, we wouldn't have whole messages in both halves.

It's not that a structuralist can't answer such a question.

But the structuralist's thesis — my old argument — must be tied together with an embarrassingly long string of maybes.

The mind-brain conundrum has many other dimensions and extends to virtually every level of organization and discourse, from molecules to societies of animals, from molecular biophysics to social psychology. Name the molecule, cell, or lobe, or stipulate the physiological, chemical, or physical mechanism, and somebody, someplace, has found memory on, in, around, or associated with it. And, in spite of the generally good to splendid quality of such research, there's probably someone else, somewhere, whose experiments categorically deny a given result.

Among those who believe, as I did, that memory is molecular, there are the protein people, the RNA people, the DNA people, the lipid people. And they're often very unkind to each other. Why? Most scientists, consciously or unconsciously, practice the principle of causality — every cause must have one and only one effect, or a causal relationship hasn't been established. If you're an RNA person and somebody finds memory on fat, that's unpleasant news. For RNA *and* fat cannot both be *the* cause of memory.

Some investigators believe that memories can be transferred from animal to animal in chemical form; that it's possible to train a rat, homogenize its brain, extract this or that chemical, and inject the donor's thought into another rat or even a hamster. The disbelievers vastly outnumber the believers, for a variety of rational and irrational reasons. Not everyone has been able to reproduce the results;[6] but memory transfer is in the literature, implicating quite a variety of alleged transfer substances.

[6] See Pietsch and Schneider, 1969.

Some research on memory doesn't implicate molecules at all. And while some data suggest that memories depend on reverberating circuits to and from vast regions of the brain, other evidence places memory in individual cells.

Who's right? Who's wrong? As we shall see later in the book, this is not the question.

Dynamics of the learning process have suggested to psychologists that two distinct classes of memory exist: *short-term* memory and *long-term* memory. Short-term memory is, for example, using the telephone number you look up in the directory and forgetting it after you've put through the call. Long-term memory operates in the recollection of the date of New Year's, or in the remembrance of the telephone number you don't have to look up. Can we find any physiological evidence to support the psychologists' claim? The reader probably knows that electroconvulsive shock (ECS) can induce amnesia. ECS can totally and permanently obliterate all signs of short-term memory, while producing only temporary effects on long-term memory.[7] Certain drugs also induce convulsions. The results are similar to those produced in experiments with ECS. Taken together, the evidence does indicate that short-term memory and long-term memory depend on different physiological mechanisms.

Some investigators employ a very interesting theory in dealing with the two classes of memory.[8] According to this theory, short-term memory is the active, working memory, and it exists in an idealized "compartment." Long-term memory is stored

---

[7] Humans exhibit this general trend, as do other animals. I am not suggesting, however, that the survival of long-term memory in laboratory animals automatically justifies shock therapy. Many variables and uncertainties exist in ECS treatment.

[8] See Atkinson and Shiffrin, 1971.

memory, and the storage "depot" differs from the working compartment. According to the theory, the working compartment receives incoming perceptual data, which create short-term memories. The short-term memories, in turn, make the long-term memories. In other words, in the learning process, information from experience moves into the working compartment, becomes short-term memory, and then goes on to the storage depot. But what good would the memory be if it were confined to storage? According to the theory, the working compartment has two-way communication with the storage depot. In the theory, when we use long-term memory, we in effect create a short-term working memory from it. And there's more. Learning doesn't depend simply on what comes into the mind. The remembered past has a profound effect on what we're learning in the present. Cognition — understanding — can't be divorced from the learning process. The working-memory theory maintains that the active memory in the working compartment is a blend of perception from the senses and memory drawn from storage. When we forget, the active memory "goes off" in the working compartment.

But the concept of two classes of memory gives rise to imponderables in the mind-brain connection. If different physiological mechanisms handle short-term and long-term memories, how do we explain their informational identities? After all, Butterfield 8 is Butterfield 8 whether we forget it immediately or remember it to the end of our days. There are other problems. The useful working-memory theory requires a more general theory to link it to reality.

Nevertheless there is a great deal of empirical evidence of a structure in the human brain that is involved in short-term memory. This structure is known as the hippocampus. Shaped like a zucchini, but about the size of a little finger, the hippocampus (Greek for sea-horse) is buried deep within the cerebrum's temporal lobe. A person with a damaged hippocampus exhibits defective short-term memory, whereas his or her long-term memory shows every sign of being intact. One clinical sign of a lesion in the hippocampus is when a person can't repeat a name or a short sequence of randomly presented numbers but can, for instance, recite the Gettysburg Address. I will say more about the hippocampus in chapter 10. For now, I want to make the point that if we take the holist's classical position, we will have to dismiss important facts about the hippocampus.

Well, then, why can't we consider the hippocampus the seat of short-term memory? I've been asked sophisticated versions of this very question by several persons who work with the brain. There are correspondingly sophisticated reasons why we can't. But let me indicate some simple ones.

First of all, there are entire phyla of organisms whose brains lack hippocampi. Yet these same creatures often have splendid working, short-term memories. I can give another example from my own laboratory. Salamanders whose cerebrums, and therefore their hippocampi, have been amputated learn as well as normal animals. Perhaps salamanders and various other forms of life are simply too lowly to count? Later in the book, I will summarize experiments whose results show that cats can learn, and thus exhibit working memory, without their hippocampi. The point, once again, is that structuralism is no more enlightening than holism, in regard to the role of the hippocampus.

I mentioned earlier that we humans require the visual cortex in order to see. But on a summer forenoon, when I look out my office window, I sometimes observe a hawk, perhaps 600 feet up, gliding in circles above our hardwooded, meadowed campus, searching the ground for a target less than a foot long. Why doesn't the hawk dive after that discarded Hershey-bar wrapper or the tail of that German shepherd? The hawk is up there in the clouds doing complicated data processing with its visual system. It's certainly seeing. Yet that hawk, unlike a human, doesn't employ a visual cortex. It doesn't even have one. For the visual cortex in the occipital lobe is a mammalian characteristic.

Birds process their visual sensations in what is called the *midbrain tectum*. (Barn owls, in addition, handle depth perception in a mound of brain, on the front of the cerebrum, called the Wulst, the German word for pastry roll. Indeed, the Wulst[9] does look like something on a tray in a Viennese bakery.)

Mammals, humans included, also have tectums, which they use in pupillary light reflexes. A human who has suffered complete destruction of both occipital lobes, and loses the entire visual cortex as a consequence, becomes blind, although some evidence indicates that this person may be able to sense very strong light. Firm evidence shows that rats, rabbits, and even monkeys can sense diffuse light following complete destruction of their occipital lobes. Perhaps the tectum and the visual cortex (and the Wulst, too, of course) comprise the seat of vertebrate vision. If a vertebrate lacks some, but not all, of these structures, it may lack certain special features of vision. If the creature lacks a tectum, a visual cortex, and a Wulst, will it have no vision at all?

The argument works, up to a point. Specific lesions in a frog's tectum produce specific deficits in its visual perception. But let me tell you a little anecdote from my own laboratory in the days before my experiments with shufflebrain.

I was doing experiments with larval salamanders. For control purposes, I had to have a group of neurologically blinded animals. That would be a cinch, I thought, since the tectum is

---

[9] See Pettigrew and Konishi, 1976.

the seat of vision in animals below mammals (the function of the Wulst hadn't been worked out yet). All I had to do, I thought, was go in and remove the tectum, which I did. Was I in for a surprise when the animals came out of anesthesia! Every single one could see! I didn't even consider publishing the results, feeling certain that I had done something wrong. But a few years later, the animal behaviorist G. E. Savage reported basically the same thing, except in adult fish.

It's not that the visual cortex and the tectum (or the Wulst) aren't important. And it's not that the vision of a squid is identical to yours and mine. The fact is that we really can't assign all vision to a single anatomical system. We can relate specific features of visual perception to certain structures in particular organisms. But we can't generalize. And if we can't generalize, we can't theorize. Which leaves mind-brain open to the holist — or to the magician.

I can't think of anyone who has contributed more to our knowledge of functional human neuroanatomy than the late Wilder Penfield. Yet mind-brain eventually forced him into mysticism. A neurosurgeon who began his career early in this century, Penfield developed and made routine the practice of exploring and mapping a region of the brain before cutting into it. He was preoccupied by the question of whether the treatment would be worse than the disease.

The cerebrum doesn't sense pain directly. Painful sensations from inside the skull travel on branches of peripheral nerves. These nerve fibers leave the skull, join their parent trunks, reenter the cranium, and fuse into the brainstem, the lower region of the brain between the cerebrum and spinal cord. Local anesthesia deadens the skull, scalp, and coverings of the brain; intracranial surgery can thus be performed on a fully conscious person, which is what Penfield usually did. With electrodes, he stimulated an area and found out, firsthand, the role it played in his patient's actions and thoughts. In this way, Penfield confirmed many suspected functions and discovered new ones as well.

During the early and middle phases of his career, Penfield was a staunch advocate of the anatomical point of view. In some of his last written words, he related how he'd spent his life trying "to prove that brain accounts for the mind." But he'd seen too many paradoxes over the years.

Take, for example, a patch of cerebral cortex you're probably using this very moment as your eyes scan this page. The patch is the size of a postage stamp, on the rear of your frontal lobe, about where a Viking's horn emerges from the side of his helmet. It's in a place called area 8 α, β, γ, or, alternatively, the frontal eye fields, or just plain area 8 for short. Penfield explored area 8 with electrodes and found that it is indeed associated with voluntary eye movements. What do you suppose happens if area 8 is cut out? The person may lose the ability to move his or her eyes, willfully, toward the opposite side of the head (smooth, involuntary eye movements are handled by the occipital lobes). But the voluntary eye movements usually return a few days after surgery. And sometimes the function doesn't disappear at all.

Memory is even more puzzling. Penfield could often elicit vivid recollections of scenes from his patient's distant past by stimulating the temporal lobe. Had Penfield tapped the seat of long-term memory? Removal of the area frequently had no demonstrable effect on the person's memory.

For Penfield, the discrepancies eventually became overwhelming. Shortly before he died, he came to the conclusion that "our being consists of two fundamental elements."[10] For

---

[10] See Penfield, 1975.

him those elements had become "brain *and* mind" (my italics).
Even the most faithful of the faithful have had trouble with
mind-brain.

Holism does not rest its case on the structuralist's dubious dia-
lectical position, but on prima facie evidence from some of the
finest research ever conducted in psychology or biology — thirty
years of exhaustive, imaginative, and carefully controlled laboratory investigations by Karl Lashley, the founder of the entire
field of physiological psychology.

Lashley investigated memory in a wide variety of species,
ranging from cockroaches to chimpanzees. But his favorite subject was the rat. His basic experiment was to train an animal to
run a maze. Then he'd injure the animal's brain at a particular
location and in a specific amount. Finally, he'd retest the animal's ability to run the maze postoperatively, comparing its performance with that of control rats whose skulls had been
opened but whose brains hadn't been injured.

Lashley found that destruction of 20 percent or more of a
rat's cerebrum could dim its memory of the maze. And increasing the damage would proportionately decrease the animal's
recall. But (and this is the single biggest "but" in the history of
brain research!) the critical thing was not *where* he made the
wound but *how much* of the area he destroyed. Lashley got the
same results by destroying the same percentages of different
lobes. Anticipating hologramic theory, he even analogized memory to interference patterns,[11] examples of which the reader can
find on pages 154–160 of this book. He had borrowed the name of
the principle — equipotentiality — from the embryologist Hans

[11] See Lashley's article "The Problem of Cerebral Organization in Vision," 1971,
p. 21.

Driesch. The term means that engrams, or memory traces, are distributed all over the region.

From chemistry, Lashley borrowed the principle of *mass action* [12] to explain how increased brain damage dulled performance. The less engram the brain had to work with, the dumber the animal seemed.

Equipotentiality and mass action became Lashley trademarks. He and his students and followers reproduced, reconfirmed, and extended their evidence. More recently, the physiologist E. Roy John has developed an extensive new line of evidence to support the principle of equipotential distribution of memory.

John and his colleagues, working with cats, perfected electrophysiological methods to monitor the learning brain. Electrical activities in the animal's brain assume the form of waves on the recording device. As an animal learns to distinguish flickering lights of different frequencies, the waves begin to change form; and after the animal has learned, the harmonic features of the waves assume distinctive characteristics, which John and his colleagues take to signify memory. And these same waves — and presumably the memory underlying the animal's reaction — show up throughout widely dispersed regions of the brain.[13]

There is always some extraneous "noise" associated with electronic waves — "blips" that are independent of the main waves. Information theorists call the main waves the signal, and an important aspect of electronic communications is the signal-to-noise ratio. John and his group have found that although the main waves are the same all over the brain, signal-to-noise ratio

---

[12] With temperature and pressure held constant, the rate of a chemical reaction is proportionate to the concentration of reacting substances.

[13] See Bartlett and John, 1973. Also, John has published a highly readable account of his research in *Psychology Today,* May 1976.

varies. John believes that variations in signal-to-noise ratio account for specific functions of different regions of the brain and explain why, for example, the occipital lobe works in vision and the temporal lobe works in hearing.

How might a structuralist explain John's research? One way is to argue that he really did not tap stored memory but instead tapped communications from long-term to short-term compartments. Another is to assume that the alleged noise is really the memory, and that the signals represent some nonspecific nerve-cell activity. I'm not faulting John's work here, incidentally, but merely giving examples of structuralist explanations of his findings.

Lashley did not resolve the mind-brain conundrum. His work sharpened its intensity, extended its dimensions, and made a whole generation of psychologists afraid even to think of behavior along physiological lines.

As I mentioned before, Lashley took the term *equipotentiality* from Hans Driesch. Driesch espoused equipotentiality because dissociated two- and four-celled frog and salamander embryos don't form fractions of animals but whole frogs and salamanders. Driesch's research led him to embrace entelechy, the doctrine of vitalism, or the belief that the first principles of life cannot be found in nonliving matter.

Driesch was a man of the nineteenth century. By the time Lashley came along, biology had fallen madly in love with chemistry and physics, and with the belief that life obeys the laws of Nature generally. Lashley had a background in microbiology and chemistry. True to a twentieth-century scientist's view of things, he resisted vitalism and sought to explain his findings by physical and chemical examples. Yet to me, structuralist and materialist that I was, Lashley's principles seemed a coverup. I believed that he engaged in a limp form of metaphysics, disguised to sound like science but lacking the practicing metaphysician's depth and scope. Until my shufflebrain research, I thought Lashley had concocted his doctrines as a verbal means of escape from the powerful vitalistic implications of his position. Lashley's ideas seemed like substations on the way to pure vitalism. The best thing to do was ignore him, which is what I did until hologramic theory emerged.

As we shall see later on, though, the hologram cannot be equated with equipotentiality. As I said in the first chapter, the hologram concerns that property of waves called phase. Phase makes for equipotentiality (when it is a feature of a hologram at all), not the other way around.

As a general theory, derived from the generic phase principle, hologramic theory does not make champions of the holists and chumps of the structuralists. Instead, hologramic theory breaks the mind-brain conundrum by showing that one need not choose between holism and structuralism. Hologramic theory will supply us with the missing idea — the thought that Hegel would have said allows thesis and antithesis to become synthesis.

But before we take our first glimpse at hologramic theory, let us consider holograms as such.

3

Holograms

"IT'S SPOOKY over there," one of my students said, gesturing toward the big room across the hall from our neuroanatomy laboratory. The next student to return mumbled something about *The Exorcist*. His lab partner came back next, made a quip about touching the thing but then went mute. I had volunteered my class for an experiment in educational-systems technology. But as my students kept returning, house-of-horrors looks on their faces, I began wondering if I might have exposed them to a hidden danger. Then it was my turn to go.

The windowless room would have been infinitely black, except for a bright emerald rod of laser light twenty feet from where the door shut out the world behind me. "Come this way," beckoned one of the experimenters. Taking my arm like an usher at a seance, he led me to a stool opposite the laser gun. "Don't look directly into the beam," his partner warned unnecessarily. The usher slipped a photographic plate into a frame in the beam's path. Instantly, a dissected human brain appeared in the space before me.

It was one of my own specimens, from my class demonstration collection. I'd made the dissection with great care the previous year and had loaned it to the experimenters a few weeks before. But I knew for certain that this specimen was now across the hallway, safely stored in a pickle jar and locked in a cabinet whose only key was in my pocket. Yet as an optical phenomenon the specimen was here in the room with the three of us.

I had known what would be in the room. At least I'd thought I knew. I understood the technical side of what was happening, as did my students. Yet I found myself wondering, as they must have, just what "real" really means. Visually, I could make no distinction between what I was seeing and the actual object. I looked down into a complexly shadowed recess where I'd dissected away the forward part of the temporal lobe and pared back the cerebrum to expose the optic tract and LGB; and I saw features not even the best stereoscopic photographs can capture. When I shifted my gaze to the right, structures I hadn't seen over on the left came into view. When I stood and looked down, I could see the top of the specimen. As I backed off, more structures filled my visual field, and their individual details became less distinct. As I moved in close, fewer structures occupied my field of view, but those that were there I saw much more clearly. Moving still closer, I made out grid-like indentations gauze had pressed into the soft cerebral cortex before the brain had been transferred to formaldehyde and hardened. And I became conscious that, from habit, I was holding my breath, anticipating a whiff of strong formaldehyde fumes. Finally, even though the scientist in me knew better, I was compelled to reach out and try to touch the brain, to convince myself the object wasn't there.

My students and I weren't hallucinating, observing trick photography, experiencing optical illusions, or skirting the edges of the occult. In the strictest technical sense we had been *looking* at the actual brain, even though it wasn't there. We had witnessed the decoding of an optical hologram.

How does a forest or a stained-glass window communicate a visible presence? How do objects let us see them? How do they impress their features on light?

Physical theory tells us that light, emitted and absorbed as photons, as particles, travels as waves of mass-energy. Light is mass-energy in extreme motion. Except for the fleeting instant when mass-energy becomes light, or ceases to be light, it is waves. Objects change waves; they warp them. The warp is the optical message, and its specific character depends first of all on what the waves were like just before they illuminated the scene, and, second, on the nature of the objects. If the object indiscriminately absorbs waves of any energy, in the way, for example, a patch of tar does, its image will appear to be dark, because little light radiates into the optical environment. If the object has little capacity to absorb energies, as is the case with the fur of an albino mink, for example, light will be warped by contours and edges, but the image will appear white in white light, blue in blue light, red in red light, and so forth. If the object absorbs particular colors or wavelengths, it will subtract those energies from a mixture and will reflect or transmit the rest. White light, which is a mixture of the colors of the rainbow, contains the waves for an infinite variety of hues. The primary colors red, green, and blue can combine to form the 500,000 or more hues a human eye can discriminate.[1] In addition, objects distort the waves relative to the sharpness, smoothness, or complexity of their contours. But the totality of the optical message travels in the form of a warp.

In all electromagnetic radiation, including light, the shorter the wavelength the greater the energy. Offhand, this may seem incorrect. But think of the pleats of an accordion. Compressing the bellows, thereby forcing the pleats together, concentrates the train of wavelets and increases their number per inch. In

---

[1] See Gregory, 1978, for an excellent discussion of vision.

electromagnetic radiation, likewise, the shorter the wavelength, the greater the *frequency,* or number of wavelets per second. Also, as wavelength decreases, the amplitude of each wavelet increases: the peaks become taller, the troughs deeper. You might say that compressed waves become more "ample." Physicists define amplitude as the maximum rise of the wave's crest from the horizontal surface, from the midpoint between peak and trough. The intensity of light is proportional to the amplitude, or the crest height.

According to Einstein, mass-energy has reached the maximum attainable velocity when it assumes the form of light. Conversely, when mass-energy hasn't reached that maximum speed, it isn't light. Energy is more concentrated in blue light than in, say, red light. Since the mass-energy can't move any faster or slower, and since something must accommodate the difference, blue light waves compress closer together than red ones; and, compared to red waves, blue waves exhibit greater amplitude and frequencies, and shorter wavelengths.

But not all waves move at the speed of light. Water waves certainly don't, nor do sound waves. Unlike light, the amplitude and frequency of these waves are independent of each other. This is why, for example, a high-pitched squeak may be of very low amplitude, and a deep, rumbling, low-frequency bass sound may be intense enough to knock you out of your seat.

But one thing is true about any wave: Put amplitude together with phase, and you completely define the wave. As mathematical physicist Edgar Kraut has written, "A complete knowledge of the amplitude and phase spectra of a function [the mathematical essentials of an equation] determines the function completely . . ."[2] He uses the term *spectra* because phase and amplitude define not only simple waves but complex ones as

---

[2] See Kraut, 1967, p. 198.

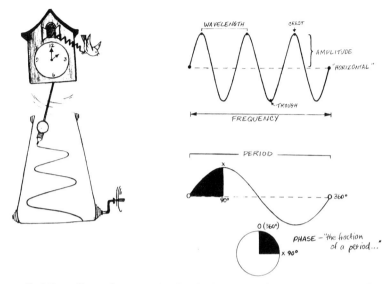

WAVELENGTH
CREST
AMPLITUDE
"HORIZONTAL"
TROUGH
FREQUENCY

PERIOD
x
0   90°   360°

0 (360°)
PHASE – "the fraction
of a period..."
x 90°

well. We will see later in the book that complex waves are made up of simple, regular waves.

What is wave phase? The formal definition of the term describes it as that part of a cycle a wave has passed through at any given instant. Engineers and physicists use the term *cycle* almost interchangeably with *wavelet*. This is because the points on a simple, regular wavelet relate directly to the circumference of a circle, or a cycle. For example, if what is known as a *sine* wavelet has reached its amplitude, it has passed the equivalence of ninety degrees on the circle.

Phase also implies knowledge of the wave's point of origin, as well as every point through which the wave has passed up to the moment of observation. And the future course of a simple regular wave can be predicted when we know what phase it is in, just as we can predict how much of a circle remains the instant we reach, say, 180 degrees. Amplitude represents the bulk mass of a wave, whereas phase defines just where or when that mass will be doing what, in space or time. Phase instantly mani-

fests to the observer the way a wave has changed since its origin, and how it will continue to change, unless outside forces
intervene.

Phase, as I have said, is a sizeless entity — sizeless in the
sense that we can't measure it with a yardstick or weigh it on a
scale. We speak of phase in terms of angles or their equivalents,
or in terms of time. And to create an angle, or to specify it, we
need more than a single entity. Phase demands a reference,
something to compare it with. Because phase is relative, we
cannot treat it, or even conceptualize it, as an absolute.

We can appreciate both the nature of phase and the problems in dealing with it by looking at the face of a clock. The revolutions of the hands around the dial describe the phase of the
hour of the AM or PM. The hands move at different rates and exhibit different phases. Yet the phase difference — relative
phase — converts the seemingly abstract, invisible, untouch-
able, ever-beginning, never-ending dimension, time, into *our*
time. Five-thirty is the phase of the morning when we must
crawl out of the sleeping bag and milk the goat. Four-fifteen is
the phase of the afternoon when the children will be getting off
the school bus expecting cookies and orange juice. Phase on the
clock has the same theoretical meaning as it does on a wavy
surface. Thus relative wave phase is a part of our everyday lives.

In an optical hologram, such as the one my students and I experienced, the encoded message exists in a special kind of
shadow, the interference pattern — alternating zones of light
and dark. (The reader may inspect simple interference patterns
on pages 154–160.) The densities of the shadows depend on the
intensity of the light, and carry the information about amplitude. How rapidly the shadows change from light to dark depends on relative phase, and thus carries the phase code. As I
mentioned earlier, objects warp light; they warp amplitude and
phase. The warp, in turn, creates the shadows. In fact, the

shadows are transformations of the wave's phase and amplitude warps to a kind of mathematical warp in the photographic plate. When the correct decoding beam passes through those shadows, they warp its waves. The shadows force into the decoding beam the very phase and amplitude changes that created them in the first place. And when the decoding beam forms an image, it is, by every physical standard, completely regenerating the scene as an optical phenomenon, even though the objects may be gone.

What about photographs? They, and all conventional pictures, capture intensities of light from a scene. Photographs encode information about amplitude but not phase.

Optical holograms encode for amplitude as well as for phase variations in the scene. The basic reason for this has to do with the nature of light, with the waves' attainment of their maximum speed. But other kinds of waves also make holograms. And the acoustical holographer Alexander Metherell some years ago had a hunch that phase was really the generic essence of the hologram. Of course we can't have phase all by itself, except in the abstract. But Metherell wondered if he might assume just one amplitude — create a constant background din — and then encode the message strictly with phase variations. It worked. And he went on to demonstrate his point with the phase-only holograms I referred to earlier.

I mention phase-only holograms at this juncture to make a point about hologramic mind. The frequencies and energy levels in the nervous system do not remotely approach those of light. For this reason we can't make a literal comparison between optical and neural holograms, at least not in using hologramic theory. Also, because of phase-only holograms, amplitude *variations* would not play a necessary and indispensable role in the storage of information in the brain. Phase is the essence of hologramic mind.

Before I supply more background on holograms, per se, let
me raise still another important preliminary question. What do
we actually mean when we use the word *wave*? Let's take an in-
trospective look.

Many of us first became acquainted with the word *wave* when
someone hoisted us from the crib or playpen, gently kissed us
on the side of the head, and coaxed, "Wave bye-bye to Uncle
Herbie!" Later, we may have thought "wave" as we pressed a
nose against the cool windowpane and watched little brother
Ben's diapers waving on the clothesline in the autumn breeze.
Then one Fourth of July or Saint Patrick's Day, our mother
perhaps gave us a whole quarter; we ran to the candy store on
the corner, and, instead of baseball cards and bubblegum, we
bought a little American flag on a stick. We ran over to the park
and waved the little flag to the rhythm of the march; then we
began to laugh our heads off when the mounted policemen
jiggled by in their saddles, out of time with each other and the
beat of the drums and the cadence we were keeping with the
little waving flag. Still later, perhaps, we learned to wave Morse
code with a wigwag flag, dot to the right, dash to the left. Up
early to go fishing, when radio station W-whatever-the-heck-it-
was signed on, we may have wondered what "kilocycles" or
"megahertz" meant. And it was not until after we began playing
rock flute with the Seventh Court that the bearded electronic
piano player with the Ph. D. in astronomy said that "cycle" to an
engineer is "wavelet" to a sailor, and that the hertz value means
cycles per second — in other words, frequency. If we enrolled in
physics in high school, we probably carried out experiments
with pendulums and tuning forks. An oscillating pendulum
scribed a wave on a revolving drum. A vibrating tuning fork also
created waves, but of higher frequency: 256 cycles per second
when we used the fork with the pitch of middle C on the piano.

Moving down an octave, according to the textbook, would give us 128 hertz.

Are our usages of *wave* metaphorical? The word *metaphor* has become overworked in our times. While I certainly wouldn't want to deny waves to poets, I don't think metaphor is at the nexus of our everyday usage of *wave*. *Analogue* is a better choice: something embodying a principle or a logic that we find in something else. (Notice the stem of ana*log*ue.)

To and fro, rise and fall, up and down, over and under, in and out, tick and tock, round and round, and so on. Cycles. Periodicities. Recurrences. Undulations. Corrugations. Oscillations. Vibrations. Round-trip excursions along a continuum, like the rise, fall, and return of the contour of a wavelet, the revolutions of a wheel, the journey of a piston, the hands of a clock. These are all analogues of waves.

Do we really mean that pendular motion is a symbolic expression of the rotations of a clock's hands? No. The motion of one translates into continuous displacements of the other. Is the ride on a roller coaster an allegorical reference to the course of the tracks? Of course not. The conduct of the one issues directly from the character of the other, to borrow a phrase from a John Dewey title. And why would we suppose that a pendulum or a tuning fork could scribe a wave? The answer is that the same logic prevails in all periodic events, patterns, circumstances, conditions, motions, surfaces, and so forth.

No, a child's hand isn't the same thing as a fluttering piece of cloth or the ripples on a pond. And yes, there's imprecision and imperfection in our verbal meanings; we wouldn't want it otherwise. Poetry may exist in all of this. Yet by our literal usages of *wave* we denote what Plato would have called the *idea* of waviness, the universal logic revealed by all things wavy. And that logic translates, completely, into amplitude and phase. And if the medium stores phase, we have a species of hologram.

Not all physics is about waves, of course. The liveliest endeavor in that science today, the pursuit of the quark, is a search for fundamental *particles* — discrete entities — of mass-energy. The photon is a light particle. Light is both particles and waves. The same is true of all mass-energy at the atomic level. The electron microscope, for example, depends on electrons, not as the particles we usually consider them to be but as the electron waves uncovered in the 1920s as the result of de Broglie's theories. And one of the tenets of contemporary physics is that mass-energy is both particulate and wavy. But when we are dealing with particles, the wavy side of mass-energy disappears; and when it is measured as waves, mass-energy doesn't appear as particles. If you want to concentrate on corpuscles of light, or photons, you must witness the transduction of a filament's mass-energy into light, or from light into some other form, as occurs in the quantized chemical reactions in our visual pigment molecules. But if the choice is light on the move between emission and absorption, the techniques must be suitable for waves.

Physics would be a side show in our times if the logic of waves had been left out of science. And waves might have been left out of science, were it not for Galileo's discovery of the rules of the pendulum. The pendulum taught us how to build accurate clocks. Without a reliable clock, astronomy would be out of the question. And how could anybody contemplate timing something such as the speed of light without a good clock? It was in 1656 that a twenty-seven-year-old Dutchman named Christiaan Huygens invented the pendular clock.

Huygens wasn't just a back-room tinkerer. His work with the pendulum was the result of his preoccupation with waves. The reader may recognize Huygens's name from his famous wave principle. He had studied the question of how waves spread to make an advancing wave front. Have you ever observed ripples diverging in ever-expanding circles from the point where you drop a rock into the water? If not, fill a wash

Huygens' Principle:

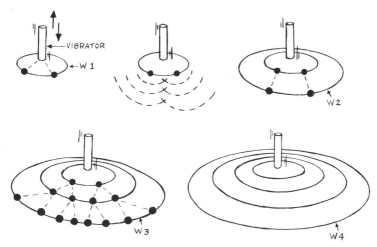

basin halfway, and then let the faucet drip . . . drip . . . drip! Huygens explained how one set of ripples gives rise to the next. He postulated that each point in a ripple acts just like the original disturbance, creating tiny new waves. The new waves then expand and combine to make the next line of ripples, the advancing wave front. A diagram in a treatise Huygens published in 1690 is still the prototype for illustrations of his principle in today's physics textbooks.

Nor is it a coincidence that Huygens, "during my sojourn in France in 1678," proposed the wave theory of light.[3] (He didn't publish his *Treatise on Light* for another twelve years.)

We can't see light waves. Even today, the light wave is a theoretical entity. And to scholars in Huygens's times, nothing seemed sillier or more remote from reality than light waves.

But on November 24, 1803, Thomas Young, M.D., F.R.S., thought it right "to lay before the Royal Society a short statement of the facts which appear so decisive to me . . .

---

[3] See Huygens, 1962, page v.

"I made a small hole in a window-shutter, and covered it with a piece of thick paper, which I perforated with a fine needle." Outside the shutter "I placed a small looking-glass . . . to reflect the sun's light, in a direction nearly horizontal, and upon the opposite wall." And with perforated cards in the path of "the sunbeam," Young produced interference patterns and demonstrated, conclusively, the wavy nature of light.

Young's experiment is a laboratory exercise in physics courses today. It involves two baffles, one perforated in the center by a single pinhole, the other with two pinholes in line with each other but off-center. The experimenter places the baffles between a tiny light source and a screen, locating the one with the single hole nearest the light. When light passes through the single pinhole and then through the two pinholes in the far baffle, interference fringes, dark and light stripes, appear on the screen. What happens if we place a finger over one

YOUNG'S EXPERIMENTS

INTERFERENCE PATTERNS

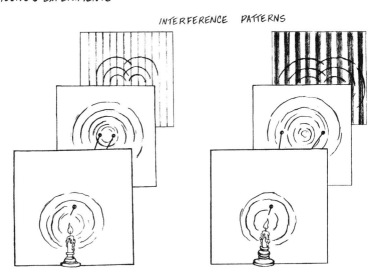

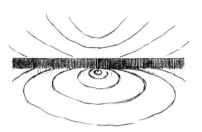

pinhole in the far baffle? Let's let Thomas Young tell us: "One of the two portions [our pinholes] was incapable of producing the fringes alone." Changes in the intensity of the light don't affect the results. Interference fringes require *two* sets of waves.

Interference patterns guarantee waves. But Young's work wasn't immediately accepted by British scientists. In fact, if he had not been active in many other fields (the range of his work is astonishing), he might never have been allowed to lay another thing before the Royal Society. Young's critics, according to his biographer, George Peacock, "diverted public attention from examination of the truth."[4]

But across the English channel, Napoleon notwithstanding, Young's work found an eloquent and persuasive champion in the person of François Arago. And by the time Victoria became Queen, even the English believed in light waves.

It wasn't Arago's original research that vindicated and extended Young's theory, however, but that of Augustin Jean Fresnel, with whom Arago collaborated.

Fresnel! When my mind says "Fray-nel!" in poor Ph.D.

[4] See Young, 1972, p. 192.

language-examination French, certain words of Charles Peirce also surface: "These are men whom we see possessed by a passion to learn . . . Those are the naturally scientific men."[5] Fresnel's work brought him little renown in his lifetime. But optical physicists today use his name as an adjective. For Fresnel demonstrated just what interference is all about.

Interference occurs whenever waves collide. You've probably seen waves of water cancel each other upon impact. This is *destructive* interference, which occurs when the rising part of one wave meets the falling part of another. Conceptually, destructive interference is like adding a positive number to a negative number. On the other hand, when waves meet as both are moving up together, the interference is *constructive,* or additive, and the resulting wave crests higher than its parents. In order to have an interference pattern, some definite phase relationship must exist between two sets of colliding waves. A well-defined phase relationship is *coherent* and is often referred to as "in step." When colliding waves are incoherent, their interaction produces random effects. An interference pattern is not random; and a basic requirement in an interference pattern is coherency.

Ordinary light is decidedly incoherent, which is why optical interference patterns aren't an everyday observation. Today, Heisenberg's uncertainty principle[6] accounts for this: wicks and filaments emit light in random bursts. Even if we filter light

---

[5] Peirce, 1957, p. 195.

[6] The uncertainty or indeterminacy principle asserts the impossibility of being completely sure of the position *and* speed of an atomic particle. In fact, the principle extends to all independent quantities. One reason is that the measuring device must distort one entity in order to allow the observer to measure the other. An illustration often used is that of the coin. Both sides must exist in order to have the coin; yet both cannot face upward at the same instant. Quantum physicists got around the problem by using large numbers of events and making highly precise estimates of the uncertain quantity. They minimized rather than tried to eliminate uncertainty. But knowledge of the speed of light would make phase itself theoretically unknowable.

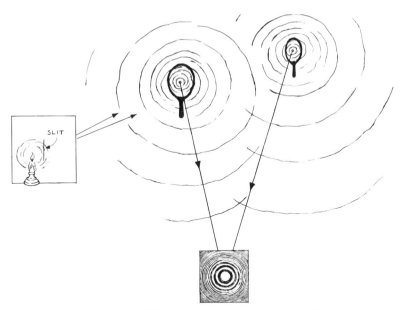

waves — screen out all but those of the same amplitude, wavelength, and frequency — we can't put them in step. In other
words, we can't generate a definite phase relationship in light
waves from two or more sources.

Young's experiment circumvented the uncertainty principle in a remarkably simple way. Recall that his sunbeam first
passed through a single pinhole. Therefore, the light that went
through both pinholes in the far baffle, having come from the
same point source, and being the same light, had the same
phase spectrum. And, coming out of the other side of the far
baffle, the two new sets of waves had a well-defined phase relationship, and therefore the coherency to make interference
fringes.

Here's what Fresnel did. He let light shine through a slit.
Then he lined up *two* mirrors with the beam, aiming them so as
to reflect light toward a screen. But he set the two mirrors at
unequal distances from the screen. In so doing, he introduced a
phase difference between the waves reflected by each mirror.
But because the waves came from the same source (the slit),

their phase differences were orderly; they were coherent. And when they interfered, they produced fringes like the rings depicted on pages 154–160 of this book.

Interference patterns not only depend on an orderly phase difference, they are precisely determined by that difference. If you're ever in a mood to carry out Young's experiment, see what happens when you change the distance between the two holes (create a phase variation, in other words). You'll find that the closer the openings, the narrower the fringes (or beats) will be and the greater the number of fringes on the screen.

The hologram is an interference pattern. The distinction between what we call hologram and what Young and Fresnel produced is quantitative, not qualitative. Now, in no way am I being simplistic or minimizing the distinction (no more so than between a penny and a dollar). Ordinary interference patterns do not contain the code for a scene, because no scene lies in the waves' paths. Such patterns do record phase variations between waves, though, which is the final test of all things hologramic. Just to keep matters straight, however, unless I explicitly say otherwise, I will reserve the term *hologram* for interference patterns with actual messages.

The hologram was born in London on Easter Sunday morning, 1947. It was just a thought that day, an abstract idea that suddenly came alive in the imagination of a Hungarian refugee, the late Dennis Gabor. The invention itself, the first deliberately constructed hologram, came a little later. But even after Gabor published his experiments in the British journal *Nature* the following year, the hologram remained virtually unknown for a decade and a half. Gabor's rudimentary holograms had none of the dramatic qualities of holograms today; perhaps as few as two dozen people, worldwide, appreciated their implications. Not until 1971, after holography had blossomed into a whole new branch of optics, did Gabor finally receive the Nobel Prize.

Gabor often related his thinking on that fateful Easter morning. He hadn't set out to invent the hologram at all. His thoughts were on the electron microscope, then a crude and imperfect device. In theory, the electron microscope should have been able to resolve atoms.[7] (Indeed, some instruments do today.) But in 1947, theory was a long way from practice. "Why not take a bad electron picture," Gabor recounted in his Nobel lecture, "but one which contains the *whole* of the information, and correct it by optical means?"[8]

The entire idea hinged on phase. And Gabor solved the phase problem with the conceptual approach Albert Einstein had taken in theorizing mass-energy and, eventually, the universe itself. No wonder we lose the phase, Gabor thought, if there is nothing to compare it with! He would need a *reference*. He would have to deal with phase information in relative, not absolute, terms.

The big technical hurdle was coherency. How could he produce a coherent source? Gabor's answer was very similar to Young's and Fresnel's: Let light shine through a pinhole. If he set a tiny transparent object in the path of the beam, some waves — object waves — would pass through it, while others would not; the waves that missed the object would still collide with the object waves downstream, and that ought to create interference patterns. Those waves that missed the object would become his reference. And the interference patterns would be-

---

[7] *Resolution* refers to the optical separation of details in an object. Thus a microscope not only magnifies, it also resolves details. A number of factors make for resolving power. But wavelength is a critical factor. The shorter the wavelength, the more the beam will resolve. Electron waves are many thousands of times shorter than visible light waves.

[8] Gabor, 1972, p. 299.

come a record of the phase and amplitude differences between object and reference waves. He'd use a photographic plate to capture that pattern, he decided.

Recall the discussion about objects warping the amplitude and phase of waves? If the interference pattern is completely determined by the amplitude and phase spectra of interacting sets of waves, then what? The hologram plate ought to contain a complete code of that warp. The hologram should retain not only amplitude changes but also the relative phase variations imposed on the object waves.

It is hard to believe that such records had already been produced by other physicists. But as a matter of fact, x-ray crystallographers' diffraction patterns are holograms. Crystallographers take the information from the x-ray diffraction patterns and use the equations Kraut was talking about to deduce the images of the atoms in crystals. Gabor realized that he could do the same thing with a beam of light. He could physically decode the image. He realized that if he passed the original light through the hologram plate, instead of through the object, the shadows in the hologram would put the warp into those waves and the *complete* image would appear where the object had been. For this would reconstruct the image-bearing wavefront. When he tried it, it worked.

The object Gabor used for his very first hologram was a tiny transparent disc with a microscopic but monumental message etched onto it. It read, "Huygens, Young, Fresnel."

Gabor did not succeed with the electron microscope. In fact, his first hologram just barely reconstructed the message. "It was far from perfect," he quipped. But it was not his reconstruction that had made history. It was the idea.

Gabor's principle is very simple, in retrospect — so simple that only a genius could have seen through the taboos of the time to find the hologram amid the arcane and abstract properties of waves.

The hologram is an interference pattern, and interference is a subject taught in high school physics courses. To engineers and physicists, the hologram is a straightforward extension of elementary optics. Even the mathematics of the hologram are fairly simple. Crystallographers for some time had been doing the construction step of holography without calling it that. And a color technique developed in 1894 (the Lippman process) suggested even the reconstruction step. How then was it possible for the hologram to escape modern science until 1947?

Science is people. Scientists seldom try out in their laboratories what they do not believe in their guts. Recording the phase of light waves would violate the uncertainty principle. And nothing yet known has withstood the incredible power of the uncertainty principle, including the hologram. There's a subtle distinction, though, between phase and a code resulting from phase. But only an extraordinary mind could see this; and only an extraordinary person had the courage to proceed from there.

Gabor was no ordinary person. And in the early 1960s, in Michigan, two other extraordinary persons entered the scene — Emmett Leith and Juris Upatnieks. A small amount of work had been done in this field after Gabor's research; but Leith and Upatnieks turned Gabor's rudimentary discovery into holography as it is practiced today. And among their long string of remarkable inventions and discoveries was one that precipitated nothing less than hologramic memory theory itself.

The germ of hologramic memory is unmistakable in Gabor's original discoveries — in retrospect. A physicist named van

Heerden actually proposed an optical theory of memory in 1963; but his work went as unnoticed as Gabor's had. As in the case of the acorn and the oak, it is difficult to see the connection, a priori. Leith and Upatnieks did for the hologram what Gabor had done for interference in general: they extended it to its fullest dimensions.

Leith had worked on sophisticated radar, was a mathematical thinker, and thoroughly understood waves; and in 1955 he had become intrigued by the hologram. Upatnieks was a bench wizard, the kind of person who when you let him loose in a laboratory makes the impossible experiment work.

Gabor's so-called "in-line" method (because object lies between plate and source) put several restrictions on optical holograms. For instance, the object had to be transparent. This posed the problem of what to do about dense objects. Besides, we actually see most things in reflected light. Leith and Upatnieks applied an elaborate version of Fresnel's old trick: they used mirrors. Mirrors allowed them to invent "off-line" holograms, and to use reflected light. The light came from a point source. The beam passed through a special partially coated mirror, which produced two beams from the original; and other mirrors deflected the two beams along different paths. One beam, aimed at the object, supplied the object waves. The other beam furnished the reference waves. They by-passed the scene but intersected and interfered with the reflected object waves at the hologram plate.

Leith and Upatnieks used a narrow beam from an arc lamp to make their early holograms. But there was a problem. The holographed scene was still very small. To make holograms interesting, they needed a broad, diffuse light. But with ordinary light, a broad beam wouldn't be coherent.

So Leith and Upatnieks turned to the laser. The laser had been invented in 1960, shortly before Leith and Upatnieks tooled up to work on holograms. The laser is a source of extremely coherent light, not because it disobeys the uncertainty

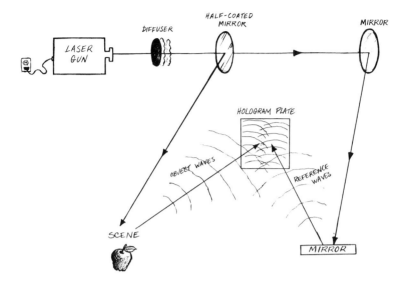

principle but because each burst of light involves a twin emission — two wave trains of identical phase and amplitude.

The insight Leith and Upatnieks brought to their work was profound. Back when holograms were very new, I had seen physicists wince at what Leith and Upatnieks did to advance their work. What they did was put a diffuser on the laser light source. A diffuser scatters light, which would seem to throw the waves into random cadence and total incoherency. Leith's theoretical insight said otherwise: the diffuser would add another order of complexity to the changes in the phase spectrum but would not cancel the coherent phase relationship between object and reference waves. Not if he was right, anyway! And Leith and Upatnieks went on to make a *diffuse-light hologram,* in spite of all the conventional reasons why it couldn't be done.

Gabor had tried to make his object act like a single point source. The encoded message spread out over the medium. But each point in the scene illuminated by diffuse light acts as though it

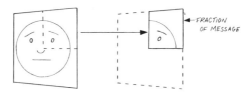

FRACTION
OF MESSAGE

DIFFUSE HOLOGRAM :

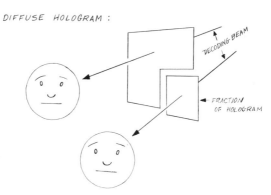

DECODING BEAM

FRACTION
OF HOLOGRAM

is a source in itself; and the consequence of all points acting as light sources is truly startling. Each point in the hologram plate ends up with the phase and amplitude warp of every point in the scene, which is the same as saying that every part of the exposed plate contains a complete record of the entire object. This may sound preposterous. Therefore, let me repeat: *Each point within a diffuse hologram bears a complete code for the entire scene.* If that seems strange, consider something else Leith and Upatnieks found: "The plate can be broken down into small fragments, and each piece will reconstruct the entire object."[9]

How can this be? We'll have to defer the complete answer until later. But recall the sizeless nature of relative phase, of

---

[9] See Leith and Upatnieks, 1964, p. 1297.

angles and degrees. The uncanny character of the diffuse hologram follows from the relative nature of phase information. In
theory, a hologram's codes may be of any size, ranging from the
proportions of a geometric point up to the magnitude of the entire universe.[10]

Leith and Upatnieks found that as fragments of holograms
became small, "resolution is, of course, lost, since the hologram constitutes the limiting aperture of the imaging process."[11]
They were saying that tiny pieces of a hologram will only accommodate a narrow beam of decoding light. As any signal carrier becomes very tiny, and thus very weak, "noise" erodes the
image. But vibrations, chatter, static — noise — have to do with
the carrier, not the stored message, which is total at every point
in the diffuse hologram. Even the blurred image, reconstructed
from the tiny chip, is still an image of the whole scene.

Not a word about mind or brain appeared in Leith and Upatnieks's articles. But to anyone even remotely familiar with Karl
Lashley's work, their descriptions had a very familiar ring. Indeed, substitute the term *brain* for *diffuse hologram,* and Leith
and Upatnieks's observations would aptly summarize Lashley's
lifelong assertions. Fragments of a diffuse hologram reconstruct
whole, if badly faded, images. Correspondingly, a damaged
brain still clings to whole, if blurred, memories. Sharpness of
the reconstructed image depends not on the specific fragment
of hologram but upon the fragment's size. Likewise, the efficiency with which Lashley's subjects remembered their tasks
depended not on which parts of the brain survived but on how
much brain the animal retained. "Mass action and equipoten-

---

[10] A physicist named Bohm has, in fact, proposed a holographic theory of the
universe.

[11] Leith and Upatnieks, 1964, p. 1297.

tiality!" Lashley might have shouted had he lived another six years.

Leith and Upatnieks published an account of the diffuse hologram in the November 1964 issue of the *Journal of the Optical Society of America*. The following spring, ink scarcely dry on the journal pages, Bela Julesz and K. S. Pennington explicitly proposed that memory in the living brain maps like information in the diffuse hologram. Hologramic theory had made a formal entry into scientific discourse.

Whom then should we credit for the idea of the hologramic mind? Lashley? He had forecast it in pointing to interference patterns. Van Heerden? He saw the connection. Pribram? The idea might not have made it into biology without his daring. The cyberneticist Philip Westlake, who wrote a doctoral dissertation to show that electrophysiological data fit the equations of holograms? Julesz and Pennington, for the courage to come right out and say so? I've spent many years unsuccessfully trying to decide just who and when. And I'm not really the person to say. But I am thoroughly convinced of this: subtract Leith and Upatnieks from the scene, and a thousand years could have slipped by with only an occasional van Heerden observing, unnoticed, how closely the hologram mimics the living brain. For the genesis of the theory recapitulates virtually the history of human thought: only after Pythagoras's earth became Columbus's world did it become perfectly obvious to everyone else that our planet was a sphere. And only after Gabor's principle became Leith and Upatnieks's diffuse hologram did science enter the age of the mind.

4

Mimics of Mind

THEORY, ABSTRACTION, AND ANALOGY are words used pejoratively by many writers, editors, and publishers of our general information, even in an age alternately sustained and menaced by the yield of theoretical physics. Yet theories provide a matrix for much of scientific knowledge. And whatever less committal synonym we may choose (principle, explanation, concept, generalization, for instance), theory is what we really demand of science when we apply the word *why* to questions about Nature.

Abstractions, in turn, are what theories really deal in: when we compare six apples with six oranges, we divide or square or multiply the numbers, the abstractions — not the pits or rinds. The test for determining a valid abstraction is: does it survive if we shift it to a new set of parochial conditions? The ninety-degree angle — the abstraction — made by the edges of a table top does not depend on oak or maple wood; it can be formed of brass, or asphalt, or two streaks of chalk.

The analogy has its intellectual justification in the first axiom of geometry: things equal to the same things are equal to each other. Things dependent upon the same abstractions are analogues of each other!

Analogy can show us what a theory *does,* but not what a theory *is.* Nor does analogy provide a rigorous test of a theory's applicability to a problem. Analogies can't serve as substitutes for experiments, in other words. Nonetheless analogies often reveal a theory's implications. They also help connect abstractions to some concrete reality; they often put us in a position to grasp the main idea of a theory with our intuition. The analogy can also expose a subject and show important consequences of a theory, even to those who do not know the strange language of the theory. The analogy can put the theory to work on a human being's familiar ground — experience. It is by way of the analogy that I shall introduce the reader to hologramic theory.

The hologram is not a phenomenon of light, per se, but of waves — in theory, any waves or wavelike events. I've already mentioned acoustical holograms. X-ray holograms, microwave holograms, and electron holograms also exist, as do "computer" holograms, which are holograms constructed from mathematical equations and reconstructed by the computer — holograms, in other words, of objects comprised of pure thought.

The same kinds of equations can describe holograms of all sorts. And the very same phase code can exist simultaneously in several different media. Take acoustical holograms, for instance. The acoustical holographer produces his hologram by transmitting sound waves through an object. (Solids transmit sound as shock vibrations, as, for example, when someone knocks on a door.) He records the interference patterns with a microphone and displays his hologram on a television tube. Sound waves cannot stimulate the light receptors in our retinas. Thus *we* would not be able to "see" what a sonic wave would reconstruct. But the acoustical holographer can still present the scene to us by making a photograph of the hologram on the TV tube. Then, by shining a laser through the photograph, he reconstructs optically — and therefore visibly — the images he originally holographed by sound.

Sound is not light, nor is it the electronic signals in the television set. But *information* carried in the phase and amplitude of sound or electronic waves can be an *analogue* of the same message or image in a light beam, and vice versa. It is the code, the abstract logic, that the different media must share, not the chemistry. For holograms are encoded, stored information. They are memories in the most exacting sense of the word — in the mathematical sense. They are abstractable relationships between constituents of the medium, not the constituents themselves. And abstract information is what hologramic theory is about.

As I said in the preceding chapter, the inherent logic in waves shows up in many activities, motions, and geometric patterns. For example, the equations of waves can describe a swinging pendulum; a vibrating drum head; flapping butterfly wings; cycling hands of a clock; beating hearts; planets orbiting the sun, or electrons circling an atom's nucleus; the thrust and return of an auto engine's pistons; the spacing of atoms in a crystal; the rise and fall of the tide; the recurrence of the seasons. The terms *harmonic motion, periodic motion,* and *wave motion* are interchangeable. The to-and-fro activity of an oscillating crystal, the pulsations in an artery, and the rhythm in a song are analogues of the rise and fall of waves. Under the electron microscope, the fibers of our connective tissues (collagen fibers) show what anatomists call periodicity, meaning a banded, repeated pattern occurring along the fiber's length. The pattern is also an analogue of waves.

Of course a periodically patterned connective-tissue fiber is not literally a wave. It is a piece of protein. A pendulum is not a wave, either, but brass or wood or ivory. And the head of a tom-tom isn't the stormy sea, but the erstwhile hide of an unlucky jackass. Motions, activities, patterns, and waves all obey a common set of abstract rules. And any wavy wave or wavelike event can be defined, described, or, given the engineering wherewithal, reproduced, if one knows amplitude and phase. A crystallographer who calculates the phase and amplitude spectra of a crystal's x-ray diffraction pattern knows the internal anatomy of that crystal in minute detail. An astronomer who knows the phase and amplitude of a planet's moon knows precisely where and when he can take its picture. But let me repeat: the theorist's emphasis is not on the nominalistic fact. It is on logic, which is the basis of the hologram.

Nor, in theory, does the hologram necessarily depend on the literal interference of wavy waves. In the acoustical hologram, for example, where is the information? Is it in the interferences of the sonic wave fronts? In the microphone? In the voltage fluctuations initiated by the vibrating microphone? In oscillations among particles within the electronic components of the television set? On the television screen? On the photograph? The answer is that the code — the relationships — and therefore the hologram itself, exists — or once existed — in all these places, sometimes in a form we can readily appreciate as wavy information, and in other instances as motion or activity, in forms that don't even remotely resemble what we usually think of as waves.

Lashley's experiments can be applied to diffuse holograms, as I have pointed out. His results depended not on *where* he injured the brain but on *how much*. Likewise, cropping a corner from a diffuse hologram does not amputate parts from the regenerated scene. Nor does cutting a hole in the center or anywhere else. The remaining hologram still produces an entire scene. In fact, even the amputated pieces reconstruct a whole scene — the same whole scene. What Lashley had inferred about the memory trace is true for the diffuse hologram as well: the code in a diffuse hologram is equipotentially represented throughout the diffuse hologram.

The loss of detail that occurs when we decode a small piece of diffuse hologram is not a property of the code itself. Blurring results mainly from noise, not from the signal. How seriously noise affects the quality of an incoming message depends on the ratio of noise to signal. If the signal is powerful, we may dampen noise by reducing volume or brightness. But with very weak signals, as short-wave radio buffs can testify, a small amount of noise (static) severely impedes reception. In optical holograms, the relative level of noise increases as the size of the hologram decreases. And in a small enough piece of hologram, noise can disperse the image.

We have already made the analogy between the survival of memory in a damaged brain and the survival of image in a marred hologram. Signal-to-noise ratio is really an analogue of the decline in efficiency found in Lashley's subjects. In other words, the less brain, the weaker the signal and the greater the deleterious consequence of "neural noise."

Loss of detail in an image produced from a small chip of hologram is a function of decoding, not of the code itself. An infinitesimally small code still exists at every point in the diffuse hologram. Like a single geometric point, the individual code is a theoretical, not a physical, entity. As with geometric points, we deal with codes physically in groups, not as individuals. But the presence of a code at every location is what accounts for the demonstrable fact that any arbitrarily chosen sector of the hologram produces the same scene as any other sector. Granted, this property may not be easy to fathom; for nothing in our everyday experience is like a diffuse hologram. Otherwise, the mind would have been the subject of scientific inquiry long before Leith and Upatnieks.

If a single holographic code is so very, very tiny, any physical area should be able to contain many codes — infinitely many, in theory.[1] Nor would the codes all have to resemble each other. Leith and Upatnieks recognized these properties early in their work. Then, turning theory into practice, they went on to invent the "multiple hologram" — several different holograms actually stacked together within the same film.

With several holograms in the same film, how could reconstruction proceed without producing utter chaos? How might individual scenes be reconstructed, one at a time? Leith and Upatnieks simply extended the basic operating rules of holography they themselves had developed. During reconstruction, the beam must pass through the film at a critical angle — an angle approximating the one at which the construction beam originally met the film. Thus, during multiple constructions, Leith and Upatnieks set up each hologram at a different angle. Then, during reconstruction, a tilt of the film in the beam was sufficient for one scene to be forgotten and the other remembered.

One of Leith and Upatnieks's most famous multiple holograms is of a little toy chick on wheels. The toy dips over to peck the surface when it's dragged along. Leith and Upatnieks holographed the toy in various positions, tilting the film at each step. Then, during reconstruction, by rotating the film at the correct tempo, they produced images of the little chick, in motion, pecking away at the surface as though going after cracked corn. Some variant of their basic idea could become the cinema and TV of tomorrow.

---

[1] Collier et al., 1971, p. 455, note that certain holograms would be able to store "50 bibles [in] one square inch."

Multiple holograms permit us to conceptualize something neither Lashley nor anyone else had ever satisfactorily explained:
how one brain can house more than one memory. If the engram
is reduplicated and also equally represented throughout the
brain, how can room remain for the next thing the animal
learns? Multiple holograms illustrate the fact that many codes
can be packed together in the same space.

Just as important, multiple holograms mimic the actual
recalling and forgetting processes: tilt the film in the reconstruction beam, and, instantly, off goes one scene and on comes
the next. A few years ago, I met a young man named John Kilpatrick who suggested that a person trying to recollect something may be searching for the equivalent of the correct reconstruction angle.

But suppose that instead of using a single reconstruction
beam, we use several. And suppose we pass the beams through
the multiple hologram at different angles. We may, in this manner, synthesize a composite scene. And the objects in the composite scene may never have been together in objective reality.
When the human mind synthesizes memories into unprece-
dented subjective scenes, we apply terms such as *thinking,
reasoning, imagining,* and even *hallucinating.* In other words,
built right into the hologramic model are analogues of much
human mental activity.

Holography does not require the use of lenses. But lenses may
be employed to produce certain special effects. Leith and Upatnieks showed in one of their earliest experiments that when the
holographer uses a lens during construction, he must use an
identical lens for reconstruction. This fact should (and probably
does) interest spies. For not even Gabor or Leith and Upatnieks
could read the holographic message directly. It is a code in the
most cloak-and-dagger sense of the word. A hologram must be

decoded by the appropriate reconstruction beam, under specific conditions. And a lens with an unusual crack in it would create an uncrackable code for all who do not possess that same cracked lens.

A combination of different construction angles and flawed lenses might also be used to simulate malfunctions of the mind. Suppose a holographer makes a hologram of, say, a bedroom wall, and onto the same film also encodes the image of an elephant, using a lens at this stage. Given the appropriate conditions, he could synthesize the bizarre scene of a pink elephant emerging from the bedroom wall. Humans hallucinate similar scenes during delirium tremens.

Leith and Upatnieks also made color part of holography. Physically, a particular hue is the result of a specific energy or wavelength. What we usually think of as light is a range of energies lying in the visible region of the electromagnetic spectrum. Molecules in our rods and cones make the visible region visible. Red light lies on the weaker end of the spectrum, while violet is on the stronger end. Thus, *infra*red waves have energies just below red and *ultra*violet waves are stronger than violet. Physicists often deal with color in conjunction with the subject known as dispersion. For when white light, say a sun ray, passes through a prism, the beam disperses into red, yellow, green, and blue light. (Dispersion also accounts for rainbows.) White light, remember, is a so-called spectral mixture. And full-color illumination of a multicolored scene requires white light.

It is possible to produce white light by mixing red, green, and blue lights. Thus the latter are called the additive primary colors. Not only will they produce white light but varying combinations of them can yield the half-million or more hues we discriminate.

The colors we see depend on which wavelengths reach the

retina. The pigment in a swath of red paint looks red in white light because the molecules absorb the other wavelengths and reflect red back to our eyes. The sky looks blue on a clear day because the atmosphere absorbs all but the energetic blue violets. The sea looks black on a moonless night because nearly all the visible wavelengths have been absorbed. Light is energy. Thus tar on a roof heats much more in the sunlight than does a white straw Panama hat; the tar has absorbed more energy than the hat and has therefore reflected less.

Photometrists use the word *additive* to describe red, green, and blue lights because *subtractive* primaries also exist: magenta, yellow, and green-blue. When magenta, yellow, and green-blue filters are placed in the path of a beam of white light, no visible light can pass through. The result is sometimes called black light. Black light is a potential product of even the three additive primary colors. For red and blue can produce magenta; green and blue can produce yellow, and, if the mix is right, some green-blue as well. And a beam of white light — a mixture of the primaries, red, green, and blue — can color a scene white, black, or anything in between, depending on the relative amounts of each primary color.

Leith and Upatnieks described how they would "illuminate a scene with coherent light in each of three primary colors, and the hologram would receive reflected light of each color." Now the hologram plate itself was black and white. For the hologram remembered not color itself but a code for color. Yet when Leith and Upatnieks passed a red-green-blue beam through the hologram, they produced, in their words, "the object in full color."[2]

Offhand, it might seem as though the reconstruction beam would have to be the same color as the original light source. But Leith's equations said something different: the reconstruction

---

[2] See Leith and Upatnieks, 1964, p. 1301.

beam's wavelength must be *equal to or shorter than* that of the
original. He and Upatnieks tested the hypothesis, and it
worked: they could change the scene from one color to another,
provided that the decoding beam's wavelength did not exceed
that of the original beam.

Let's put this property to use in our analogies.

Color manipulations permit us to mimic a number of mental activities. For example, suppose we construct a hologram with
green light. During reconstruction, suppose we use light with
wavelengths longer than green — red, for instance. The rule for
"remembering" the scene is to use a wavelength equal to or
shorter than the original. Thus the red light cannot regenerate
the scene. But the hologram still has a memory of the scene,
doesn't it? We simply can't decode with red. As is the case with
construction angles in the multiple hologram, displaying the information means satisfying certain conditions — wavelength, in
the case of color.

Kilpatrick's scanning model might employ wavelength as
well as angle of tilt to simulate the act of recalling a memory.
(Indeed, the use of both would make a more versatile model.)
Suppose we use a blue reconstruction beam, which has a
shorter wavelength than green. Then we would produce a scene
from a hologram constructed with green light, although the
color of the scene would be blue instead of green. Suppose we
don't know the original color. If we began scanning from the
red end, we would pass through a considerable portion of the
visible spectrum before any scene at all appeared. But once into
the green zone, we would reconstruct the scene through a vast
range of greens, blues, and violets and never know what wavelengths we used during construction.

Think of our own recollection process. How often have you
scanned your memory to recall a past experience and, having

recalled it, seen it in your mind's eye with different details from those of the experience itself? We almost never remember things perfectly. What would happen if we used red-green-blue in our model? We could vary the reconstruction wavelengths over a vast range indeed. We might contrive a wavelength mixture where, suddenly, everything seems to go blank. These properties give the hologram many features that Freud and his followers envisaged for the human mind.

Can we actually simulate the subconscious with holograms? A model is implicit in what I have already described. To illustrate it further, let's return to our green hologram. Suppose that during scanning we move off into ultraviolet wavelengths, beyond the visible region of the spectrum. The wavelengths there are shorter than green, and thus fully able to regenerate an image. But beyond the visible spectrum, the image would be invisible; and we would have to use special film or meters in order to detect it. Invisible or not, the image would burn itself into our retinas if we were foolish enough to look in its direction long enough, for the same reasons that we can suffer severe sunburns on cloudy days. Likewise, our physiology can come under incredible stress from thoughts, feelings, and so forth that do not surface in the conscious mind.

Acoustical holographers also do very interesting things with color. In an excellent *Scientific American* article in 1969, Alexander Metherell reported his methods for making full-color holograms. He used sonic waves of three different frequencies, but frequencies whose *ratios* corresponded with red-green-blue. He then used mixtures of light to reconstruct multicolored scenes. Sound is not light, of course. Nor are sonic frequencies colors. Metherell's experiments dramatize the truly abstract nature of the hologram's code. He encoded color not with wavelengths but with *ratios of wavelengths*.

Metherell's experiments suggest many features of mind we have already discussed. In addition, they hint at a physical model of language.

Modern theoretical linguists believe that languages do not evolve pell-mell from the raw sound-producing capabilities of our voiceboxes, tongues, cheeks, teeth, and so on; all languages, they believe, follow certain general rules of syntax. Still, German is not Korean. In Metherell's experiments, ratio was the rule. But to reconstruct a specific color, Metherell did have to pay attention to specific wavelengths. Wavelength ratio can serve as an analogue of the general rules of syntax, and specific wavelengths can be models of the particular features of a language.

But Metherell's experiments go beyond the spoken word. They contain the elements of translation: translation from sound to light. Built into his system is a whole scene-shifting, from one medium to the other, with an abstract code to do the remembering. We are constantly shifting our language modalities — writing notes at a lecture, dictating words destined for print. Consider the many forms English may take: script, sound, shorthand, print, Braille, Morse code, American Sign Language. We need abstract codes — like those in Metherell's holograms — to move among the analogues on a whole-message basis.

Color holography and multiple holograms also supply models for the results of split-brain research. Recall that persons who underwent the split-brain operation behaved as though their right and left cerebral hemispheres knew different things. Yet the operation did not derange them; they remained, as Gazzaniga said, "just folks." A hemisphere knew *whole* messages.

Suppose we decide to construct two holograms of an elephant, on the same piece of film, using two different angles, with, say, red at one angle and blue at the other. Remember that the reconstruction beam must contain wavelengths equal to or shorter than the original. During reconstruction with blue light, either angle will reproduce our elephant's image; but red will work at only one angle. Still, whenever we do reconstruct the elephant's image, it is a whole image, not a tusk here, a trunk there. Wavelength manipulations, in other words, allow us to simulate the observations reported by split-brain researchers.

We can envisage another model for split-brain. Suppose we shade the left side of the film during one step of construction. Obviously, we would be able to reconstruct scenes from the right side that we would not get from the left. Gazzaniga's observations hint at the possibility that humans learn to direct certain information to only one hemisphere. Active inhibition occurs on a grand scale in the nervous system, and at levels from individual cells to whole lobes. It is not inconceivable that shading in our experiment would serve as an analogue of inhibition.

A toddler I once knew went into a gleeful prance whenever her young father entered the room. Around the perimeter of her playpen she would march, damp diaper at half-mast, singing "Dadadada!" until the man rested his chin on the rail next to her little face to receive a moist kiss. One day he came home wearing new eyeglasses. The toddler began her routine but then broke off, frowning, on the first "Da," as she apprehended the change. When he bent down, she placed a wet finger on one of the curious lenses, and, maintaining the frown, continued, "dadadada!" at a puzzled pace.

No physical hologram, multiple or otherwise, matches the complexity of that toddler in action. But holograms used in the materials-testing industry suggest one feature of her behavior, namely, the instantaneous — and simultaneous — recognition of both the familiar and unfamiliar attributes in a scene. The technique is known as interference holography and involves looking at an object through a hologram of it. The light waves coming from the object and the hologram superimpose interference fringes on the object's image. Any locus where the object has changed since its hologram was made will reflect light differently than before. And in that area the interference patterns converge toward the point of change. The method is extremely sensitive. Even the pressure of a finger on a block of granite shows up immediately. The observer is immediately aware of the change but can also recognize the object in the background.

In a splendid article they wrote for *Scientific American* in 1965, Leith and Upatnieks made an interesting comparison between holograms and FM signals. FM is, of course, the abbreviation for frequency modulation, and it is the form in which TV and FM radio stations broadcast. Frequency, remember, refers to the number of cycles occurring during a given period of time. In FM, the amplitudes of the radio waves stay constant while their frequencies vary, or modulate, to carry the message. As waves contract or expand, their peaks, or amplitudes, shift. Phase, remember, specifies the location of amplitude. As many engineers describe it, and as Leith and Upatnieks point out, FM is in effect *phase modulation,* the generic feature of all holograms.

Physiologists have known for some time that neural signals involve frequency modulation (see Brinley), and therefore variations in phase. The reason for this has to do with the nature of the main neural signal carrier, the nerve impulse.

A nerve impulse shows up on the physiologist's oscilloscope as a traveling electronic wavelet. What's on the scope represents a wavelike voltage flux on the exterior of the neuron's membrane, and is often called a "spike." Now the impulse obeys what is called the all-or-none law. This means, first of all, that the cell must absorb stimulation at or above a particular threshold, or else it won't fire an impulse; second, that the impulse travels at a constant rate and maintains uniform amplitude throughout its passage along the membrane; third, that increasing the stimulus above threshold will not make the impulse move faster or become stronger. Also, immediately after the appearance of the spike, and for a brief duration as the cell recocks itself, the membrane won't carry an impulse. This interval is called the absolute refractory period. The refractory period prevents impulse additions. With threshold in the van and the refractory period in the wake, the impulse becomes a wave of constant amplitude. What's left to turn impulses into signals? The *number* of impulses per unit of time — frequency or phase modulation, the fundamental principle in hologramic theory.

Groups of neurons, some firing (ON), others inhibited (OFF), can produce arrays of ON-OFF in the nervous system. This is very conspicuous on the retina and in the LGB. Some time ago, Karl Pribram, going counter to conventional thinking, analogized such ON-OFF arrays to interference patterns — implicating phase modulation, and, of course, the hologram. In more recent years, physiologists have been finding what Pribram suggested. Today, phase has become a major topic in sensory physiology, especially in vision research.[3]

Thus we do not have to search very far or long to make analogies between the generic principle of the hologram, wave phase, and the physiology of the brain.

My purpose is not to oversimplify the mind. The important

[3] See Finlay and Caelli, 1979; Pollen et al., 1971, 1979; De Valois et al., 1979; and earlier references in Pribram, 1971*b*.

question is: Do we find nonliving analogues of ourselves out there? The answer is yes.

But analogy is too casual and conjectural a process to suit scientific verification. A theory must justify itself in experiments. And this is where shufflebrain comes into the story.

5

Shufflebrain

HOLOGRAMIC THEORY can explain the otherwise paradoxical body of facts about brain damage. The theory also accounts for Lashley's findings. But neither his experiments nor the volumes of anecdotal information on the injured brain provide critical tests of hologramic theory's most important predictions. Let me illustrate this with an imaginary experiment. Envisage three or four transparent plastic sheets on which we have photocopied and reproduced the message: ANATOMY. As in a diffuse hologram, our message is redundant. But it is not hologramic, not truly "distributed" as in an interference pattern. ANATOMY is "anatogramic," as I once thought memory was.

Think of the space each letter occupies as a specific, independent "set" on the sheet. The meaning of our message devolves from the relationship *among* a sheet's sets. We can even define "meaning" from the organization — the anatomy — of the sheet: What's in each set? How do the sets interrelate? The specific answers define the specific message.

How do we simulate the brain with our sheets? More specifically, what can we do to model structural order among the several redundant sheets? The simplest way is to stack all sheets in exact correspondence or, as the printer says, perfect register.

The first thing we want to do is to *observe* our system —

look at its output or readout, as information theorists call the display. The output, the analogue of behavior, is what we see on the surface. With the sheets of the stack in perfect register, the output is obviously ANATOMY. But how many messages do we have in the system? We already know the answer for our imaginary system. But the brain is an unknown.

What happens when we remove the first sheet? Obviously, we still read ANATOMY at the surface; a little lighter, perhaps, but with its meaning quite intact. Does it make any difference which sheet we remove? Obviously not. Suppose we erase or snip off the "TOMY" on the first sheet? Suppose we take "ANA" away from the bottom sheet and "TOMY" away from the second? We may introduce subtle variations in intensity, but the meaning of our message survives as long as we maintain the equivalence of a sheet's worth of ANATOMY. We can only destroy meaning at the surface if we clean out every last sheet of a particular set.

Our experiments model Lashley's experiments and lead to his basic conclusions. The important consideration is not *where* we erase or cut but *how much*. And there is nothing equipotential about our system. (The set on the left certainly isn't the same as that on the right!) These imaginary experiments served as my intellectual justification for rejecting Lashley's conclusions long before the hologram came along. They illustrate the theory I believed would account for regeneration as well as memory.

In designing an adequate test of hologramic theory, it is useful to ask why we were able to simulate Lashley's findings. The major reasons are these: First, our message is redundant. Second, we can preserve the analogue of structural order by keeping the stack in register. Third, by subtracting or erasing we can create the equivalents of empty or blank sets. We did nothing to the carriers of *meaning,* or to the free access surviving sets had to the readout. If our system had been an unknown, our subtraction experiments would merely tell us of its

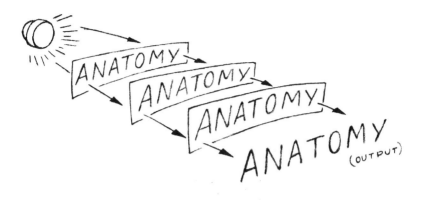

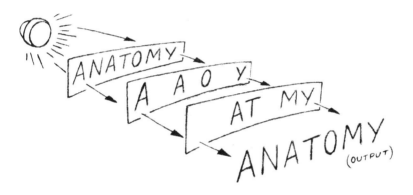

redundancy, and this property of the brain's information has been recognized since ancient times.

Suppose that instead of erasing sets, we rotate one of our sheets 180 degrees. Obviously, this manipulation will change the quality of our readout. Or suppose we switch the Y with the T? And what would happen if we simply gave the stack a shove and knocked the sheets out of register? The moment we alter the carriers of meaning, or anatomy, we distort the message.

But in a hologram, the carrier of meaning, or phase, cannot be reached with an eraser or a knife. Unlike our sheets, the hologramic code ought to survive any anatomical changes we

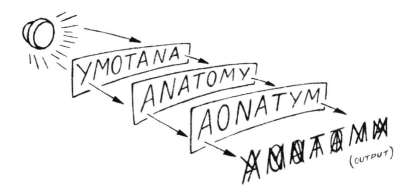

make. Herein is hologramic theory's most astonishing prediction: *shuffling the brain will not scramble the mind!* And how might we shuffle a living brain? The answer is embodied in the salamander.

Salamanders are amphibians, taxonomically one step up from fishes and a half-step down from frogs and toads. They begin life as aquatic creatures, and, a few species excepted, they undergo metamorphosis, become land-dwelling animals, and only return to the water to make new salamanders. As larvae — the equivalents of toad and frog tadpoles, and before metamorphosis — salamanders of the genus I work with range down in size from the proportions of a six-year-old child's index finger, their digits barely discernible to the naked eye. Under a stereoscopic dissecting microscope, you can see blood corpuscles racing, scarlet, through vessels beneath transparent tissues, turning crimson as they reach the brushlike external gills on either side of the head. The external gills, which they lose at metamorphosis, take oxygen from, and give carbon dioxide to, the clear spring-water environment. The larva does have lungs, but they are functionless little cellophanelike bags, until the animal gets ready to move onto land. The larva's coloration recapitulates the basins and banks of its native woodland waters in the sunlight of an early spring morning: a thousand continuous hues of soft yellow; browns that range from almost-black through Dutch chocolate to the shades on the belly of a fawn; silver, in spots and patches, glinting like a slick of frost or a drop of dew. The larva's brain, textured like lightly polished Carrara marble and narrower than the letters on this page, can slip through the eye of a needle. Nevertheless, the tiny brain has the same major anatomical subdivisions as our own: cerebrum, diencephalon, midbrain, cerebellum, medulla. And within those minuscule neuroanatomical entities, somewhere, lie the programs for a range of complex, if primitive, behaviors.

Aside from flight, the most conspicuous manifestation of a salamander larva's mind is the quest for food. The salamander is a carnivore, but it is programmed to eat only living organisms. If it is hungry — and it usually is — the salamander will attack and devour whatever moves and can fit between its jaws. Indeed, it is to a crimson threadlike tubifex worm, or a dainty daphnia, what a hungry wolf is to a careless pack rat or a stray lamb: imminent death.

Salamanders are born with the instinct to hunt. In the embryo stage, yellow-white yolk fills their stomachs and intestines. Traces of yolk persist into the early larval periods; but within hours after the last molecules of the yolk have been consumed, thus clearing the alimentary passageway for a meal, the larva is ready to strike at any prospective quarry. Although feeding seems instinctive, behavioral nuances may be imprinted during early encounters with prey. The greater the struggle at the stage when feeding begins, the more finesse the larva shows in subsequent attacks. But animals deprived of early attack experiences still hunt later on, only with less elegance and efficiency.[1]

The active nature of the salamander's feeding is apparent

---

[1] I made these observations during preliminary experiments in an unsuccessful effort to produce nonfeeding subjects.

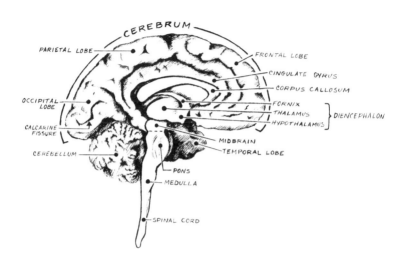

CEREBRUM

PARIETAL LOBE

FRONTAL LOBE

CINGULATE GYRUS

CORPUS CALLOSUM

OCCIPITAL LOBE

FORNIX
THALAMUS
HYPOTHALAMUS
} DIENCEPHALON

CALCARINE FISSURE

MIDBRAIN

TEMPORAL LOBE

CEREBELLUM

PONS

MEDULLA

SPINAL CORD

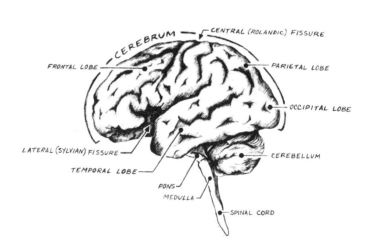

CEREBRUM

CENTRAL (ROLANDIC) FISSURE

FRONTAL LOBE

PARIETAL LOBE

OCCIPITAL LOBE

LATERAL (SYLVIAN) FISSURE

CEREBELLUM

TEMPORAL LOBE

PONS

MEDULLA

SPINAL CORD

in its movements in relation to different kinds of prey. When it is preying on water fleas, daphnia, or brine-shrimp embryos — any creature that jets through the water in jerky little spurts — the salamander larva waits motionlessly, poised, until the victim comes close to its snout. Then, snap! The larva's move is quick, sudden, accurate, and deadly. Then it settles down to wait for more.

But with wriggling worms, such as the threadlike crimson tubifex or their cousins, the milk-white encyhtreas, the salamander's response is quite different. When it first senses a worm, it freezes, hangs suspended in the water, or stands stock still at the bottom of the bowl. Moments may pass as it seems to be fixing the location of the worm. Then, slowly, it turns, usually pausing again, perhaps to recheck the azimuth of the prospective course. Half-walking, half-swimming, it now glides cautiously toward the fated worm. At its destination, it usually pauses once more, and carefully, deliberately, moves its head

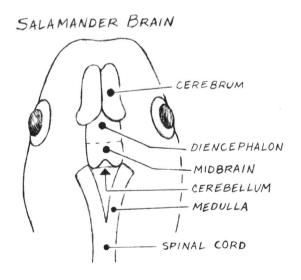

SALAMANDER BRAIN

CEREBRUM

DIENCEPHALON

MIDBRAIN

CEREBELLUM

MEDULLA

SPINAL CORD

back, forth, and around the undulating mass, as though computing the tensor algebra of the quarry's ever-varying geometry. I have seen this sizing-up stage last thirty or forty seconds. The salamander takes one last momentary pause. Then comes the strike. And into it the salamander throws every bit of its might. The attack is not the "blip," as with brine shrimp or daphnia, but a ferocious, violent assault that would knock down a building, if the salamander were the size of a tiger shark. It locks the worm in its jaws and hangs on, no matter what escape maneuver the squirming victim tries; and it swallows the worm, live, bit by bit. If the worm is relatively short, it goes down quickly. If not, the process may take minutes, the salamander holding on with such tenacity that it can actually be lifted from the water by the free end of the catch.

Salamander larvae sense their prey in three known ways: sight, touch, and sonar — shock-wave detection via what is called the lateral line system. The larva has the anatomy for smell, but by all indications it doesn't use this sense until it becomes a land animal. It can use its other senses singly and in combinations, but has a very strong predilection for the eyes, when it has them. For example, an animal with only one eye will turn, twist, and aim the eye for a good look at a worm before making a strike. Yet an eyeless salamander can use either sonar or touch to launch a completely successful attack.

The salamander's capacity to endure massive injury has fascinated biologists ever since 1768, when Lazzaro Spallanzani published the fact that they regenerate lost appendages. In larvae, a fully functioning replica replaces an amputated leg or tail in a month to six weeks; in adults, the process may take a year or more. Regeneration occurs again and again following subsequent amputations, as Spallanzani reported. Other organs and tissues regenerate as well. A severed optic nerve, for example, reestablishes contact with the brain, and the eye can see again. In fact, almost all their nerve fibers grow back. Following an incision into the brain, new nerve fibers quickly sprout and soon reknit a completely functional patch across the rift.

Larval salamanders are also excellent recipients of tissue and organ transplants. They do possess tissue-rejecting mechanisms, but rejection is very sluggish and inefficient, and often fails completely, the foreign graft becoming a permanent part of the host animal.

The larva's small size necessitates the use of a dissecting microscope for operations. With experience, the surgery becomes routine and requires only a few inexpensive tools. An anesthetic (MS 222), dissolved in the water, renders the animal unconscious.[2] A cream-colored Vermont marble clay lines the bottom of the operating dish, the clay molded to complement the contours of a salamander's belly. Ordinary straight pins, plunged into the clay and then crossed, truss the animal into the desired position. A needle with its point honed serves as the scalpel. But I use iridectomy (iris) scissors for most of the cutting, and "Genuine du Mont et fils" Swiss watchmakers' forceps for grasping, manipulating, and blunt dissecting.

The larva's skull cap consists of two microscopically thin translucent membranes, the forerunners of bony plates. The membranes meet at a midline seam, or raphe, and an upward longitudinal stroke with the tips of the iridectomy scissors quickly separates them, thus exposing the brain. Even after the skull ossifies into bone, the opening up of the cranium requires no more force than does clipping a fingernail. Hemorrhage is not serious, and is no problem at all with larvae. Working under

---

[2] What if the anesthetic only paralyzes the salamanders and they merely can't display signs of agony? I lived with this unpleasant thought for many years, until a graduate student in my lab began probing salamander brains for electrical activity in response to tactile and visual stimulation. He found, to my relief, that MS 222, at concentrations that immobilize the animals, turns off stimuli-related electrical activity of the brain.

the dissecting microscope, the operator can see and avoid the tiniest blood vessels. When the experiment makes cutting a vessel necessary, clots form rapidly and plug the leaks quickly. Unlike the organs of higher animals, those of the salamander can survive for days without a blood supply, particularly in a cool environment. In fact, the animal may be bled entirely and yet remain alive for a time. (In the early 1950s the embryologist Meryl Rose actually raised a colony of bloodless tadpoles.) The chilled animal's slowed metabolism reduces its demand for oxygen. After surgery, the thin skin lets sufficient oxygen pass in from the water to keep a transplanted organ alive until the host's vasculature hooks into it.

For operations on larvae, sutures are unnecessary. But it is essential to cover a wound with skin. When gently pressed together, the cut edges of the skin adhere and send battalions of cells over the incision. Within days the line of incision has disappeared completely. (Adult skin may require stitches, however.)

The salamander larva was an excellent candidate for shufflebrain experiments on an additional count. After the healing period, messages would relay freely between the spinal cord and the shuffled brain. How did I know this? Some of my confidence grew out of an extensive series of preliminary experiments I will mention briefly in a moment. But as a student trying to teach myself the art of transplanting tiny organs, I assigned myself exercises involving the larval salamander's brain. First, I would make a tunnel in the jellylike connective tissue of the dorsal fin. Then I would amputate the brain, and store it in the tunnel. The animal, of course, went into a stupor. How did I know whether the brain had survived (whether I had passed or flunked my test)? After some days, I would return the brain to the cranium. Most animals survived. And in eight to twenty days, they recovered consciousness.

Preliminary to shufflebrain experiments, I conducted a systematic investigation of the salamander larva's medulla, the transition zone between the rest of the brain and the spinal cord. When I destroyed the medulla, the animals became unconscious and died within two weeks. If I left the medulla intact, and amputated the brain immediately in front of it, the animals went into permanent stupor but remained alive for many months.

To interpret my experimental results, I had to control variables associated with brain regeneration. Other investigators had reported that a larval salamander's cerebral hemispheres regenerate but that lower regions of its brain do not.[3] I repeated and confirmed these observations: cerebral hemispheres regenerated in about six weeks, and I found no restoration of lower parts of the brain, even after several months. Six weeks was plenty of leeway for shufflebrain, for I knew from student days that two pieces of brain tissue could easily weave a functional bridge within three weeks. My results would be harvested well before regeneration became a factor. Still, I wanted a more positive way to eliminate regeneration, just in case long-term experiments became necessary. A grafted organ can prevent regeneration of a lost part. Reattach an amputated limb, for example, and, if it heals properly, no new parts regenerate. I had performed many such experiments. Perhaps I could prevent regeneration if I grafted the spinal cord in place of the amputated cerebrum. I experimented. Indeed, the spinal-cord segment quickly attached to the stump, and no new cerebrum developed. In fact, I found that any portion of the central nervous system would quickly weave fibers into the stump, and substitute for, and prevent regeneration of, any other part of the brain. The transplants retained their original anatomy.

---

[3] The salamander embryo's midbrain regenerates; see Detwiler, 1948.

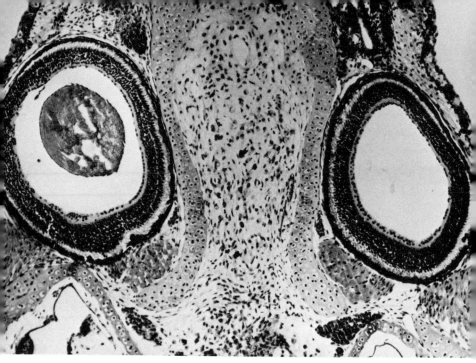

A section through the head of an essentially brainless salamander larva, an example of "blanking." The large circular objects toward the left and right edges of the photograph are the eyes. The zone between them should be filled with brain. In this specimen, connective tissue cells fill the cranium. This animal lived for many months after its brain was amputated and was "behaviorally inert" during the entire period.

My first formal plunge into shufflebrain experiments involved repetition of Lashley's basic operation. I mapped the brain into regions. Then, in an extensive series of operations, I replaced given map regions with pieces of spinal cord, systematically moving down the brain, region by region, among the various subgroups of experimental animals.

The animals invariably fed the moment they recovered from postoperative stupor, no matter which region I removed.

Massive destruction of the brain reduced feeding but did not stop it. Clearly, there was no exclusive repository of feeding programs in any single part of the salamander's brain.

My next series of experiments involved interchanging right and left hemispheres. Feeding survived. Next, I tried rotating the cerebral hemispheres 180 degrees around their long axes so that up faced down and down faced up. I did this with each hemisphere separately and then with both simultaneously. Feeding survived. Next I turned the cerebral hemispheres around so that the front faced to the rear. Feeding survived.

I then moved down to the diencephalon, where the optic nerves enter the brain. I knew from my own observations and from the vast literature on the subject that disturbing the diencephalon might affect vision. But I was sure that touch and sonar from the lateral line system would enable the animal to sense the worm. My first experiments in this series involved removing the diencephalon and fusing the cerebral hemispheres directly onto the midbrain. As I had expected, surgery blinded the animals. They were also much less active than before. But when worms came close, the salamanders would attack and eat them.

In the next series of experiments with the diencephalon, I either rotated the part 180 degrees or reversed it front to back. These animals did recover vision. But often, when they struck (or seemed to strike) at a worm, they'd move in the wrong direction. At least this was how I interpreted their strange behavior toward worms, on the basis of eye rotation experiments performed by Roger Sperry in the 1940s. However, when I dimmed the lights and forced the salamanders to use sonar and touch, they were able to attack the worms.

My next experiments involved the exchange of brain parts. For example, I switched the diencephalon with the cerebrum. I moved the midbrain up front, and either the cerebrum or the diencephalon to the rear. I performed every operation I could think up. But nothing eradicated feeding. Let me describe one series of rather drastic operations in more detail.

I decided to see what effect an extra medulla would have on feeding. The best approach, I thought, would be to take the entire brain of one animal, down to and including its medulla, and fuse it to the medulla of the host. The available space inside my prospective host's cranium, however, wasn't sufficient to accommodate this amount of brain — not if I used a sibling as a donor (which I most frequently did). Therefore I decided to use a large tiger salamander larva (*Amblystoma tigrinum*) as the host and a little marble salamander larva (*Amblystoma opacum*) as the donor. The operations went well. A week to ten days later, all five of the animals in the group were awake and feeding again. And no facet of their behavior even hinted at the bizarre contents of their crania.

I suspect that most experimentalists suffer, from time to time, from what I call janitor-induced paranoia — the certainty that in the middle of the night the janitor, or someone, has exchanged the labels on test tubes, cages, or salamander dishes. I certainly suffered a bad case of the syndrome while observing the behavior of members of the tiger-marble salamander experiments. I repeated the operations and got identical results. But my disbelief simply would not go away. Here was a brain in a foreign head, plugged into the medulla of a different species — a brain with *two* medullas, no less. And yet the beast behaved like a normal salamander. And every time I checked a salamander's vision (with mirror images of worms), the animal showed that it could see, which meant that the transplanted brain could process visual perception delivered by the foreign eyes of its host. One Sunday morning I finally gave up, pickled some of these animals, and dissected their brain cases. There was no question about it. Each had two medullas, one plugged into the other. And I could trace the host's optic nerve into the transplanted brain. Even if Lashley had been our janitor, I would

A dissection of a tiger salamander larva whose brain was amputated in front of its medulla and replaced by the entire brain — including the medulla — of a smaller marble salamander larva. The donor brain is the deep gray structure between the specimen's two eyes; the host's medulla is the large whitish trough behind it. The behavior of these animals was identical in all respects to that of the controls.

have been forced to conclude that shuffling the brain had not scrambled feeding activity.

Even after the tiger-marble series of experiments, I still clung feebly to the hope of impugning hologramic theory by means of some ingenious anatomical transformation. I formulated this last-ditch working hypothesis: Assume that the medulla is the seat of feeding programs. Suppose, furthermore, that the brain anterior to the medulla merely gives the animal consciousness and nothing else. Obviously an unconscious animal can't carry out an attack. Perhaps all a transplant did, then, was to awaken the creature and allow feeding programs in its medulla to come into play. Clearly I needed another experiment. I had to eliminate feeding memories from the graft but at the same time revive the host. And so I turned to the frog.

The adult leopard frog is a notorious carnivore. Yet as a young tadpole it is a vegetarian. When the tadpole bothers a tubifex at all, it is only to suck algae and fungi from the worm's wriggling flanks.

I called the first member of this series Punky. Punky the tadamander! He had the body of a salamander (*Amblystoma punctatum*), but the brain in front of his medulla had come into this world in a *Rana pipiens*.

The first and most obvious question about Punky was whether or not a frog's brain would even connect, anatomically, with a salamander's medulla. But this question had to wait. To answer it for certain, I would have to kill Punky. Meanwhile, it was only my hunch that his new brain would reinstate overt behavior. If he ever came around, I'd actually have to observe him eat a worm in order to vindicate my hypothesis.

By seventeen days after surgery, Punky had fully regained

his ability to stand and swim. Within a few days after that, he had become the liveliest animal in my colony. (Tadpoles are more active than salamanders.) He was blind, but his sonar and sense of touch were in splendid working order. When I dropped a pebble into his bowl, the "clink" would alert him and bring him swimming over immediately. And so would a newly presented tubifex worm.

But the worm was completely safe. Punky would inspect the squirming crimson thread for perhaps a minute or two. Then he would execute a crisp about-face and swim away. And this continued for the next 68 days, while I virtually camped at the edge of his dish. A conscious, alert, and responsive little fellow he remained throughout. But not once during that time did Punky even hint at an attack, despite the fact that a fresh worm was always available for the taking. Worms were now objects of lively curiosity, not of furious assault. If feeding programs were present in Punky's medulla, their presence would have to be accepted on the strength of divine revelation, not experimental fact. My last-ditch hypothesis failed the pragmatic test of truth: it didn't work.

I had performed an even dozen tadamander operations. None of the tadamanders fed, but eight must be discounted because, although they lived for months, they never regained consciousness. I also introduced a number of control operations into the study. In one control series, I evaluated variables of surgery by transplanting the same regions of the brain I had transplanted to form the tadamander, but with salamanders as donors, instead of tadpoles. These animals regained typical salamander feeding behavior in less than three weeks. What about the possibility that tadpole tissue had some general inhibitory effect on salamander feeding? I controlled this by transplanting various tadpole tissues (brain or muscle or diced tadpole) to salamanders' tail fins or abdominal cavities. These salamanders exhibited no changes in feeding habits. But perhaps frog-brain tissue had an active inhibitory influence on salamander feeding behavior. To test this, I transplanted portions of tadpole brain in place of the salamander's cerebral hemispheres, leaving the rest of the host's brain intact. These animals ate the worms. Because tadamanders would not eat spontaneously, I had to force-feed each one, which became a major undertaking. Twice a week, I lightly anesthetized each tadamander and inserted fresh meat into its stomach. Of course I also had to control the feeding procedure. What if the meal satiated the animal or the anesthetic dulled its appetite? I anesthetized and force-fed normal animals, but neither the anesthetic nor the meal affected their appetites.

The extra work had made Punky's season a long one. And I might have terminated the experiment much sooner had I not grown fond of him.

One morning I arrived in the lab to find all the active tadamanders except Punky displaying signs of something I had dreaded from the outset — transplant rejection! Fortunately, Punky was still healthy. But I doubted that he would last very long. And I could not risk losing the critical anatomical data to be found inside his cranium.

I stained alternate slides of Punky's tissues in two different ways. One procedure, a widely used all-purpose method known as hematoxylin and eosin, enabled me to judge the overall health of the tissue at the time of preservation. The other method, called Bodian's protargol stain, involved depositing silver salts on very fine nerve fibers, fibers that otherwise do not show up under the microscope. Bodian's stain is tricky. And the moment these slides were ready, I selected one at random merely to check quality. But that very slide had the answer I sought. A cablework of delicate nerve fibers connected the tadpole brain to the salamander medulla. It is irrational, I confess, but I date my belief in hologramic theory from that first look at Punky's brain.

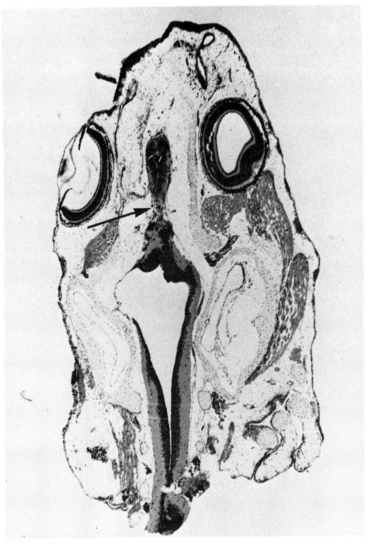

A photomacrograph of one of Punky's sections. The plane of sectioning is parallel to the ground. The arrow points to a neural cablework connecting Punky's frog brain, in the upper part of his head, with his salamander medulla below. There is a more detailed photograph of him in the next picture.

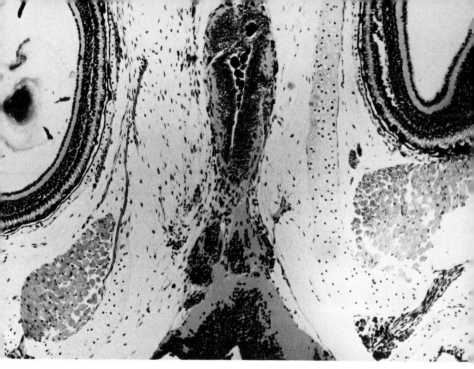

A low-power photomicrograph (40× on the microscope) of Punky. The next two photographs in this sequence show, respectively, his frog and salamander brain cells at high magnification.

The picture on the upper part of the page at the right is a high-power micrograph showing cell nuclei in Punky's frog brain; the lower picture is of nuclei in his salamander medulla. To a trained eye, these cells are as different from each other as a cow and a horse.

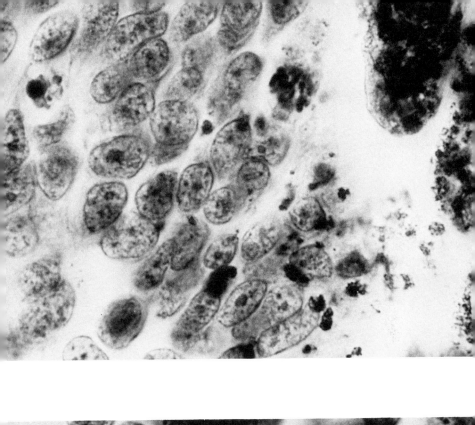
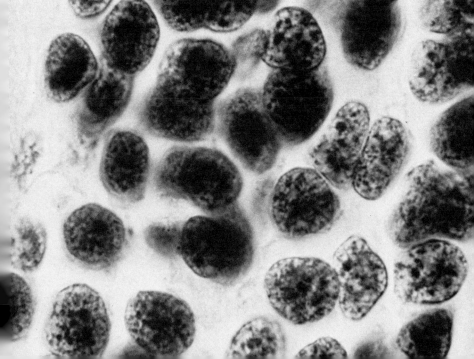

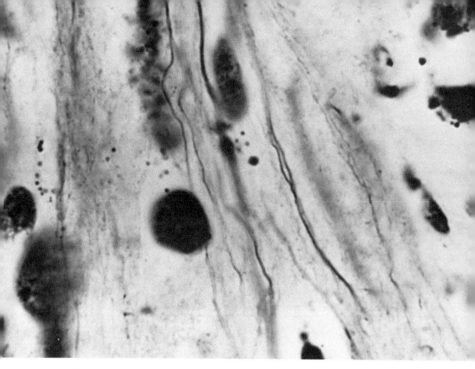

The neural cablework passing between Punky's frog brain and his salamander medulla, in a section stained especially to highlight fine nerve fibers (they do not show up in general staining). Many of the punctate bodies in the picture are what are known as lipofucsin granules (the larger spheres are various cell nuclei). Such granules herald the onset of brain-graft rejection in the salamander. Not only did Punky's sections tell me that the transplant had set up neurological connections; they also indicated that I preserved him just in the nick of time. He would have died in a day or so.

6

The Hologramic Deck

IN FORMAL TERMS, Punky was just a control. Indeed, in a technical paper I eventually delivered on shufflebrain at the Anatomy Meetings, he became a nameless item in a table of data, a slide on a screen, and a dependent clause of passive-voice prose. But Punky had made my structuralist partisanship vulnerable to the overwhelming case my own data had produced in support of hologramic theory. He had humbled me, Punky had. My narrow notions no longer seemed appropriate to the situation. I think I had begun to appreciate for the first time what science might be but seldom is in our day: the privilege of seeing Nature's secrets unfold, rather than an exercise in right and wrong.

Yet my ego was not anchored to hologramic theory. It was not *my* theory. I would remain aware of this fact at all times, as a hedge against new prejudice that might seep in and occupy the void left by removal of the old one. Yes, I believed hologramic theory, in my guts, but I believed it as I do the theory of evolution and the laws of thermodynamics: not as icon, not as an oath I couldn't disclaim if Nature should reveal something better.

Before Punky, I sought only to refute hologramic theory. Afterward, I began to look at the theory as a whole. And the range of its implications set my imagination on fire.

I soon began to realize how lucky I was that the salamander's feeding behavior had obeyed Lashley's dictum so well. For hologramic theory must also take into account what multiple holograms exhibit. From our imaginary experiments in chapter 4, we learned that by shading we can keep some codes out of certain parts of the photographic plate, and we can construct a multiple hologramic system without having every code exist in every single part; no a priori mandate in hologramic theory rules out such possibilities in any given brain. What might I be writing now, had feeding programs been confined to, say, the salamander's left cerebral hemisphere? Equipotentiality is something we can know only after the fact.

What principles do account for the survival of feeding after shufflebrain? How can we explain the retention of the salamander's mental codes despite its scrambled neuroanatomy? There are two major explanations. The most obvious one is that various pieces of brain must have housed *whole* codes. Let's call this the wholeness principle. The second explanation, a much less obvious one, is that each piece of brain must have made its own *independent* contribution to the animal's behavior. We'll call this the independence principle. If codes had been partially represented in a piece of brain, or if pieces mutually depended on each other to construct meaningful sequences, I could never have swapped, flipped, rotated, deleted, reversed, or added parts of the brain — all parts! — without jumbling feeding behavior.

The imaginary experiments we performed earlier with transparent sheets illustrate the wholeness principle rather well. It is not difficult to appreciate that if feeding codes had been spread out like ANATOMY, my operations would have had a different meaning.

The independence principle seemed much more subtle and warranted further investigation. Besides, the independence principle predicted that I should be able to transplant new thoughts into a brain. The new codes ought to become integral parts of the host's mental mix and add new features to the animal's behavior.

Punky's behavior certainly suggested the independence principle, but only indirectly. Demonstrating it required *two* active minds. Punky only had his donor's. But he did show that a salamander's behavior can display totally foreign phase codes.

Before I describe the actual experiments, let's look at the independence principle by way of another imaginary experiment. This time, instead of transparent sheets let's imagine a deck of cards. Let's begin with a conventional nonhologramic message, using a single card as a set for storing one letter. The meaning of our message — let's use DOG — depends on the relationship between our cards: *where* each card lies in relationship to the others when the deck is at rest, or *when* a card turns up during the deal. If we shuffle the deck, we obviously run the risk of scrambling the meaning of our message. DOG might become GOD, for instance. Just as with our message, ANATOMY, on the transparent sheets, the message in our conventional deck is made up of *inter*-dependent elements.

The hologramic deck of cards is far different. Here each card contains a *whole* message. And if the same message is on each card, just as the same feeding message is in each part of the salamander's brain, then shuffling will not alter the deal.

But each card is an *independent* carrier of our hologramic code. What's to stop us from slipping in cards with new codes? Certainly not the codes per se. Cards are independent. Therefore, old and new codes can coexist in the same deck without distorting each other's meanings. And nothing in the information itself would prevent us from constructing a compound hologramic deck, or mind, if hologramic theory really does work. The big "if" is the readout: What happens in reconstruction? Which independent codes activate and drive an animal's behavior?

In the bleak Michigan January of 1969, in anticipation of tests of the independence principle, I began a series of preliminary experiments to find out how well a salamander larva would tolerate the brains of guppies. I had not yet begun worrying about the behavioral side of the study — which fish traits to look for in the hosts, in other words. My major concern was tissue rejection. How long would I have before the salamander's immunological defenders ruined my experiments?

Under the dissecting microscope, one can actually see through the transparent tissue of the larva's dorsal fin. I decided, therefore, to place the heart of a guppy into a tunnel in the jellylike tissue of the fin. The guppy's heart would continue beating, and I could take its pulse, visually, until rejection caused it to stop. While I was at it, I also transplanted guppy flank muscle or liver to salamander fins or abdominal cavities. And during one operating session, I decided to see what would happen if I actually replaced a salamander's cerebrum with that of a guppy. I called the animal in this experiment Buster.

As I said, my attention focused on the operative side of the upcoming study. I had not yet done any hard thinking about behavior. And what Buster showed me was the result not of my prowess but of a series of lucky accidents.

In those days, I had a light-tight inner sanctum specially built within my main laboratory. Equipped with a heavy-duty air conditioner, double doors, and insulated walls, it could serve as a temperature-regulated darkroom (where I sometimes coated radioactive slides with photographic emulsions). I designed the inner sanctum to provide a cool environment, 15–16 degrees centigrade, so as to approximate the temperature of the woods at the time the species of salamanders I work with are young feeding larvae. This procedure seems to prevent premature metamorphosis. In addition, cool temperatures retard the growth of a troublesome fungus; and the inner sanctum turned out to be an excellent post-operative recovery room. As the animals grow a little older, they seem to tolerate higher temperatures more readily. At any rate, I always maintained my stock animals in the inner sanctum. I conducted my operations there, and it was where my dissecting microscope was located. The inner sanctum was too small to accommodate all my animals, and I had gotten into the practice of keeping most experimental subjects out in the main lab, where the temperature was 20–21 degrees centigrade. Because the dissecting microscope was in the small room, I took animals there if I had to inspect them under magnification. This was necessary in order to monitor the pulse of transplanted guppy hearts. The temperature changes had not affected the outcome of my experiments. But as a precaution, I brought all animals of a group — controls and experimentals — into the cool room together, whether or not they had to be examined. I also made it a practice to feed the animals immediately after my daily inspection of a group, and before returning them to the main lab.

Since Buster was a member of a guppy-heart group, he went into the cool room daily. He had taken surgery well, had righted himself on the following day (usual with injury confined to the cerebrum, which his was), and had fed normally from the moment he could walk. One afternoon, three weeks after Buster's operation, I had just finished taking pulses and was rinsing off some juicy-looking tubifex worms in a jet of spring water when I was startled by the building fire alarm. The decibel level of that siren left only two choices: go mad or immediately cover your ears with both hands and flee outdoors! I put down the tubifex and fled.

When the drill was over, it was almost quitting time. The siren had interrupted my ritual, and I had completely forgotten

Buster and company, unfed in the cool inner sanctum. As a matter of fact, it was not until the following day, when I took out my liverwurst sandwich, that I remembered my hungry little pals on the other side of the wall opposite my desk. I stuffed the sandwich back into the bag and went in to make amends.

As I was stacking the salamander dishes on the tray for transfer back into the main lab, I noticed that Buster had not taken his worm. This was impossible! My first thoughts were profanities against the fire-alarm siren. Perhaps the noise had affected my animals. But all the other animals had already devoured their worms. I checked the stock animals, and their appetites were fine too. But Buster wasn't taking. Yet he was frisky enough and looked very healthy.

Now I had a suspicion. I ran into the main lab, filled two beakers with spring water from a carboy, and transferred six feisty-looking stock guppies into each beaker. One group I set beside the fish tank to fast overnight, at 20 degrees centigrade. The second group I chilled to 15 degrees centigrade by swirling the exterior of the beaker in cracked ice. When the thermometer hit the fifteen-degree mark, I transferred these guppies into the cool room and set them down next to Buster.

I allowed the guppies to acclimate for about an hour, using this time to check the feeding responses of the stock salamanders and the recipients of guppy hearts and then to wolf down my stale lunch. Finally it was time to check the chilled guppies.

I placed each guppy in a dish by itself. Then I dropped in a worm for each. The fish swam over and inspected the worm but, like Buster, would not attack.

There was nothing unusual about a tropical fish refusing to eat live meat at cool temperatures. Their digestive enzymes become inefficient in the cold. Had my guppies' ancestors back in Trinidad ignored sudden drops in temperature and gone on eating worms they couldn't digest, the species would have vanished via natural selection eons before my experiments with Buster's brains. The salamander, on the other hand, in a cool pond in early spring or late fall, can't afford to pass up a meal. General considerations notwithstanding, I held off on any conclusions, because I did not know the particulars — the details necessary to make this story ring true. I decided to leave Buster and the guppies in the cool environment overnight. And I placed a fresh worm in each dish.

When I arrived the next morning, the first thing I did was check out the fasting guppies in the main lab. They went into a frenzy when I held worms above the beaker. When I released the squirming ball, it vanished almost as soon as it hit the surface of the water, as though attacked by a school of piranhas. The control fish kept at 20 degrees were hungry indeed.

Next, I went into the cool room to see what had happened there during the night. All the tubifexes in the dishes with Buster and the chilled guppies had survived. Everybody was still lively and healthy, by every criterion I could apply. But Buster and the guppies simply were not taking worms. Again, I checked feeding among the stock and the guppy-heart recipients. They attacked the worms immediately.

But wait! I wanted more data. Now came a critical test. For the next step was like backchecking addition with subtraction. I transferred Buster and the guppies into the main lab, placed them in fresh water — 20.4 degrees centigrade — from a carboy there, gave each a fresh worm, set the entire bunch on my desk, recorded the time in my notebook, and then sat down to watch.

Sixty-one minutes from the time I changed his water, Buster devoured his worm. It took 101 minutes for a guppy to make the first nibble; by 111 minutes, not a worm was left in any of the bowls. Warming the water had revived their cooled appetites.

But like a crapshooter on a hot streak, I couldn't stop. I added to the experiment salamanders with guppy flank muscle transplanted to their abdominal cavities. I added some new guppies. And I transferred the group back to the cool room, where I fasted them for forty-eight hours before adding worms. When testing time came, all the control salamanders ate their worms. But Buster and the guppies did not. I decided to allow the trial to run an additional twenty-four hours, leaving Buster and the guppies each with a worm. Still they failed to take the prey. When I repeated the warming phase of the experiment, Buster went after his worm in 58 minutes and the guppies averaged an hour and a half.

I set up an entire series of guppy-to-salamander cerebral transplants to answer a number of subsidiary questions about what I was now calling "temperature-dependent feeding behavior." How often would it occur? About 70 percent of the time. What was the critical temperature? I determined that it was 17–18 degrees centigrade — for the donors as well as the hosts. When, postoperatively, did temperature-dependent feeding emerge? In a little more than two weeks. Checking Buster's records, I realized that had the fire drill taken place perhaps a day or two earlier, I never would have made the observation.

Then one day, six weeks after his operation, after having fasted twenty-four hours in the cold, Buster hauled off and ate a worm. For a moment I was sick enough to cry. Had it all been just a fluke? But that same day, the transplanted guppy hearts beat their last beats. Rejection! And five to six weeks after the new batch of guppy-to-salamander hosts had been operated on, they too reverted to feeding at low temperature. I was sorry to see the trait disappear. But its disappearance made the story as complete as it could possibly be.

Buster exemplified the independence principle. Punky gives us no basis to judge it. Buster's feeding behavior was a composite of salamander and guppy traits. Punky merely used his salamander body to display his tadpole mind. Buster's failure to attack worms at low temperatures did not mean that he lacked the necessary memories. The stimulus, a cool environment, had prevented his use of those memories. His reaction at cool temperatures was negative, but an "active" negative. Punky's refusal to attack worms during those 68 days stemmed from different causes entirely: his negative response was passive. As a control for my experiment with Punky, I performed operations in which I left most of the host salamanders' brains in place and substituted only the cerebrums with those of tadpoles. These animals, unlike Punky, always attacked worms. Thus I had to conclude that in preparing Punky for his transplant, in amputating his original salamander midbrain, diencephalon, and cerebrum, I had removed his carnivorous memory, which his new tadpole brain did not restore to him. Placing the active-passive comparison in the context of our earlier analogy with the deck of hologramic cards, Buster's failure to attack was similar to dealing out an inappropriate hand. When Buster's environment was warmed, we found that attack was in his deck after all. But no possible deal could have turned Punky into a killer; attack was not among his cards.

Are Buster and Punky too remote from us to suggest anything about the human condition? During embryonic life, we develop through stages in which we look and act like fish, salamanders, and tadpoles. Embryonic development provides convincing evidence for the theory of evolution. One principle of embryology, von Baer's law, holds that ontogeny recapitulates phylogeny, meaning that as we develop, we go through our own individual mini-evolutions, revealing our close kinship to other vertebrate creatures. Behavior doesn't start when we slide out onto the obstetrics table. We're live cargoes in the womb. And we behave long before we're born.

An old-time Georgia country obstetrician, Richard Torpin, used to show up every year at the meetings of the American Association of Anatomists with all sorts of novel and ingenious exhibits of human behavior *in utero*. From stillbirths and detailed records on his patients, Doc Torpin would reconstruct what led to a particular fetus's undoing. Using rubber bands and plaster of paris, he produced models to illustrate various prenatal problems. One year he demonstrated how a restless fetus could get its fingers and toes tangled, and eventually lost, in loops of umbilical cord. (He had found bits of fingers in the inner wall of the placenta.) In another exhibit, he showed how a swimming fetus had found and swallowed its umbilical cord, much as a salamander or a guppy would down a worm.

The movement within a pregnant woman's uterus can't be equated to the simple push-pull action-reaction of a hydraulic shock absorber. It is behavior. Just as the embryo's lungs, heart, eyes, face, and brain gradually develop through fishlike, froglike, and ratlike stages into what we might be willing to call a "baby," so the primitive mind we start out with must gradually and *continuously* evolve into a human mentality. The course our development takes runs right by the junctures where our aquatic vertebrate cousins stopped evolving. And when one of us gets off course too soon, what we do en route to the formaldehyde jar is fishlike, salamanderlike, or ratlike, depending on the point of departure.

Yet in spite of an unbroken thread running all the way back through our development, we emerge from the uterus infinitely different creatures from when we first implanted into its soft, warm, sticky inner wall. How do we become so different during development? The independence principle, remember, permits new codes to be added virtually at will to the pre-existing deck. Buster serves as a precedent for such additions.

The independence principle also frees us from having to assume fundamentally different laws of Nature in order to explain how experience can add to our mental stores what development builds into us spontaneously. In hologramic theory, one general principle serves all the codes, whether we call them memories or instincts, learned ideas or innate thoughts, a priori or a posteriori knowledge. An examination of this prediction of the theory was the next phase of my research.

I lost my job at the beginning of 1970, before shufflebrain was a complete story. A depression had begun in the sciences during 1969 (indeed, it persists even as I write). Shortly after I was fired, a staff writer for *Science* magazine came to the conclusion that what many scientists were calling a "Ph.D. glut" was really a myth. True, the article conceded, the really good jobs were getting hard to find. Competition had intensified, and there was no doubt that the federal government was spending significantly less on science. But the article implied that only the Willie Lomans of science were driving taxi cabs, washing dishes, freelancing, and drawing unemployment checks. Directly or through friends, I soon contacted the anatomy department of every medical school in the United States and Canada, without success. And wherever else I looked, there were no jobs, not for me at least. Perhaps it was the *Science* article, which I believed at the time; perhaps it was the serious economic plight of my family (the oldest of our four children had had to miss a semester at the University of Michigan); perhaps it was my still-incomplete shufflebrain research, or the fact that my unemployment insurance was running out. In any case, when a friend eventually arranged an interview for me at Indiana University's optometry school, I found it psychologically impossible to negotiate seriously for anything. Had my pride been operative, I would have rejected their job offer, which carried lower rank and less pay than my former job. And I would never have worked as a scientist again.

But by the autumn of 1970, I was drawing real wages once more. I had a splendid office overlooking the most beautiful campus I had ever seen. Although my lab had nothing in it, my morale was excellent. I had applied to the university's grant committee for a few thousand dollars to tide me over until I could secure federal funds. When I got four hundred dollars instead, I was still too euphoric to bitch. And I set about doing what scientists of the generation before mine had done routinely: I made do.

Making do included scrounging salamanders from a wonderful man, the late Rufus Humphrey. Humphrey had retired to Indiana University from the anatomy department of the University of Buffalo (now the State University of New York at Buffalo). I had joined that department, myself, for a brief period in the early 1960s. After taking over some drain tables Humphrey had once used for his salamanders, I had written him to tell him that his picture still hung in the microscopic anatomy lab at Buffalo. Thus we began a lasting correspondence. Humphrey studied the genetics of a salamander known as the axolotl. Some of his purebred strains ran back to 1930. His colony was famous, worldwide, among people who work with amphibians. Even if I had not been on a scrounging mission, one of the first things I would have had to see in Indiana was Humphrey's axolotl colony.

Another item I needed was a dissecting microscope. There wasn't one lying around in Optometry, and I couldn't afford to buy one out of my wife's tight budget. I learned of a new ecology program starting up over in Biological Sciences, however, and dissecting microscopes were part of the equipment for the forthcoming teaching lab. The course, though, wasn't scheduled to begin until the first of the year. Could I arrange a loan? The answer was yes.

Making do also meant giving up the live tubifex worm as staple for my colony. Detergents and chemical pollutants have driven these once-ubiquitous worms from all but a few waters. Since the early 1960s, I'd not been able to collect them in the field, but had had to fly them in from New York or Philadelphia, which was totally out of the question on a make-do budget. Thus I began feeding young larvae on freshly hatched brine-shrimp embryos, which could be purchased dry by the millions for a quarter in any pet shop. When the axolotl larvae reached about 40 millimeters, I weaned them onto beef liver swiped from my wife's shopping basket.

Feeding animals on beef liver does take time. The animals must first be taught to strike. Even after they acquire the necessary experience, though, you still can't fling a hunk of meat into the dish and forget it, as you can a ball of live tubifex worms. The liver rots at the bottom of the dish, while even the experienced feeder starves.

Now there was a federal program called Work-Study, whereby the government paid all but 20 percent of the wages for students who had university-related jobs. Just as I was weaning a group of about fifty axolotls onto liver, an optometry student, Calvin Yates, came around looking for a Work-Study job. One duty I assigned him was feeding liver to the axolotls.

Calvin now practices optometry in Gary, Indiana. If his treatment of people matches the care he gave my salamanders, I am sure he is an overwhelming success. Calvin had what Humphrey once called a "slimy thumb" — the salamander buff's equivalent of the horticulturist's green thumb. In Calvin's presence, living things thrived. A few days after he took over the job of weaning, the axolotls were snapping like old veterans. Calvin also introduced a clever trick into his feeding technique. He would tap the rim of an axolotl's plastic dish and then pause a few seconds before presenting the liver. In a few days, tapping alone would cause the larva to look up, in anticipation of the imminent reward.

I paid only the most casual attention to Calvin during that

time. For I had learned that my favorite species of salamander, *Amblystoma opacum,* lived in the area. Opacum was one of the three principal species I had been using in my shufflebrain experiments. Luckily, the female opacum lays her eggs during the autumn. Finding them can be tricky, though. Fortunately, I met a man who happened to have 50 eggs he was willing to let go for two dollars. And by the time Calvin was weaning the axolotls, the opacum larvae had grown to just the right size for me to put the finishing touches on my shufflebrain project.

The opacum belongs to the same genus as does the axolotl (*Amblystoma mexicanum*). Opacum is a shrewd little animal, the smallest member of the genus but easily the most elaborate and efficient hunter. And what a fascination to watch! But its small size made liver-feeding impractical, which was also lucky for me.

One afternoon at the tail end of an operating session, I realized that I had anesthetized one too many opacum larvae. It is against my standard procedures to return such animals to stock. Yet I don't like to waste a creature, make-do budget or not. On impulse, I decided to see how well an axolotl's forebrain would work when attached to an opacum's midbrain. And I took an animal from Calvin's colony to serve as the donor.

The fateful moment came ten days later. I had taken my time getting to the lab that morning, walking slowly through the crisp autumn air, admiring the trees, saying several "good mornings" to students along the way, and had seated myself perfunctorily at the operating table, thinking much more about the world in general than about science. I usually keep recuperating animals near the microscope and check their reflexes daily until they come out of their stupor. That morning, I came in merely to take a routine daily record.

To check a salamander's reflexes, I flick the edge of the

dish. When an animal has recovered from postoperative stupor, it usually jumps in response to the noise. As I placed the opacum larva with the axolotl brain on the stage of the microscope, I noticed that he had righted himself and was standing on the bottom of the dish. I gave a light flick, expecting him to give a little jump and then swim out of the microscopic field. Instead, he slowly arched his little back and looked directly up into the barrel of the microscope, right into my eyes. My heart missed a beat. I had observed this looking-up response in only one other place — over on the table among Calvin's axolotls, where the donor had come from. Immediately I jumped up, went over and flicked every last dish on the axolotl table. Every axolotl there looked up in response.

Next I checked out the stock opacum larvae. Flicking only caused them to scurry around in their dishes. Not one stock opacum looked up.

Now back to the operating table. Again, I flicked. Again the opacum with the axolotl brain looked up. I tested the other subjects that had had operations. They did not look up. Again I tried the axolotl recipient. Again it worked. Unwittingly, I had discovered that a learned response can be added to the hologramic deck.

My little experimental animal reminded me of a sermon I had heard decades earlier in a down-at-the-heel church at the corner of 111th Street and Lexington Avenue in New York City. The sermon had been about gratitude, and the preacher had used an anecdote from his Ohio farmboy youth to illustrate the theme. His father used to let hogs into the apple orchard to clean up windfallen fruit, according the story. It always amazed him that the hogs would devour every last apple on the ground but never once look up at the trees, the source. Looking up! I haven't practiced the religion of my boyhood for a long time. Nature has taken its place. But often, very often, in the laboratory, at the moment of a new discovery, I have felt intense gratitude, not for being right — for I've had the emotion when I was completely wrong — but simply for being there. Looking down at my talented opacum, I felt that same gratitude, to an almost overwhelming degree. And thus I gave this new paradigm its name: "looking up."

Before I had the chance to carry out a decisive investigation of looking up, good fortune seemed to disappear. The opacum died of a fungus infection. Something happened to the tap water, and the brine shrimp were hatching in minuscule quantities, forcing me to abandon the opacum stock in order to maintain the experimental subjects. Then the time came to surrender the borrowed dissecting microscope. The optometry school had rooms full of junked optical equipment from which I jerry-rigged a substitute. But under it, I committed butchery. Then the National Institutes of Health rejected my application for research funds. I finally began to lose confidence, and I would have closed the lab permanently had not Calvin's job depended on feeding the axolotls. But I could not go near the lab.

Although I could not yet make a public case for "looking up," I was now privately convinced that hologramic theory applied to learned as well as instinctive behaviors and that the abstract rules were indeed the same for both. I felt that the time had come to make the main part of the shufflebrain story known. And I was convinced that my days in the laboratory were over at last. If what I wrote was going to be a swan song, why say it in the stiff, lifeless prose of science and bury it in unread archives? If the story was as interesting as it seemed to me, perhaps a popular magazine would take it. *Harper's* eventually accepted my article and published it in their May 1972 issue.

But once again, the calamity was only apparent. On the elevator one day, Art Jones, a colleague of mine, asked if it was true that I did not have a dissecting microscope. He said "hmm" when I said yes. A few weeks later, I was busy preparing a lecture when someone began kicking on the door. I opened it and there stood Art Jones, a brand new dissecting microscope in each hand and a big grin on his face. He had convinced the dean that our graduate program required dissecting microscopes. And would it be an inconvenience to store two of them in my laboratory? I still wonder if he saw the tears in my eyes.

I felt like making do again.

Unlike other species of salamanders I work with, the axolotl spends its entire life in the water. Because of a genetic quirk, it fails to metamorphose into a land-dweller. It does undergo changes as it develops into an adult, but not the drastic transformations other salamanders go through. Metamorphosis usually wipes out my colony for the season. The axolotl, however, passes into adulthood uneventfully, and lives five or six years, and sometimes longer, under laboratory conditions. By the time I was ready to experiment again, Calvin's axolotls had not only become adults but had been looking up for well over a year. If I had had a dissecting microscope, I would have used every last one of them much earlier, and they wouldn't have been around for what happened next.

Shortly after my article appeared in *Harper's,* I received a phone call from Igor Oganesoff, a producer for the CBS News program "60 Minutes." The people at CBS had liked the article, he said, and he asked if I would perform experiments in front of the camera.

With the wrong camera angle, my experiments could easily

come out looking like *Grandson of Frankenstein* filmed in Indiana, which would have been unfair to Punky and Buster as well as the audience. Yet I couldn't envisage Igor Oganesoff wanting to produce a horror movie. I vividly recalled two pieces he had produced for "60 Minutes": one had portrayed the world inside a Carmelite cloister in California, and the other captured an aspect of chessmaster Bobby Fisher that no one had suspected. I was sure Igor could do justice to shufflebrain. And with the opportunity to reach fifteen million people, I decided to do it.

Technicalities worried me, I said, trying to imagine what would work in a visual medium. Did I remember the work done with microscopes during Walter Cronkite's "21st Century"? Oganesoff asked. The cameraman Oganesoff had in mind, a man named Billy Wagner, had taken those pictures. With a camera in his hand Wagner becomes a genius. There was, I said, a double-headed microscope that enabled two people to view the same microscopic field simultaneously. But I didn't have one of those expensive instruments. Details like that, Oganesoff said, were his worry. As we were talking, I thought about Calvin's large, well-trained axolotls. It was time I did some experiments with adults anyway. Their brains could be seen even without a microscope, if worse came to worse. Yes! I thought it might be quite feasible. After a preliminary visit, Igor made plans to film the operations in July and the results in August, between the two political conventions.

Meanwhile, I scrounged a fresh batch of axolotl larvae from Humphrey. I also carried out a few preliminary operations with adult axolotls, to work out technical nuances and get my hands back in shape.

Calvin had graduated, and another student had taken his place. He lacked Calvin's touch with animals and couldn't seem to get the knack of weaning larvae onto liver. I undertook the chore myself, and while at it decided to study the looking-up response carefully.

Looking up is surprisingly easy to induce. The quickest way is to put the larva in an opaque cylindrical container and give it a sort of tunnel view of the world above. Then, with one session a day, for four or five days, the use of a brisk, discrete tapping of the dish, followed in a second or two by a reward, will instill the trait. After this, looking-up behavior persists for weeks, even after the reward has been withheld. Once the animal has been trained, the looking-up response is virtually guaranteed. I decided to put looking up on "60 Minutes."

The experiment I performed on camera involved three animals: two naive axolotl larvae and a trained adult "looker-up" from Calvin's old colony. The anterior part of the trained adult's cerebrum replaced the entire cerebrum of one naive larva. Would the host become a looker-up? The other naive larva served as a donor animal, and I transplanted its entire brain into the space left in the adult's cranium. Would the transplant "confuse" the adult? Mike Wallace eventually called the second larva "the loser." For it received no brain transplant.

I decided not to call the viewer's attention to looking up, and instead focused attention on the survival of feeding after shufflebrain operations. I had no doubts about feeding. But looking up was still very new. Something could have turned up to change my mind. If the paradigm turned out to be a fluke, trying to correct the misinformation broadcast on television would be like attempting to summon back an inadvertently fired load of buckshot.

CBS broadcast the show a year later. In the interim, I had carried out enough testing and had conducted sufficient control experiments to be sure of the results. Within about one week, a previously naive recipient of a trained looking-up animal's cere-

brum becomes a looker-up itself, without training. And these animals retain the looking-up trait for the remaining months, or even years, of their lives. Controls, animals with transplants from the brains of naive animals, do not show this response. While the initial experiments — like those I performed on camera — were with the cerebrum, I obtained the same results with pieces of midbrain and diencephalon.

The trained cerebral-donor animals were very interesting. As soon as the effects of anesthesia wore off, these animals demonstrated that they remembered the signal to look up. In other words, looking-up memories existed in the donated as well as the retained parts of these animals' brains. What was true of innate feeding behavior worked for looking up: memory wasn't confined to a single location in the brain.

I had also repeated Mike Wallace's "loser" experiment. I

found that true to the principle of independence, the extra brain parts did not "confuse" the host.

Meanwhile, a group of Israelis, working with the brains of adult newts, had demonstrated that dark-avoidance memories can be transplanted from one animal to another.[1] When the "60 Minutes" show did air, I had no doubts about looking up. Sitting in my living room, a member of Igor's audience myself, I felt that someone else was on the screen doing my experiments. Indeed, someone else *was* at the microscope. The intervening year had been a full one.

---

[1] See Hershkowitz et al., 1972. In more recent years, several laboratories have successfully demonstrated that small foci of mammalian brains can be transplanted from one animal to another. See Lund and Hauschka, 1976; Kromer et al., 1979; Perlow et al., 1979.

7

Waves of Theory

UNTIL NOW, we have been investigating hologramic theory from the outside, looking at its implications in terms of what we can understand in the realm of experience, testing its predictions to see if they can possibly work, asking ourselves if the hologram mimics the living brain sufficiently to warrant a serious probe into the subject's rational aspects. Until now, our questions have concentrated on what a hologramic mind has the capacity to do, and we have been able to pursue the answers in the world most real to us. But now we must turn to the question, What *is* hologramic mind? To find the answer, we must enter the ideal, abstract, unfamiliar domain of the hologram itself. And to make the journey, we will need to borrow concepts from mathematics.

What is mathematics? Charles Peirce, who gave contemporary science its philosophical backbone, observed, "The common definition . . . is that mathematics is the science of quantity."[1] But, citing his mathematician father, Benjamin Peirce, Charles went on to assert that it is actually "the science which draws necessary conclusions." Thus the numbers are not what make a mathematical statement out of $1 + 1 = 2$; rather, the conclusion forced from 1 and 1 by the plus sign does. If we ex-

---

[1] See Peirce, 1957, p. 256.

tend Peirce's characterization to our own quest, the payoff ought to be a clear understanding not only of what we mean by "hologramic mind" but also of why hologramic mind does what it does.

The reader probably can think of many specific examples, though, in which adding one thing to another does not necessarily yield two. In preparing scrambled eggs, for instance, combining two beaten yolks produces one entity. Bertrand Russell helps us with problems such as this, and in so doing furnishes us with an essential caveat: "The problem arises through the fact that such knowledge [mathematical ideas] is general, whereas all experience [egg yolks or salamander brains] is particular." [2]

Our search will uncover hologramic mind not as a particular thing but as a generalization. We will begin the quest in this chapter with a theoretical look at waves. And we will continue our search through the next two chapters. Our objective will be not the geography but the geometry of mind.

The central idea for our examination of waves originated in the work of an eighteenth-century Frenchman, Pierre Simon, Marquis de Laplace. But it was a countryman of his who in 1822 explicitly articulated the theory of waves we will call upon directly. His name was Jean Baptiste Joseph, Baron de Fourier.

In chapter 3, I mentioned that in theory a compound irregular wave is the coalesced product of a series of simple regular waves. This is the essence of Fourier's theorem. With a few modest restrictions, the theorem works for all waves.[3] The out-

---

[2] See Russell, 1959, pp. 84–85.

[3] I use Fourier's theorem in a somewhat broader sense than do most mathematics textbooks. Related theorems allow us to skirt certain technical restrictions in Fourier's basic idea. The most widely used of such methods is called the Laplace transform.

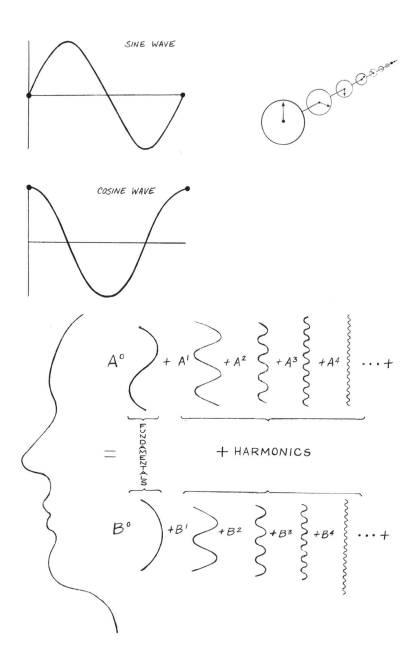

SINE WAVE

COSINE WAVE

A^0 + A^1 + A^2 + A^3 + A^4 ··· +

= FUNDAMENTALS + HARMONICS

B^0 + B^1 + B^2 + B^3 + B^4 ··· +

line of a human face, for example, can be represented by a
series of what are called sine and cosine waves. This series is
called a Fourier series, and the Fourier series of one person's
face differs from that of another.

We are not simply talking about waves, however. As J. W.
Mellor wrote in a classic textbook, *Higher Mathematics,* "Any
physical property — density, pressure, velocity — which varies
periodically with time and whose magnitude or intensity can be
measured, may be represented by Fourier's series."[4] Therefore
let's take advantage of the theory, and, to help our imagery, let's
think of the compound irregular wave as a series of increasingly
smaller regular *cycles;* or better, as wheels spinning on the
same axle; or perhaps better still, as the dials on an electric
meter or gas meter. Waves, after all, are cycles. And wheels or
dials are circles. Now imagine our series with the largest wheel,
or slowest dial, as the first in line, and with the smallest, or fast-
est, back at the tail end of the line. The intermediate wheels
progress from large to small, or slow to fast. The smaller the
wheel, the faster it will spin, relatively speaking. Or the faster
the dial, the more cycles it will execute in, say, a second. In
other words, as we progress along the series, frequency increases among cycles. If we were to transform our cycles back
to wavy waves, we would see more wavelets as we progressed
along the series. In fact, in a Fourier series, the frequencies go
up — 1, 2, 3, 4, 5, 6, and so on.

But wait! If the frequencies of your face and mine go up 1,
2, 3, 4, 5, and so forth, how can our profiles be different? What
Fourier did was calculate a factor that would make the first regular wave a single cycle that covered the period, or recurrent
duration, of the compound wave. Then he calculated factors, or
coefficients, for each component cycle — values that would

---

[4] Mellor, 1955, p. 470.

make their frequencies 2, 3, 4, 5, 6 or more times that of the first cycle. The individual identities of our profiles depend on these Fourier coefficients. The analyst uses integral calculus[5] to determine Fourier coefficients. Fourier analysis is the name applied to this process. And the analyst represents his compound wave as a Fourier series so that he can determine the coefficients. Once he has the coefficients, he can make a graph and plot, say, amplitude versus frequency. A graph can be represented by an equation. And an equation using Fourier coefficients to represent a compound wave's amplitude versus frequency is called a Fourier transform, which we will discuss in the next chapter.

But wait! Isn't there something fishy about the coefficients? Isn't Fourier analysis like making the compound wave equal 10, for instance, and then saying $10 = 1 + 2 + 3 + 4$? And if the components don't come out right, we'll just multiply them by the correct amount to make sure the series adds up to the sum we want. Mellor even quotes the celebrated German physicist and physician Ludwig von Helmholtz as calling Fourier's theorem "mathematical fiction."[6] But this belief did not stop Helmholtz and many others of his day from using Fourier's theorem. Fourier's ideas gave new meaning to theoretical and applied mathematics long before all the underlying conditions and proofs had been established. Why would anyone use an unproven formula that had shady philosophical implications? The answer is very human. It worked.

An extremely complicated wave may be the product of many component waves. How many? An infinite number, in

---

[5] Integral calculus involves merging or integrating the infinitely small parts of a curve. Waves are so-called periodic curves. Technically, the Fourier coefficients make the higher frequencies *integral* multiples (meaning their infinitely small parts will sum up) of the fundamental frequency.

[6] Mellor, 1955, p. 470.

theory. How, then, does the analyst know when to stop analyzing? The answer to this question suggests another powerful use of Fourier's theorem. The analyst synthesizes the components, putting them back together to make a compound wave. And when the synthesized wave closely matches the original one, the analyst knows he has all the coefficients necessary to calculate his Fourier transform equation. This synthesis is known as Fourier synthesis. Conceptually, Fourier synthesis has much in common with the decoding of the hologram. But before we can talk about this process, we must know more about the hologram itself. And before that, we must dig deeper into the theoretical essence of waves.

The first regular wave in a Fourier series is often called the fundamental frequency, or, alternatively, the first harmonic. The subsequent waves, the sine and cosine waves, represent the second, third, fourth, fifth, etc., harmonics. Most large computers have programs to calculate up to the ninth harmonic, which is usually much more than enough to approximate even compound waves that have very large numbers of components. As the analysis proceeds, the discrepancy between the synthesized wave and the original wave usually becomes so small as to be insignificant.

These terms may seem quite musical to the reader. Indeed, harmonic analysis is one of the many uses of Fourier's theorem. Take a sound from a musical instrument, for example. The first component represents the fundamental frequency, the main pitch of the sound. Higher harmonics represent overtones. There are odd and even harmonics, and they correspond to the sine and cosine waves in the series. I present these terms from harmonic analysis only to illustrate one use of Fourier's theorem. But the theorem has such wide application that it has become a virtual lingua franca among persons who deal with

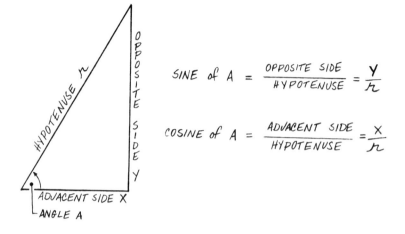

$$\text{SINE of } A = \frac{\text{OPPOSITE SIDE}}{\text{HYPOTENUSE}} = \frac{y}{r}$$

$$\text{COSINE of } A = \frac{\text{ADJACENT SIDE}}{\text{HYPOTENUSE}} = \frac{x}{r}$$

periodic events, patterns, motions, surfaces, and so forth. I see no particular reason why the reader should dwell on terms like "fundamentals" and "odd-and-even harmonics." But for our purposes, it is highly instructive to look into why the component waves of a Fourier series bear the adjectives "sine" and "cosine."[7]

The trigonometrist uses sines and cosines as *functions* of angles, "function" meaning something whose value depends on something else. A function changes with changes in whatever determines it. Belly fat changes as a function of too many peanut-butter cookies changing location from plate to mouth. Sines and cosines are numerical values that change from 0 to 1 or from 1 to 0 as an angle changes from 0° to 90° or from 90° to 0°. The right triangle helps define the sine and cosine. Sine is the side (Y) opposite an acute angle (A) in a right triangle, divided by the diagonal or hypotenuse (r): $\sin A = Y/r$. The cosine is the side (X) adjacent, or next to, the acute angle, divided

---

[7] There are special forms of the Fourier series in which components go by names other than "sine" and "cosine" wave; but these special forms can be converted to "sine" and "cosine" waves.

by the hypotenuse: cos $A = X/r$. The famous and ancient Pythagorean theorem holds that the square of the length of the hypotenuse of a right triangle equals the sum of the squares of the lengths of the two sides ($r^2 = X^2 + Y^2$). Suppose that we give r the value of 1. Of course r^2 is still 1. Notice that with X^2 at its maximum value of 1, Y^2 is equal to 0. Thus when the cosine is at its maximum, the sine is at 0, and vice versa. Sine and cosine, therefore, are opposites. If one is odd the other is even.

Now imagine that we place the right triangle into a circle, putting angle A at the center and having side X run along the equator. Imagine also that we rotate r around the center of the circle and make new triangles. Since r is the radius, and therefore will not vary, any right triangle we draw between radius

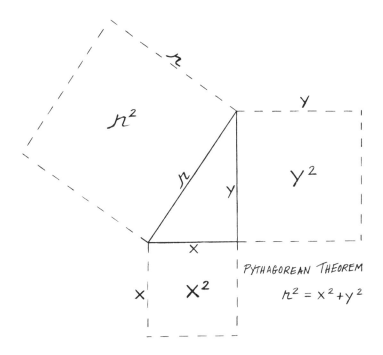

PYTHAGOREAN THEOREM

$$r^2 = x^2 + y^2$$

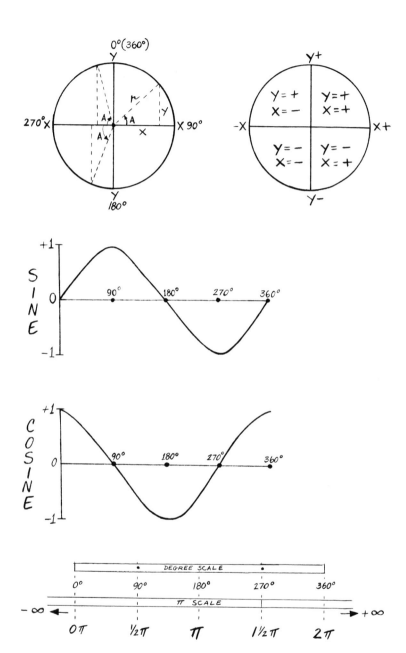

and equator will have a hypotenuse of 1, the value we assigned it before. Of course angle A will change, as will sides Y and X. Now the same angle A can appear in each quadrant. If it does, the result is two non-zero values for both sine and cosine in a 360-degree cycle. But there is a simple trick that will enable us to avoid the ambiguity. We can let all values of Y above the equator be positive; below the equator, we can let side Y be represented by negative values. We can do essentially the same thing for X, this time using the vertical line: to the right, let X be positive, and to the left, let X be negative.

If we plot a graph of sine or cosine values for angle A versus degrees on the circle, we get a wave. The cosine wave starts at +1, drops to 0 at 90°, plunges to −1 at 180°, and returns to +1 at 360°, the end of the cycle. Meanwhile, the sine wave starts at 0, swells to +1 at 90°, drops to 0 again at 180°, bottoms to −1 at 270°, and returns to 0 at the completion of the 360-degree cycle.

We don't really need the triangle anymore; the circumference suffices. But the degree scale gets to be a pain in the neck after a single cycle. Roulette wheels, clocks, meter dials, orbiting planets, components of higher frequency, and the like don't stop at a single cycle. There's a simple trick for shifting to a more useful scale. Remember the formula for finding the circle's circumference, $2\pi r$? Recall that π is approximately 3.14, or $^{22}/_7$. But when r is 1, the value for the circumference is simply 2π. This would convert the 90° mark to $\frac{1}{2}\pi$, the 180° mark to π, and so on. When we reach the end of the cycle, we can keep on going up the π scale as long as the baker has the dough, so to speak.[8] But we end up with a complete sine or cosine cycle at every 2π.

---

[8] In actual practice, the measure mathematicians use is called a π radian. $\pi = 3.14$ (approximately); π radian = 180°; thus 1 π radian = $180/\pi$ = 180/3.14 = approximately 57°. While radians lend ease in calculations, the π scale itself explicitly applies to the concept of the cycle. Since we are interested in ideas, not calculations, we will stay with the rarely used but heuristic π scale.

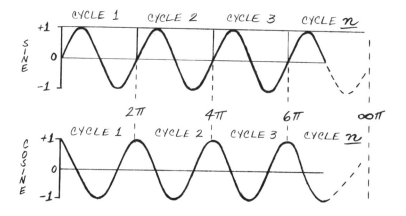

With regard to a single sine or cosine wave on the π scale, what is amplitude? Recall that we said it was maximum displacement from the horizontal plane. Obviously, the amplitude of a sine or cosine wave turns out to be +1. But +1 doesn't tell us *where* amplitude occurs, or whether we have a sine or a cosine wave — or any intermediate wave between a sine and cosine wave. This is where phase comes in, remember. Phase tells where or when we can find amplitude, or any other point, relative to the reference or to zero. Notice that our sine wave reaches +1 at $\frac{1}{2}\pi$, $2\frac{1}{2}\pi$, $4\frac{1}{2}\pi$, and so forth. We can define the sine wave's phase from this. What about the phase of the cosine wave? It reaches 1 at 0π, 2π, 4π, etc.

If someone says, "I have a wave, amplitude +1, phase spectrum $\frac{1}{2}$, $2\frac{1}{2}$, $4\frac{1}{2}\pi$," we automatically know that we're dealing with a sine wave. In other words, our simple, ideal system gives us very precise definitions of phase and amplitude. We can also see in the ideal how these two pieces of information, phase and amplitude, actually force us to make what Benjamin Peirce called necessary conclusions. Phase and amplitude spectra define our regular waves.

Now let me make a confession. I pulled a philosophical fast one here, in order to give the reader a precise look at phase and

amplitude. We know the phase and amplitude of a wave the
moment we assert that it's a sine or a cosine wave. Technically,
our definition is trivial. To say "sine wave" is to know exactly
where amplitudes occur on our π scale. But let's invoke
Fourier's theorem and apply it to our trivia. If a complicated
wave *is* a series of sine and cosine waves, and those simple
waves *are* their phase and amplitude spectra, then knowing the
phase and the amplitude spectra for a complicated wave means
having a complete definition of it as well. Our trivial definition
leads us to a diagrammatically simple explanation of how it is
that phase and amplitude completely define even the most complicated waves. It is not easy to explain the inclusiveness of
phase and amplitude in the "real" world. But look at how simple
the problem becomes in the ideal. First, phase and amplitude
define sine and cosine waves. Second, sine and cosine waves
define compound waves. It follows quite simply, if perhaps
strangely, that phases and amplitudes define compound waves
too. But there's a catch.

We can define the phase and amplitude of sine and cosine
waves because we know where to place 0π, the origin or reference. We know this location because we put the 0 there
ourselves. If we are ignorant of where to begin the π scale, we
don't know whether even a regular wave is a sine or cosine
wave, or something in between. There are an infinite number of
points between any two loci on the circumference of a circle,
and thus on the π scale. The pure sine wave stakes out one
limit and the cosine wave the other, while in between lie an infinite number of possible waves. Without knowing the origin of
our wave, we are infinitely ignorant of its phase.

Suppose, though, that instead of a single regular wave, we
have two waves that are out of phase by a definite amount of π.
We still can't treat phase in absolute terms. But when we have

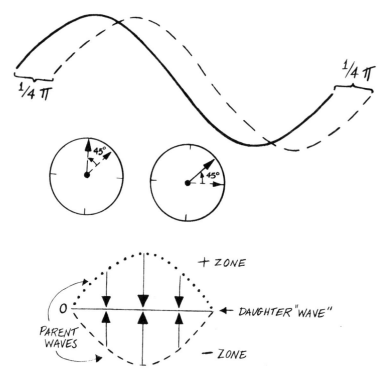

$\frac{1}{4}\pi$

$\frac{1}{4}\pi$

45°

45°

+ ZONE

O

PARENT
WAVES

← DAUGHTER "WAVE"

− ZONE

DESTRUCTIVE OR SUBTRACTIVE INTERFERENCE

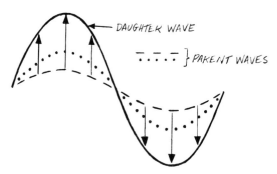

DAUGHTER WAVE

$\left.\begin{array}{c}-\ \cdot\ -\ \cdot\ - \\ \cdot\ \cdot\ \cdot\ \cdot\ \cdot\end{array}\right\}$ PARENT WAVES

CONSTRUCTIVE OR ADDITIVE INTERFERENCE

two waves, we can deal with their phase *difference* — their relative phase — just as we did in chapter 3 with the hands of the clock. And even though we may not be able to describe them in absolute terms, we will not be vague in specifying *any* phase difference in our system: our two waves or cycles are out of phase by a definite value of π. If we transfer our cycles to the circle, we can visualize the phase angle. In Fourier analysis, phase takes on the value of an angle.

In other words, relative phase has a well-defined meaning. That well-defined meaning can become a part of our intuitions most readily, in the ideal. And we need a clear intuitive idea of relative phase.

What about relative phase in compound waves? Let's approach the problem by considering what happens when we merge simple waves to produce daughter waves. In effect, let's analyze the question of interference, but in the ideal. Consider what happens if we add together two regular waves, both in phase and both of the same amplitude. When and where the two waves rise together, they will push each other up proportionally; likewise, when the waves move down together, they'll drive values further into the minus zone. If the amplitude is $+1$ in two colliding waves, the daughter wave will end up with an amplitude of $+2$, and its trough will bottom out at -2. Except for an increased amplitude, the daughter will look like the parents. This is an example of pure constructive interference; and it occurs when the two parents have the same phase, or a relative phase difference of 0. The outcome here depends strictly on the two amplitudes, which, incidentally, do not have to be identical, as in the example.

Next let's consider the consequences of two waves that are out of phase by π, 180 degrees, but have the same amplitude. They'll end up canceling each other at every point, just as when we add $+1$ to -1. The value of the daughter's amplitude will be 0. In other words, the daughter won't really be a wave but will

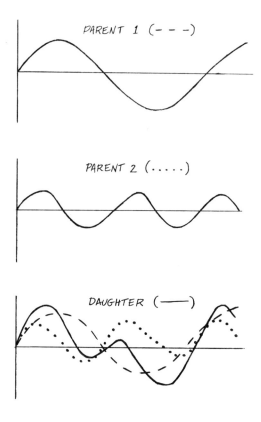

be the original horizontal plane. This is an example of pure destructive interference, which occurs when the colliding waves
are equal but of opposite phase.

Now let's take the case of two waves that have equal amplitude but are out of phase by something less than π, that is, 180
degrees. In some instances the point of collision will occur
where sections of the two waves rise or fall together, thus con-
structively interfering with each other — like the interference
that occurs when we add together numbers of the same sign. In
other instances, the interference will be destructive, like adding
+ and − numbers. The shape of the resulting daughter be-

comes quite complicated, even though the two parents may have the same amplitude. Yet any specific shape will be uniquely tied to some specific relative phase value.

Now let's make the problem a little more complicated. Suppose we have two regular waves, out of phase by less than π; but this time imagine that they have different amplitudes. The phase difference will determine where constructive and destructive interferences occur, but the magnitude of the resulting daughter at that point will depend on the amplitudes of both parents. Remember, though, that any daughter resulting from the collision of two regular waves will have a unique shape and size; and the resulting shape and size will be completely determined by the phase and amplitude of the two parents. In addition, if we know the phase and amplitude of just one parent, subtracting those values from the daughter will tell us the phase and amplitude of the other parent.

Suppose we coalesce three waves. The result may be very complicated, but the basic rules won't change: the new wave will be completely determined by the phase and amplitude of the three, four, five, six, or more interacting waves. Or the new compound wave will bear phase and amplitude spectra that have been determined completely by the interacting waves. How does this example differ from Fourier synthesis? For the most part, it doesn't. Fourier synthesis reverses the sequence of analysis. The process is an abstract form of a sequence of interferences that produce the original compound wave. But the compound wave, no matter how complicated it is or how many components contributed to its form, is an algebraic sum of a series of phases and amplitudes.

A moment ago when we were talking about simple waves, I pointed out that we could always figure out the values of an unknown parent wave if we knew the phase and amplitude of the other parent and the daughter. Why couldn't we do the same with an unknown compound wave? Why couldn't we introduce a known simple wave, measure the phase and amplitude spectrum of the new compound wave, and derive the unknown amplitudes and phases? It might take a long time, but we could do it, in theory. In fact, the holographer's reference wave is a kind of "known." The reference wave is a relative known in that its phase and amplitude spectra are identical to those of the object wave, before the latter strikes the scene and acquires complicating warps. The holographer's "known" results from coherency — a well-defined phase relationship. But the phase and amplitude spectra in the object wave, upon reacting with those of the reference wave, will completely determine the outcome of interference. And the results of that interference, when transferred to the hologram plate, create the hologram.

In dealing with waves, theoretical or physical, it is always critically important to remember their continuous nature. True, the physicist tells us that light waves are quantized, that filaments will emit light, and that detectors will absorb light as photons. We can look upon the quantized transfer of light as the emission or delivery of complete cycles of energy. But the light wave itself is still a continuum. Thus when we do something to part of the continuum, we do it to all of it. If we increase the radius of a circle, the entire circle increases. And we see the change just as readily in a wavy plot. Also, the change would affect the outcome of the union of that cycle with another cycle. If we change, say, the Fourier coefficient on the second cosine wave in a series, we would, potentially at least, alter the profile of the compound wave. And the effect would be distributed throughout the compound wave. For the components do not influence just one or two parts of the compound wave. They affect it everywhere. The continuous nature of waves is the reason that in Leith and Upatnieks's diffuse hologram every point in the object wave front bore the warping effects of every point in the illuminated scene.

As I have mentioned numerous times, relative phase is the birthmark of all holograms, and thus the central issue in hologramic theory. Remember that phase makes a sine wave a sine wave and a cosine wave a cosine wave, once there's any amplitude to work with. We can come to the very same conclusion for the compound wave: the amplitude spectrum will prescribe how much, but the phase spectrum will determine the distribution of the amplitude spectrum. Thus our profiles, yours and mine, are as recognizable on the surface of a dime as they would be on the face of Mount Rushmore. And your profile is uniquely yours, and mine mine, because of unique phase spectra.

In this chapter, we have examined waves in the ideal. For only in the ideal can we free our reason from the bondage of experience. We are about to extend our thoughts into the hologram. Using reason, we will enter an abstract space where phase information lies encoded. This space is most often called Fourier transform space. The entry fee for crossing its boundaries is the Fourier transform (the equation I mentioned earlier in the chapter) that Fourier analysis yields. We make this journey in the next chapter.

8

Ideal Mind

IN THE LAST CHAPTER, we learned some of the basic vocabulary of hologramic theory. Now we begin the process of constructing a language, of assembling vehicles to convey brand new thoughts about the universe within the brain. In this chapter and the next, we will raise questions about the mind that no one could have articulated just a few years ago. Let me forewarn the reader, though, that our answers will not take the form of *the* physiological mechanism, *the* chemical reaction, *the* molecule, or *the* cellular response. Hologramic theory denies the assumption implicit in questions that demand the answer as bits of brain.

What *is* hologramic mind? What *is* the nature of the phase code? What *is* remembering? Recalling? Perceiving? Why does hologramic theory assert that parts of the brain, as such, do not constitute memory, per se? Why does hologramic theory make no fundamental distinction between learning and instinct? Why does hologramic theory predict the outcome of my experiments on salamanders? We have touched on these issues already, but in an inferential, analogous, and superficial way. Now we are on the brink of deriving the answers directly from hologramic theory itself. We will start by reasoning inductively from waves to the hologram and on to hologramic theory. Then, having done that, we will deduce the principles of hologramic mind.

The coordinate system we used in chapter 7 exists on an ideal plane, but one we can easily superimpose on the surfaces we experience. We can draw sine or cosine axes vertically on, say, the bedroom wall, or scribe a π scale on a paper towel. If we equate sine values with something such as lumens of moon-light, and place 29 ½-day intervals between each 2π on our horizontal axis, we can plot the phases of the moon. Alternatively, we could put stock-market quotations on the ordinate (sine or cosine axis) and years on the abscissa (our π scale), and get rich or go broke applying Fourier analysis and synthesis to the cycles of finance. Ideal though they were, our theoretical waves dwelt in the space of our intuitive reality. I shall call this space "perceptual" space, whether it be "real" or "ideal."

I mentioned in the last chapter that in analyzing the compound wave as a Fourier series of component regular waves, the analyst calculates Fourier coefficients — the values required to make each component's frequency part of a continuous, serial progression of frequencies. I also mentioned that the analyst uses the coefficients to construct a graph, or write its equation. This is known as the Fourier transform. From Fourier transforms, the analyst calculates phase, amplitude, and frequency spectra.

In general usage, "transform" is a verb; and it sometimes is in mathematics. Usually, though, the mathematician employs "transform" as a noun, as the name for a figure or equation resulting from a transformation. Mathematical dictionaries define transformation as the passage from one figure or expression to another.[1] While "transform" has specialized implications, its source, transformation, coincides with general usage. In fact, a few mathematical transformations and their resulting transforms are a part of everyday experience. A good example is the

---

[1] See James and James, 1968; also, *The International Dictionary of Applied Mathematics.*

Mercator projection of the earth, in which the apparent size of the United States, relative to Greenland, has mystified more than one school child, and in which the Soviet Union, split down the middle, ends up on opposite edges of the flat transform of the globe. We have made use of transformation ourselves, by moving from circles to waves and back again. In executing a Fourier transformation, in creating the Fourier transform of components, the analyst shifts the values from perceptual space to an idealized domain known as a *Fourier transform space*. Sometimes the analyst's objective is to simplify calculations. Operations that would require calculus in perceptual space employ multiplication and division in transform space. Also, many events that don't look wavy in perceptual space show their periodic characteristics when represented as Fourier transforms, and as their more abstract cousins, the Laplace transforms. But my reason for introducing transform space has to do with the hologram. Transform space is where the hologram's message abides. The Fourier transform is our link to transform space.

We cannot directly experience transform space. Is it pure construct of reasoning? Or alternatively, is it a "place" in the same sense as the glove compartment of a car? I cannot say, one way or the other. But though we may not *visualize* transform space on the planes of experience, we can nonetheless establish its *existence* within our intuition; we can connect it to our awareness; and we give it an identity among our thoughts.

Have you ever looked through the teeth of a comb, in soft candle light, and observed the halos, the diffractions of light, at the slits? If not, you might try this: hold the tips of your thumb and index finger close to your eye; bring them together until they almost touch. You should notice that the halos overlap and occlude the slit before your fingers actually touch. Those halos are physical analogues of Fourier and Laplace transforms. In principle, the edges of your fingers do to the light waves what the Fourier analyst does with numerical values: they execute a transformation from perceptual to transform space. What is transformed? The image the light waves would have carried to your eyes, if the halos hadn't transformed each other.

If the transform exists, the transform space containing it also exists. I say this not to propound a principle but to give the reader an impressionistic awareness of transform space. We have to intuit the ideal domain much as we would surmise that a sea is deep because a gigantic whale suddenly bursts from its surface.

Now I will put forth a principle. Although we cannot literally visualize the interior of a transform space, we can grasp the logical interplay of transformed entities. And very often, with the correct choice of a specific transform space, we can greatly simplify the meaning of an otherwise arcane idea. Let me demonstrate this point by introducing a process called convolution, whose ramifications and underlying theorem — convolution theorem — we will soon call upon.

Convolution refers to the superimposition of independent sets, planes, or magnitudes. Consider two initially separated sets of dots, A and B, in perceptual space, as depicted in the figure on page 146. (My description is a highly modified version of one in Holmes and Blow, 1966.) The dots of A line up on the horizontal axis at intervals of 5 units, say, inches. Those of B lie 2 inches apart and run obliquely upward from left to right. If we "convolute" A and B, we create a two-dimensional lattice. And if we use an asterisk to indicate the convolution operation, we may define the lattice as A^*B, which we would read "A convoluted on B." But what do we mean by *convolute*? And just how does the operation produce a lattice? The answers are quite complicated in perceptual space, but are very simple in what is called a reciprocal space ($1/$ space).

We create $1/$ space from Fourier transforms. The Fourier transform of a line of dots is a grating; that is, a series of uniform lines. In $^1/$ space the transform of A, let's call it $T(A)$, is a grating made up of vertical lines whose spacings are the reciprocal of 5 inches — $^1/_5$ or 0.2 inches. The transform of B, $T(B)$, is oblique lines running downward from left to right, with ½ or 0.5 inch spacings — the reciprocal of 2 inches. We can actually superimpose the planes represented in $T(A)$ and $T(B)$. Because the transforms are lines, we can see that the superimposition of the two creates a grid, something we could not observe with dots. The abstract operation corresponding to our superimposition is the same as the uniting of height and width to produce the area of a rectangle. This operation is multiplication.

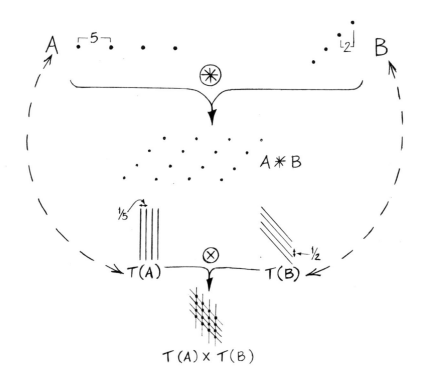

$T(A) \times T(B)$

And we can define the grid simply as $T(A) \times T(B)$. Now let's take stock.

First, perceptual and $^1/$ space are reciprocal transformations of each other. Second, A and $T(A)$ are transforms of each other, as are B and $T(B)$. Therefore, the mysterious A^*B — the lattice produced by the convolution of A and B in perceptual space — is simply the reciprocal of $T(A) \times T(B)$. In other words, the asterisk in perceptual space is the equivalent of the multiplication sign in $^1/$ space. We can't say that convolution is multiplication. But we can see for ourselves that multiplication is the transform of convolution. Now multiplication is so much a part of our everyday lives that we hardly think of it as an act of pure reason. But that's precisely what it is. And in opting for transform space, we made a small sacrifice in terms of intuition, for a substantial gain in what we could make available to pure reason: simple arithmetic.

The convolution *theorem,* which we are about to employ, is the mathematical proof that indeed convolution is what we said it is — an arithmetic operation on transforms. The critical lesson in our exercise is that while transform space is as remote as it ever was, it is far from incomprehensible. Fourier series have their corresponding Fourier transforms. And when attributes of waves do become incomprehensible to the intuition, in perceptual space, the appropriate transformation will put those attributes within the reach of reason.

When objects distort the phase and amplitude of light, the resulting warps add up not to an image of the object but to the object's transform. The cornea and lens — the eye's optical system — *transform* the transform into the object's image. The convolution theorem shows that the Fourier transform of the *Fourier transform* of an object yields the image. I'm sorry about the double talk. But the convolution theorem explains how the eye, a projector, or a microscope can turn the wave's warps into an image: the objects transform the carrier waves, and the lens system transforms the transforms from transform to perceptual space. Now I must apologize for triple talk. But think back for a moment to the halos. They are transforms of transforms right at your finger tips. Because your eye performed a third transformation, you saw transforms instead of images of the tips of your fingers.

Just as the Mercator projection and the globe are different ways of representing the same thing, so Fourier transforms and Fourier series provide different perspectives on periodic phenomena. We can use what we learned in chapter 7 to understand the ideas we're formulating now. Think of the visible features of a face, a dewdrop, or a stand of pine trees as a potential compound wave in three dimensions. The interaction between carrier waves and objects is comparable to Fourier analysis — to the dissection of the compound wave into a series of its components, except in transform space instead of perceptual space. In other words, the first transformation is much like producing a Fourier series. The second transformation — the one that occurs at the eye and shifts the components from transform space to perceptual space — is comparable to Fourier synthesis, to synthesis of the series of components into a compound wave.

The hologram captures the transform of an object, not the object's image. The interference of object and reference waves shifts their components into transform space. To conceptualize the reaction, let's form our imagery around waves, in perceptual space, but let's use reasoning alone for events occurring in transform space. Visualize the components of the compound object wave as strung out in a row, as we might draw them on a piece of graph paper in perceptual space. Along come reference waves that collide and interfere with each component. Each collision produces a daughter wave whose phase and amplitude are the algebraic sums of the phase and amplitude of the particular component plus those of the reference wave; or the reference wave and each component superimpose on each other. But the reactions take place in transform space, remember, and not in the perceptual space we use to aid our imagery. Therefore, we would observe not the image carried in the object wave, but an interference pattern, the transform — the hologram.

By imagining the components of a transform to be a Fourier series, we provide ourselves with something to "picture." This analogy could create the false impression that the object wave loses its continuity, that each component congeals into an isolated little unit in transform space. A continuum is a system in which the parts aren't separated; and the hologram is a continuum. We can appreciate its continuous nature by observing diffuse-light holograms, any arbitrarily selected piece of which will reconstruct a whole image of the scene. Although the reference must act upon each of the object wave's components, as in our conceptualization, the interference pattern represents the whole.

Of course, no interference patterns or holograms can develop unless the reference and object waves have a "well-defined" phase relationship. Recall that the optical holographer, using Young's and Fresnel's old tricks, produces orderly phase relationships by deriving object and reference waves from the same coherent source. What do we mean, though, by "well-defined?" Let me invoke a strange but powerful theorem of topology that will take us into the general meaning of "well-defined" — a theorem known as Brouwer's fixed-point theorem.

Brouwer's theorem is at the foundations of several mathematical ideas, and it is implicit in a great many more. The interested reader will enjoy M. Shinbrot's excellent article on the fixed-point theorem, which I list in the bibliography. Here, I will simply state the theorem without probing its simple but tricky proof.

Brouwer's theorem guarantees that in a continuous distortion of a system — as in stretching without tearing a rubber sheet, or stirring without splashing a bowl of clam chowder — at least one point *must* remain unchanged. This point is the fixed point. Shinbrot describes how variants of the theorem have actually been used to predict contours on the ocean's floor from characteristics of the water's surface. The absence of a fixed point is enough to deny a truly continuous relationship between two entities or magnitudes.

What is an object wave? In terms of frequency, it is the reference wave plus the changes imposed by the object. Before the object wave arrives at the object, its frequency is identical to that of the reference wave. The object imposes a spectrum of new frequencies on the object wave. But, invoking Brouwer's theorem, we note that one point in the object wave is not changed as a result of the collision, and the frequency at that point is the same before and after the object. In other words, the frequencies in the object wave will vary, but relative to the invariant frequency at the fixed point. Because the reference and object waves once had identical frequencies, the fixed point in the object wave must have a counterpart in the reference wave. Through the fixed point, the frequency spectrum in the object wave varies — but relative to the frequency of the reference.

We must take note of an important difference between object and reference waves, namely the phase variation resulting from their different paths. Let's call this phase variation D. D will vary for each object component vis-à-vis the reference. But because of the fixed point, one of those D's will have the same value before and after the reference and object waves interfere; and all the other D's will vary relative to the invariant D. Variation relative to some invariant quantity is the general meaning of "well-defined," including "well-defined" phase relationships in interference phenomena. And a well-defined spectrum of *D*'s in transform space is the minimum condition of the hologram. The minimum *requirement* is a fixed-point relationship between object and reference waves. A specific hologram is, at minimum, a particular spectrum of well-defined *D*'s in transform space.

Reconstruction of the images from the hologram involves transforming the transform, synthesizing the original compound wave, and transferring the visible features of the scene back to perceptual space. This statement is a veritable reiteration of how the object originally communicated its image. In theory, the hologram regenerates what the object generates. In order for a wave to serve reconstruction, it must interact with all the components and must also satisfy the fixed-point requirement.

What then *is* a memory? Transferring the principles we have developed to hologramic theory, and using the language we have developed thus far, we can define a specific memory as a particular spectrum of *D*'s in transform space. What are *D*'s? They are phase *differences* — relative values, relationships between and among constituents of the storage medium, the brain. Thus, in hologramic theory, the brain stores mind not as cells, chemicals, electrical currents, or any other entities of perceptual space, but as relationships at least as abstract as any information housed in the transform space of a physical hologram. The parts and mechanisms of the brain do count; but the *D*'s they establish in transform space are what make memory what it *is*. If we try to visualize stored mind by literal comparisons with experience, we surrender the chance of forming any valid concept at all of hologramic mind, and quite possibly yield all hope of ever establishing the existence of the noumenon where brain stores thought.

In hologramic theory, the utilization of series of D's during covert or overt behavior, in recall or thoughts or feelings or whatever, *is* transforming the transform into perceptual space.

This is a good point at which to examine the theoretical meaning of a percept. A percept, the dictionary tells us, is what we're aware of through our senses or by apprehension and understanding with the mind. In hologramic theory, a percept is a phase spectrum, a series of D's, in perceptual space. An activated memory, a reminiscence, is a back-transformed series of D's that have been moved from transform to perceptual space. In terms of the phase code, then, perception and reminiscence involve the same basic information, the difference being the sources of the D's: the percept is analogous to image generation by the object, while the activated memory is analogous to the reconstruction from the hologram. But both synthesize the message in the same *theoretical* way: the percept is a transformed transform of signals from the sense organs; the activated memory is the back-transformed series of D's stored in transform space. Just as the hologram regenerates what the object generates, memory regenerates what perception generates, as Karl Pribram asserted in a lecture some years ago.

The specific character of the activated memory depends on the particular readout. A useful analogy here would be to the holographer's use of light instead of sound to decode an acoustical hologram, except that the nervous system has many more options than does the engineer. The activating signal would determine the special features of the transformed transform, but the phase spectrum — the basic series of D's — would be the same whether the imagination or the fist punched somebody in the nose. In other words, through the code in transform space, behavior is a transduced version of perception. I will expand upon this idea more fully in a later chapter, after we've extended hologramic theory beyond where we are now. But we've already come far enough for me to say that hologramic theory provides a unified view of the subjective cosmos. There's not a box over here labeled "perception" and one over there marked "behavior," with fundamentally different laws of Nature governing each. One abstract set of rules works ubiquitously.

Frequency in perceptual space depends on time. Thus the Hz (hertz) value specifies cycles per *second*. In an interference pattern, however, frequency refers to how many stripes or beats occur in a given area. And whereas frequency assumes a temporal character in perceptual space, it takes on spatial meaning in transform space.

We can draw an insightful corollary from the preceding paragraph. The phase difference between two interfering sets of waves determines the frequency of beats or stripes within the interference pattern. An intimate relationship exists, then, between phase and frequency. In FM (frequency modulated) radio, a specific message is a particular spectrum of phase variations. In waves with frequency independent of amplitude, as is true in the nervous system, the phase-difference spectrum in transform space *is* the stored memory. Earlier we used Metherell's phase-only acoustical holograms to postulate phase codes as the character of hologramic mind. But we have just deduced this conclusion directly from the theory itself.

Karl Pribram suggested in the 1960s that visual perception may be analogous to Fourier transforms. He had in mind the hologram. Rather recently, a couple named De Valois and their collaborators developed a computerized system for calculating Fourier transforms of checkerboard and plaid patterns. They used the system to analyze neurons of the visual cortexes of monkeys and cats. Are these cells coded to perceive structural elements of the patterns? No. The neurons in the visual cortex responded to Fourier transforms of the patterns, rather than to

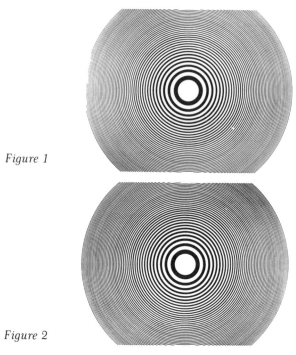

Figure 1

Figure 2

Figures 1–9 photographed by Jacque Kubley

the patterns' structural elements. The De Valois's results "were not just approximately correct, but were exact" within the precision of their system.[2] As Pribram had predicted, the retina sends the brain not a literal rendition of the image, but a transform of the image. To phrase this in the language of hologramic theory, the phase codes stored in cells in the visual cortex transform the transform into images in the perceptual space of the conscious mind.

◇   ◇   ◇

[2] De Valois et al., 1979, p. 501.

Mathematicians discover the properties of their theorems by manipulating equations, by bringing different terms together in novel ways. We will manipulate phase codes. Instead of equations, though, we will do our "calculations" in the "real" world, with pictures.

Notice the identical sets of rings in figures 1 and 2. They're optical analogues of the crests of ripples on a pond. I superimposed these two sets of rings out of phase to produce the moiré patterns in figures 3 and 4. The moirés are interference patterns, and the phase difference is how off-center the two sets are relative to each other. If we compare figures 3 and 4, it is apparent that the frequency of beats, as well as their widths and spacings, vary with the phase shift. When the two centers lie closer together, as in figure 3, the stripes are coarse, widely spaced and of low frequency. Where the phase difference is great, as in figure 4, frequency is high, spacings are narrow, and the stripes are thin. The stripes are precisely determined by the phase shift. And these stripes represent the phase code in transform space.

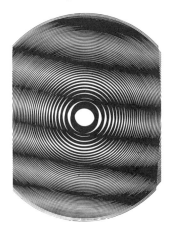

Figure 3   *Figure 4*

Figure 5   Figure 6

Figure 7

Are the stripes memories of the phase spectrum in the rings? The answer is yes, when the stripes reach high frequency. But let's not take my word for it. Let's turn the statement into a hypothesis and test it. If stripes encode for rings, we should be able to back-transform to rings from stripes alone. We ought to be able to overlay stripes on a set of rings and make new rings in perceptual space. Figure 5 is the putative memory, figure 6 its posited transform, and figure 7 the actual result of the test. New rings do indeed back-transform into perceptual space when we superimpose only stripes on them.

What do we mean by stripes? They are beats, yes. But stripes are periodic patterns of light and dark, a harmonic array of alternating densities. Given this, the memory of rings shouldn't literally be confined to stripes. The memory is a *periodicity,* a wavy logic. We should be able to back-transform rings from, say, dots. Figure 8 shows that dots on rings will indeed create new rings.

Figure 8

I am presenting this dot experiment for another reason as well. Perhaps the rings are just a matter of luck. Maybe the various dots are spaced fortuitously to interact with the correct arcs. If we look at figure 8 carefully, we see that not all rings are the same. In fact, those on opposite ends of the vertical and horizontal axes, thus lying on perspective arcs of the same circles, are mirror images of each other: where one ring has a dark center, the corresponding ring is light. If the "maybe" speculations above were right, these rings would be identical. But they are not.

The dots also show something I hadn't foreseen but can't resist pointing out, for it illustrates perception and memory so well. I mentioned in chapter 4 that we often have difficulty remembering something exactly as we originally experienced it. Have you ever fumbled around with several vivid recollections that are similar, and wondered which is the correct one? Even our simple optical patterns seem to have this difficulty. Of course, taking a look at one's notes or using a fresh percept for comparison usually solves the problem much better than does memory alone. Likewise, with our dot system we merely have to compare the various readouts with the rings in the center. Figure 8 shows the cross-correlation of two series, thus indicating the apprehension part of perception.

In hologramic theory, reasoning, thinking, associating, or any equivalent of correlating is matching the newly transformed transform with the back-transform. (The technical term for such matching is autocorrelation.)

Let's shift our focus back to the nature of the phase code, which in our ring system is the preservation of ring information by periodic patterns. The ring memory is not limited to dots and stripes. When we react rings with too great a distance between their centers, we do not produce stripes. Instead, something interesting happens. Inspect figure 9, and notice that rings are forming in the regions of overlap. Built into the higher-frequency rings is a memory of rings closer to the center. Let me explain.

First of all, as I have pointed out, the phase code is not literally stripes or dots, but rather a certain periodicity, a logic. Our rings are much like ripples on a pond; they expand from the center just as any wave front advances from the origin. Recall from Huygens's principle that each point in a wave contributes to the advancing wave front. The waves at the periphery contain a memory of their entire ancestry. When we superimpose sets of rings in the manner shown in figure 9, we back-transform those hidden, unsuspected "ancestral" memories into perceptual space. Figure 9 shows that no necessary relationship exists between the nature of a phase code and how the code came into being. The "calculation" represented by figure 9 shows why hologramic theory fits the prescriptions of neither empirical nor rational schools of thought. In figures 3 and 4, the system had to "learn" the code; the two systems had to "experience" each other within a certain boundary, in order to transfer their phase variations into transform space. But the very same code also grew spontaneously out of the "innate" advance of the wave front. These are the reasons I would not define memory on the basis of either learning or instinct. Memory *is* phase codes: whether it's "learned" or "instinctive" has no bearing on its mathematical, and therefore necessary, features.

Consider something else our stripes, dots, and rings reveal about the phase code. We can't assign memory to specific structural attributes of the system. In hologramic theory, memory is without fixed size, absolute proportions, or particular architec-

Figure 9

ture. Memory is stored as abstract periodicity in transform space. This abstract property is the theoretical basis for the predictions my shufflebrain experiments vindicated, and for why shuffling a salamander's brain doesn't scramble its stored mind. My instruments cannot reach into the ideal transform space where mind is stored. Hologramic mind will not reduce directly to constituents of the brain.

9

The Hological Continuum

NORBERT WIENER, the mathematician who founded cybernetics just after World War II, once observed, in reference to electronic computers, that "the energy spent per individual operation is almost vanishingly small," and he went on to warn scientists that "Information is information, not matter or energy. No materialism which does not admit this can survive at the present day."[1] Wiener equated contemporary materialism with the doctrine of mechanism, with the idea that life depends on chemistry and physics. And he realized that reducing the message to the medium would eventually force the repeal of the powerful laws of thermodynamics. Wiener knew that information couldn't exist on nothing. But to insist that information and mass-energy are one and the same thing would quickly put the natural sciences in an untenable philosophical position, for the reason Wiener mentioned. Abstract relationships within mass-energy create, encode, and store information, not matter or energy as measured by the pound or the erg.

With respect to the hologram, we have already arrived at Wiener's conclusions: functional *relationships* within the media encode phase information. Thus vastly different physical entities, widely varying absolute energies, or basically dissimilar

---

[1] Wiener, 1961, p. 132.

chemical reagents can construct, store, and decode the same hologram — as information. Initially, and by implication, we extended this principle to hologramic mind. But at the end of the last chapter, we reached this very same conclusion directly, from hologramic theory itself. A mind, the theory asserts, is not specific molecules, particular cells, certain physiological mechanisms, or whatever may serve as its media. It is phase information — relationships displayed in time and in what we have termed perceptual space, and stored as a function of time in transform space. We have a subtle but pivotal distinction to make, then. Molecules, cells, mechanisms, and the like must create, maintain, or display those phase relationships. But the relationships are not reducible to the molecule, cell, or mechanism any more than, say, the message on this page is reducible to ink and paper. And when we investigate mind in molecules, cells, or mechanisms, we have to be very careful in choosing a verb to describe the results we expect. Conjugates and equivalents of "to do" are what we want when we use test tubes, microscopes, or electrodes. But when we ask what mind *is*, we must turn to theory.

Does hologramic theory demand that different constituents and mechanisms of the brain house memory? The answer is no. As Bertrand Russell maintained, theory is general. The moment we begin talking about parts, we shift to the particular, to issues the experimentalist must pursue. What hologramic theory does, though, is account for how more than one class of things or events may serve as a medium for the same memory. If a protein encodes the same spectrum of phase variations as occur in a feedback loop around, say, the hippocampus, the same memory exists in or on both the protein and the feedback loop.

The test tube, the microscope, and the electrode work only in perceptual space. Of course, this restriction doesn't minimize their value, nor does it undermine the importance of experience. But to get inside hologramic mind, to unravel its logic, discover its plan, figure out how it works, we must use abstract tools. For only with reason and imagination can we cross the boundary between the real and the ideal.

Yet we can use imagination to resynthesize in our own reality the relationships our reason uncovers in realms beyond. We did this with transforms and series. The holographer also does it with reconstruction beams. Pribram did it and continues to do it in the remembering brains of monkeys. I did it with shufflebrain, unwittingly at first. If we use our theory with art as well as science, not only do we extend our comprehension beyond experience, but we avoid imprisonment in the ideal, and exile from our own reality. Hologramic theory does not dispense with the brain. Activated mind does operate in perceptual space.

In its present form, though, hologramic theory will not serve our needs. Fourier transform space is too cramped for us to appreciate, for instance, the similarities and differences between our own mental cosmos and the minds of other creatures. It is too linear to explain the nonlinear relationship between the time we measure by the clock and the intervals that elapse in dreams, for example. Nor can we readily envisage the smooth, continuous movement of information from sensations to perceptions to memories to behavioral acts to whatever. How can the information be the same while the events retain their obvious differences? Described in the language of the Fourier theorem, mind seems more like the inner workings of a stereo set than the subjective universe of a living creature. If the reader has already felt that something must be wrong with our picture, it's because he or she knows very well that we living organisms aren't squared-off, smoothed-down, case-hardened gadgets.

Thus far, the constraints on our understanding have two primary causes. First, our theory is now anchored to the axioms and postulates of Euclid's geometry. Second, we haven't yet given sufficient *theoretical* definition to the particular, having been too preoccupied with escaping from experience to give it the attention it really deserves. In this chapter, I will first reassemble hologramic theory free of the assumptions employed in previous chapters. Then I will draw the realm of the particular into the picture.

June 10, 1854, was an important moment in the history of thought. It was also a very important day in the brief life of a mathematician named Georg Friedrich Bernhard Riemann. It was the day he stood before the distinguished professors of Göttingen's celebrated university and delivered his formal trial lecture as a probationary member of the faculty. Entitled "On the Hypotheses Which Lie at the Foundations of Geometry," the lecture attacked a dogma that had ruled rational belief "From Euclid to Legrendre."[2]

"It is well known," began the twenty-eight-year-old *Privatdozent*, "that geometry presupposes not only the concept of space but also the first fundamental notions for constructions in space as given in advance. It gives only nominal definitions for them, while the essential means of determining them appear in the form of axioms. The relation [logic] of these presuppositions [postulates of geometry] is left in the dark; one sees neither whether and in how far their connection [cause-effect] is necessary, nor a priori whether it is possible."

In the detached *bon ton* of scholars then and now, Riemann was in effect saying that mathematicians and philosophers had simply assumed that space is just *there*. Like the gods in *The Iliad* who had external views of the mortal realm, mathematicians and philosophers had inspected space in toto, had immediately brought rectilinear order to the nullity, with the flat planes of length, width, and height, and thereby had

---

[2] See Riemann, 1929*b*, pp. 411–425.

known at a glance how every journey on a line, across a surface, or into a volume must start, progress, and stop. Geometric magnitudes — distance, area, volume — followed automatically.

Ever since Newton and Leibniz had invented calculus, infinitely small regions of curves had been open to mathematical inquiry; but points on the straight line had eluded the mathematician and philosopher alike. Riemann doubted that the same fundamental elements — points — could obey fundamentally different mathematical laws in curves as opposed to lines. He believed that points in flat figures had become enigmas because geometry had been constructed from the top down, instead of from the bottom up: "Accordingly, I have proposed to myself at first the problem of constructing a multiply extended [many-dimensional] magnitude [space] out of the general notions of quantity." He would begin with infinitely small relationships, and reason out the primitive, elementary rules, instead of assuming them; then he would follow the trail he had discovered, and not assume that he knew the course before his journey had begun.

I might note here that the first formal principle of quantity remains to be found, if one really exists at all. Even Riemann's genius had to be ignited by intuition. Intuitively speaking, the basic notions of quantity imply measuring something with something else. As in our experiments with optical transforms, in the last chapter, measuring, to Riemann, "consists in superposition of the magnitudes to be compared." As is the case with the reference and object waves in the hologram, superposition of the two magnitudes or quantities occurs "only when the one is part of the other."[3] Riemann was speaking about continuity in the most exacting analytical sense of the word.

---

[3] If Riemann's words sound like the fixed-point theorem we used in the last chapter, there is a very good reason. In a later investigation, he virtually laid the groundwork for modern topology. His lecture contains the germ of his later work.

Where can we find continuity? More important, how can we guarantee its existence in the relationship of, say, X and Y? To satisfy Riemann's requirements, we would have to show that at least one of the elements involved *necessarily* affects the other. Thus a frog on a lily pad won't do, especially when the animal is just sitting there enjoying the sunshine. We would have to find out whether any *change* in either the animal or the plant guarantees a concomitant variation in the other. Thus the first requirement for establishing continuity is to get away from static situations and focus on dynamic or variable relationships.

Suppose, though, that one unit of change in X produces a one-unit change in Y; in other words, that Y =X. If we graph Y versus X, the plot will be a straight line. In a linear relationship, the ratio of Y to X remains constant, of course, no matter how large or small the values become. This constancy made mathematicians before Riemann shy away from points on the straight line. For an infinite number of points exist between any two regions of the line, even as the values of X and Y approach zero: we never close the infinite interval between two *points* on a straight line.

The curve is another story. What is a curve? My handworn 1964 edition of *Encyclopedia Britannica* characterizes it as "the envelope of its tangents." Remember that on a circle, the very embodiment of curvature, we draw a tangent to a single point on the circumference. The same holds for tangents to a curve; and we do not draw a tangent to a straight line. A tangent is also a function of an angle, remember. We might even think of it as a functional indicator of a specific direction. The points on a straight line all have the same direction; therefore a tangent to the straight line would yield no information about *changes* in direction. Neighboring points on a curve, by contrast, have different relative directions. Each takes its own tangent; and the tangent to the curve will tell us something about how the directions of one point vary relative to other points.

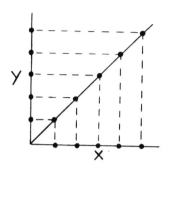

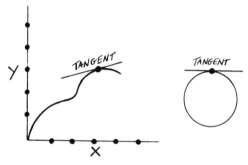

Imagine that we draw a tangent to a single point on the X-Y curve. The bend in the curve at that point will determine the slope of the tangent. If we could actually get down and look at our X-Y point, we would find that its direction coincides with our tangent's slope. Of course, we cannot reach the point. But we can *continuously* shrink X and Y closer and closer to our point. As we get nearer and nearer to the point, the discrepancy between the curvature of the curve and the slope of the tangent becomes smaller and smaller. Eventually, we arrive at a vanishingly tiny difference between curve and tangent. We approach what Isaac Newton called — and mathematicians still call — a "limit" in the change of Y in relation to X. The limit — the point-sized tangent — is much like what we obtain when we convert the value of π from $^{22}/_7$ to 3.14159 and on and on in decimal places until we have an insignificant but always persisting amount left over. The limit is very close to our point. The continuous nature of the change in Y to X allows us to approach the limit.

Finding limits is the subject of differential calculus. The principal operation, aptly called differentiation, is a search for limit-approaching ratios known as derivatives. The derivative is a guarantee of continuity between Y and X at a point. The existence of the derivative, in other words, satisfies Riemann's criterion of continuity: Y is part of X. The derivative is strictly a property of curves. For the derivative is a manifestation of changing change in the relationships of a point to its immediate neighbors. Derivatives, minuscule but measurable relationships around points, were the basis from which Riemann developed the fundamental rules for his new geometry.

Derivatives are abstractions. With one valuable exception, we can gain no impression of their character by representing them in perceptual space. The exception, though, permits me to illustrate how Riemann discovered measurable relationships among points.

The exceptional derivative signals itself in most mathematics books by an italicized lower-case e.[4] The numerical value of e is $2.718218 \cdots$ (to infinity). It goes on and on forever, like π. The curve of e is smooth in contour and sigmoid in shape, and it relates Y to X in the following manner: $Y = e^X$. In other words, Y equals $2.718 \cdots$ if X is 1; the square of e, if X is 2; the cube of e, if X is 3; and so forth to infinity. In the latter expression, e to some power of X is a function of X, meaning that e has a variational relationship to Y. But what makes e so very special to us is that its derivative equals the function. In other words, when we look at a sigmoid curve, we see what we would see if we could

---

[4] The exceptional derivative is the base of natural or Naperian logarithms.

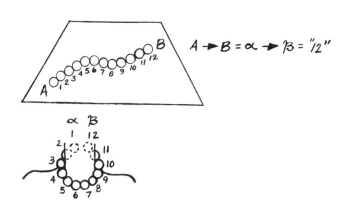

$$A \rightarrow B = \alpha \rightarrow \beta = "/2"$$

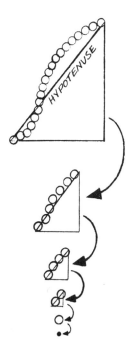

HYPOTENUSE

actually plot $Y = e^x$ at a single point. Thus what we represent in perceptual space as an S-shaped curve has validity for what we can't actually see at the point.

Imagine now that we have undertaken the task of exploring geometric figures. Assume that, like Riemann, we don't know the rules in advance, and that our only metering device is e. For the sake of imagery, envisage e's as a string of pearls. Assume that we can bend, increase, or decrease the number of e's but can neither break nor stretch the string.

Suppose we come upon a flat surface, and find two points, A and B. What would be the shortest distance between them? Remember, we have to base our answers on what we can measure. Gauged by our string of pearly e's, the shortest path is the least number of e's between A and B.

Suppose the distance from A to B is 12 pearls. Now imagine that we put the string around someone's neck. Clearly, a path of 12 pearls remains unchanged even though the new surface curves. Or, with e's as a gauge, we can relate a flat surface to a curved surface merely by finding their respective least curvatures — the least number of e's. In our imaginary universes, round and square thus become variants of a common theme.

Let's return to the flat surface. This time, imagine that we find a large right triangle. If we place a string of e's on the hypotenuse, we find a sizable discrepancy. The string fits very loosely, and we cannot gauge the length of the hypotenuse very accurately. Suppose, though, that we make the triangle and the string of pearls smaller and smaller. As we do, the discrepancy shrinks and shrinks. Eventually, the difference between the hypotenuse and the string of e's becomes so small as to be insignificant. Despite all the proscriptions of tradition, the hypotenuse — which is a straight line — has begun approaching a limit, *relative to our pearls*. We do not want to assert that the hypotenuse and our pearly e's are "the same thing." If we do, we create the contradiction that the hypotenuse and the sigmoid curve look alike, which we know is false. But at infinity, the one is part of the other. The measurable part is *e*. Thus a *point* in the hypotenuse has a measurable feature in common with a point in our pearls of *e*. And that measurable feature is curvature.

Riemann arrived at such an inference, but in a much more general, inclusive, and rigorous way. "About any point," he discovered, "the metric [measurable] relations are exactly the same as about any other point." A straight line, flat surface, or rectilinear space consists of the same fundamental elements as a curve, circle, or sphere; and magnitudes, round or square, "are completely determined by the measure of curvature." Riemann showed that "flatness in smallest parts" represents "a particular case of those [geometric figures] whose curvature is everywhere constant." Flatness turned out to be zero curvature. In other words, a geometric universe constructed for elementary *measurable* relationships among points becomes an infinite continuum of curvatures, positive and negative as well as zero.

Riemann demonstrated that "the propositions of geometry are not derivable from general concepts of quantity, but . . . only from experience." Out went the absolute prohibition against dealing with infinitely small regions of straight lines.[5] Out went the notion that parallel lines *never* cross. Out went the universal dogma of even our own day that the shortest distance between points is *always* a straight line.

The prohibition against points on lines was an artifact of trying to approach points from a flattened-down, squared-off universe; and the same had been true about parallel lines. And where did we ever get the notion that the shortest distance is the straight path? Our ancestors, noticing the curved shape of the sky, wisely made their measurements on the ground. That

---

[5] A contemporary mathematician, Benoit Mandelbrot, has discovered entities he calls "fractals," which lift the restrictions even further. See bibliography.

was before Columbus. Afterward, and in our own times, the argument in favor of straight lines has had its vindication in the peroration of my little sister's ontology: "Because the teacher said!"

But how can this be? Why don't the bridges all fall down?

The irony is that Riemann's system is not anti-Euclidean. As he pointed out, Euclid's geometry belongs to the realm of experience. It is the geometry we invent and use for distances neither very great nor very small, for uncomplicated planes, for simple spaces, for universes of noncomplex dimensions. With Riemann's system as a guide, Euclid's propositions even acquire a valid a priori foundation. (See the article by Paul Cohen and R. Hersh for more details on the latter point.) Their limitations no longer hidden from our understanding, Euclid's rules continue to serve us. Infinitesimally small regions of a straight line are beyond the Euclidean approach; parallel lines don't cross on a Euclidean plane; and as far as the shortest distances are concerned, we must keep the protractor, the ruler, and the T-square for geometric tasks within the span of experience. For in a Riemannian universe, the shortest distance between points is the path of least curvature. In the Euclidean realm of experience, that least curvature is zero curvature, and it coincides with the straight line.

I once worked on a maintenance crew with a brilliant philosophy graduate student everyone called Al the Carpenter. Older and wiser than the rest of us, Al hardly let a day go by without an enlightening observation or an anecdote. "I met a little boy this morning," he once told us, "while I was making picnic tables outside the recreation hall. 'Is the world really round?' he asked me. 'To the best of my knowledge,' I answered. 'Then tell me why you cut all the legs the same length. Won't your tables wobble?' "

Yes, the tables would wobble, Al replied, if the legs were cut an identical length. But the wobble would be so infinitely minuscule as to be only theoretical. Likewise, imperfections in length figured insignificantly in the end result, he explained. "If you want to hear philosophical questions," Al said, "pay attention to the children."

A theory fashioned to fit the planes of experience will also wobble when we attempt to force it onto a very large, exceedingly small, or extremely complex body of information. Until now, we have viewed hologramic mind along Euclidean axes. But an understanding of hologramic mind requires the freedom only Riemann's simple but powerful ideas can give it.

Riemann's name and influence pervade mathematics and physics, and the reasons for this are evident in his lecture. The seeds of his subsequent work are present there. The elementary relationships at points later became the means by which physicists learned to conceptualize invariance. Toward the end of the lecture, Riemann even anticipated general relativity. Einstein's four-dimensional space-time continuum is Riemannian. Where did Riemann's insight come from? What intuitive spark caused his genius to push against the outermost fringes of human understanding? I'm not sure I know the answer, and I only raise the question because my suppositions will aid in our quest of hologramic mind.

Riemann, I believe, had a vivid concept of what I will call "active" zero, the 0 between $+1$ and -1, the set we cross when we overdraw from the checking account, not the one a philosophy professor of mine used to call "what ain't." Riemann had a clear intuitive idea of zero space, and even negative space. Let's try to develop such a concept ourselves. But so that what I say will have theoretical validity, let me make a few preliminary remarks.

There is an important principle in logic known as Gödel's incompleteness theorem; it shows, basically, that we cannot prove every last proposition in a formal system. It's a sort of uncertainty principle of the abstract. We'll obey it by always leav-

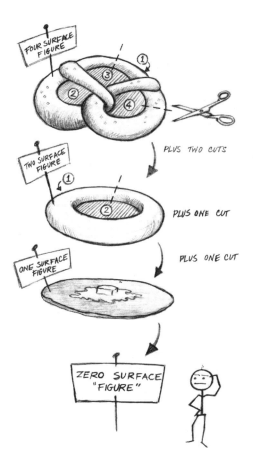

ing at least one entire dimensional set beyond our reach. In fact, let's throw in two uncountable dimensions, negative and positive infinity, which, by definition, are the sets beyond our reach.

Now let's consider a doughnut and a pretzel. To keep the discussion simple, imagine them on a plane. Our doughnut has two apparent surfaces, the outside and the lining of the hole. Our pretzel has four visible surfaces. Let's assume that all things that have the same number of surfaces belong to the same species, and let's not worry about whether the doughnut is round or oval or crushed down on one side. Also, let's consider surface to be a manifestation of dimension.

How can we convert a pretzel into a doughnut, and vice versa? With the pretzel we could make the conversion with two cuts between two apparent surfaces. To go the other way, we can employ the term *join*.

Now we have said that at either end of our universe, there is a dimension we can't reach. Thus, as we move up the scale, there will always be one dimension more in the continuum than we can count. If we actually observe two surfaces on the doughnut, we know our overall system has at least three dimensions: the two we can count plus the one we can't. What happens when we go in the other direction, when we add one cut to our doughnut? We create a pancake with one surface. But since we have the surface, we know that over on the left there must be another dimension. And that dimension is active zero.

We can't do that! you may say. But look at it this way. We admitted that we couldn't count to infinity. If we don't put those two extra dimensions into our universe, then either we can't count at all or we can reach unreachability, both of which are contradictions. We can see for ourselves that it is possible to cut or join to make pretzels and doughnuts into each other. Thus when we turn a doughnut into a pancake, we must subtract two dimensions to get there, and this brings us to active zero.

Suppose we apply a cut to the pancake — eat it up, for instance. Then we have a choice between "what ain't" and a minus-one-dimensional universe. We can define a negative universe from our counting system. But how can we define "what ain't"? If we try to define it, we'll not have "what ain't" anymore. And if we don't define it, it will disappear from the argument, leaving us with good grammar and minus-one dimension.[6]

---

[6] The reader who enjoys ideas of this sort will benefit from Martin Gardner's book, cited in the bibliography, especially chapter 3.

If we can conceive of a zero-dimensional universe, we can certainly appreciate a zero-curvature without making it "what ain't." And the zero-curvature, as part of a continuum of curvatures, is the curvature of the Euclidean world of experience.

Before we begin to place hologramic mind in a Riemannian context, I would like to emphasize three important principles. First, Riemann's success lies in his approach. He did not begin with an already-assembled coordinate system; he built the coordinates before he tried to describe what they were like. In a system formulated from Riemann's basic approach, the elements define the coordinates, rather than the other way around, as is usually the case.

The second principle is related to the first, but it is a direct outgrowth of Riemann's discovery that measurable relations in the vicinity of a point are the same as those around any other point. What does this mean in terms of different coordinate systems? If we find those relationships in different coordinates, as we did in our imaginary experiments with pearly e's, the corresponding regions can be regarded as transformations of each other.

The third principle, an extension of the second, underlies our experiment with the pearly e's. An entire coordinate system becomes a transformation of any other complete coordinate system via their respective paths of least curvature. Thus the entire abstract universe is a single continuum of curvatures. Curvature is an abstraction; but we can always mimic it in our thoughts by imagining pearly e's.

Now let's make a preliminary first fitting of hologramic mind to the world of Riemann.

In terms of our search, a periodic event in perceptual space is a transformation, as a least curvature, to any other coordinates within the mental continuum. The same would be true of a series of periodic events. Since phase variation must be part of those events, memory (phase codes) becomes transformable to any coordinates in the mental continuum. A specific phase spectrum — a particular memory — becomes a definite path of least curvature in transformations from sensations to perceptions to stored memories to covert or overt behaviors, thoughts, feelings, or whatever else exists in the mental continuum. Calling upon our e's for imagery, the least pearly path will not change merely because the coordinates change. Behavior, then, is an informational transform of, for instance, perception.

Transformation within the Riemann-style mental continuum is the means by which hologramic mind stores itself and manifests its existence in different ways. But we need some way of carrying out these transformations. For this purpose, I must introduce the reader to other abstract entities, quite implicit in Riemann's work but not fully developed until some years after his death. These entities are known as *tensors*.

The mathematician Leon Brillouin credits the crystal physicist W. Voigt with the discovery of tensors.[7] When placed under stress or strain, a crystal's anatomy will deform. But certain relative values within the crystal remain invariant before and after deformation. Like Riemann's invariant curvature relationships, the relative values that tensors represent will survive transformation anywhere, at any time. Just in time for Einstein, mathematicians worked out theorems for tensors. In the process they found tensors to be the most splendid abstract entities yet discovered for investigating ideal as well as physical change. Ten-

---

[7] Brillouin, 1964, p. 3.

sors provided a whole new concept of the coordinate. And they furnished Einstein with the language to phrase relativity, as well as the means to deal with invariance in an ever-varying universe. And with regard to their power and generality, Brillouin tells us: *"An equation can have meaning only if the two members are of the same tensor character."* [8] Alleged equations without tensor characteristics turn out to be empirical formulas, and lack the necessity Benjamin Peirce talked about.

Tensors depict change, changing changes, changes in changing changes, and even higher order variations. Conceptually, they are very closely related to relative phase. Tensor relationships transform in the same way relative phase does. This feature affords us an impressionistic look at their meaning.

Examine figure 8 on page 157, and keep a finger there for ready reference. Notice the three similar rings on the diagonal running from lower left to upper right. If you inspect the dots carefully outside the zone of overlap you'll see that we can draw a similar diagonal line between them — from lower left to upper right, as on the corresponding rings.

Now, while looking at figure 8, rotate the page until the similar rings on the diagonal lie horizontal. Also watch what happens to the arrays of dots. Notice that the dots come to lie in horizontal rows like the rings.

The rings and dots are transforms of each other. The fundamental direction of change remains constant in the transform as well as its back-transform. And in rotation, the basic orientation of rings and dots remains invariant. Absolute values differ greatly. But as we ourselves can observe, relative values transform in the same way. This is the essence of the tensor: it preserves an abstract ratio independent of the coordinate system. If we stop to think about this, we realize that if tensors carry their

---

[8] Brillouin, 1964, p. 3.

meaning wherever they go, they should be able to define the coordinate system itself. And they do.

Ordinary mathematical operations begin with a definition of the coordinate system. Let's ask, as Riemann did, what's the basis for such definitions? With what omniscience do we survey the totality of the real and ideal — from outside, no less — and decide a priori just what a universe must be like? The user of tensors begins with a humble attitude. He begins, as Riemann did, ignorant of the universe — and aware that he is ignorant. He is obliged to calculate the coordinate system only after he arrives there, and is not free to proclaim it in advance. Tensors work in the Cartesian systems of ordinary graphs. They also work in Euclid's world. But it is almost as though they were created for travel in Riemann's abstract universes.

There are two senses of change: *co*variation, where changes proceed in the same direction, as when a beagle chases a jackrabbit; and *contra*variation, as occurs in the ends of a stretching rubber band. Tensors depict either type of change, or both simultaneously. If the beagle gains on the jackrabbit, when the quarry fatigues, for instance, or if the rubber offers more and more resistance as tension is increased, then the changes assume a higher order of complexity. Thus not only do covariant, contravariant, and mixed tensors exist, they can also attain higher ranks. Thus, packaged into one entity, there can be an incredible amount of information about how things change. Ordinary mathematics become cumbersome and eventually fail when dealing with such degrees of complexity.

You may think that it would take pages to write representations of tensors. But the mathematician has invented very simple means of representing them: subscripts denote covariance and superscripts indicate contravariance. Thus R_t means a covariant tensor, or rank one. R^{kt} is a rank two contravariant tensor, and R_{ijk}^{h} is a mixed tensor, once contravariant, thrice covariant — a simple statement of a very complicated situation.

In tensor transformations the mathematician applies formal rules to make, for instance, R_i in one coordinate equal, say, R^m in another. If, having applied the rules and performed the calculation, R_i doesn't equal R^m, then the changes aren't really a tensor and represent local fluctuations peculiar to the coordinate system; they have an empirical, not an analytical, meaning. If the mathematician even bothers with such parochial factors at all, he'll call them "local constants."

Many features of holograms cannot be explained by ordinary transformations. In acoustical holograms, for instance, the sound waves in the air around the microphone don't linearly transform to all the changes in the receiver or on the television screen. Tensors do. The complete construction of any hologram can be looked upon as tensor transformations, the reference wave doing to the object wave what transformational rules do to make, say, R_{ij} equal R^{nm}. Decoding, likewise, becomes much easier to explain with tensors. We can drop the double and triple talk, especially if we work within Riemann's continuum. The back-transformation of phase codes from transform to perceptual space becomes, simply, the shift of the same *relative* values from a spatial to a temporal coordinate of the same continuum.

We imagined mind as a version of Riemann's theoretical world, a continuous universe of phase codes. Now we add the concept of tensors to the picture. Tensors represent phase relationships that will transform messages, independent of any coordinates within the system. Indeed, phase relationships, as tensors, will define the coordinates — the percept, memory, or whatever.

A universe constructed from Riemann's guidelines is an exceedingly abstract entity. Diagrams, because of their Euclidean features, undermine the very abstractions they attempt to depict.

But just as we did with perceptual and transform space, let's let our imaginations operate in a Euclidean world and, with reason, cautiously, step by step, think our way beyond our intuitive reality.

Imagine two points, *A* and *B,* on our Euclidean world. But instead of joining them with a flat line, let's connect them with two curves. And let's imagine that the path describes a circle, with *A* and *B* lying 180 degrees apart. Now let's begin a clockwise journey from *A.* But when we get to *B,* instead of continuing on around to 360°, and without reversing our forward motion, let's extend our journey into another circular dimension, this time a dimension of slightly greater size. We end up with a figure 8. Although the bottom cycle is larger than the top one, the relative values remain the same.

Notice that we "define" our universe by how we travel in it. On a curve, remember, we move continuously over each point. When we get to *B,* we have to travel out onto that second dimension, if it is there. If we don't, and elect not to count it, it might as well be "what ain't." But if the dimensions join, then a full cycle from point *A* out and back again is quite different from a journey around a single dimension. Notice that we would have to go through *two* 360-degree cycles to return to *A.* The point I want to stress is that while curvature is our elemental rule, and while the relative values remain unchanged, an increase in dimension fundamentally changes the nature of our system.

Suppose we add another dimension, at the bottom of the lower circle, for instance, increasing its absolute size even further to produce a snowman. Again our fundamental rules hold, and again relative values transform unchanged, but again the course and nature of our excursion is fundamentally unlike what we experienced with one and two dimensions. For although we have a single curved genus of figures, each universe is a new species.

We can grow larger and larger circles along the bottom of the figure. But why restrict ourselves to point *B* and its counterparts? We chose *B* arbitrarily. We can pick any point around our original circle, and extend off in any direction. Nor are we limited to a plane. A new cycle may extend up or down or obliquely or in any direction. And what limits us to larger cycles? We can make them smaller, or proceed in the negative direction. The point is that we can evolve incredible variety from a very simple rule.

I used circles for the sake of imagery. But let's get rid of literal circles and replace them with the concept of a pair of curvatures. In whatever direction we grow our universe, it's not a matter of circles or ellipses, but an abstract relationship. The *relative* values of the curved, mutually referencing pairs will remain invariant no matter where we extend our universe. To handle this idea, we must resort to reason.

Let me summarize hologramic theory at this point, and connect it to what we've been discussing in this chapter. First, we conceive of mind as information, phase information. And we put that information into an ideal, Riemann-like universe, a continuum of unspecified dimensions, whose fundamental rule is curvature. A relative phase value — a "piece of mind" — is the ratio of curvatures. We give phase ratios expression in the form of tensors. And the modalities and operations of mind then become tensor transformations of the same relative values between all coordinates within the continuum. We dispose of our need to distinguish perceptual space from Fourier transforms and kindred transform spaces because we do not set forth the coordinate systems in advance. Coordinates come after, not before, the transformation.

For illustrative purposes, we can consider hologramic mind as analogous to operations on a pocket calculator. The buttons, display, battery, and circuitries — counterparts of brain — can produce the result, say, of taking the square root of 9. The calculator and its components are very much a part of the real world. But the operations, the energy *relationships* within it, belong to the ideal world. One of those ideal coordinates coincides with experience.

I appreciate the demands Riemann's world must make on the reader. Therefore, allow me to construct a metaphor to assist our imagination.

Let's imagine a system whose rules apparently violate Riemann's curvature, a system that seems to be governed by straight lines, sharp corners, and apparent discontinuities everywhere. Imagine a giant checkerboard, on which each square is square like the whole. Now imagine that one square is subdivided into smaller red and black squares. Take one of those small squares and imagine that it is made up of still smaller squares. The pattern repeats itself again and again and again, throughout all levels. The various levels can be seen as the equivalents of dimensions within our curved continuum. Thus we can model the same red-black phase spectrum at any level. And, because we can subdivide any square as much as we please, we can make two checkerboards carry vastly different specific internal patterns.

Now that we have created the imagery we want, let's get rid of the metaphor, but with reasoning rather than by fiat.

We said that the red and black squares were infinitely divisible. Assume that we approach the dimensions of a single point (as we did with the hypotenuse and our pearly *e*'s). If the system is infinitely divisible, there ought to be a *single* unreachable point-sized square, at infinity. If there are two squares down there, then our system is not infinitely divisible; and if it's not infinitely divisible, where do we get the license to divide it up at all? Thus we must place a single square at infinity, so that

we can keep on subdividing to create our metaphor. But what kind of square occupies infinity? Red or black? The answer is, both red *and* black. At infinity our apparently discontinuous system becomes continuous: red and black squares superimpose and, as in Riemann's universe, become part of each other. This is a hidden continuity that underlies the true nature of the repetitive pattern, and it is the reason why we can deal with the pattern systematically at all. Our checkerboard metaphor of hologramic mind turns out to be a disguised version of Riemann's universe.

Now that we have a general system, let's use it. Let's answer a few questions with it.

How do we really account for the results of shufflebrain experiments? How could Buster's fish codes blend in so smoothly with his own? How was it that Punky's salamander medulla could receive the tadpole messages from the rest of his brain? The same questions exist for "looking up" and the rest of my experiments. Why weren't the experiments like trying to pound a square peg into a round hole? Continuity had to exist. And phase transformations had to define the coordinate system, rather than the other way around.

Consider another question, now that I've mentioned salamanders and the mixing of species. How can we explain the similarities and the differences between them and us? Hologramic mind, constructed as a version of Riemann's universe, supplies the answer in two words: curvature and dimension. We share the rule of curvature, but we and they are totally different universes by virtue of dimension. (I will return to dimension in the next chapter when discussing the cerebral cortex.)

And how can we sum together phase codes of learned and instinctive origins, if fundamentally different abstract rules govern, say, a reflex kick of a leg and a 6/8-time tarantella? We'd move like jerk-jointed robots if our inner universe were a series of discontinuous pieces. How could we condition a reflex if we couldn't blend the new information smoothly with what's already there?

Speaking of robots, we are vastly different from the digital computer. The computer's mind is a creature of the linear, Euclidean world of its origin. Its memory reduces to discrete bits. A bit is a binary choice — a clean, crisp, clear, yes-no, on-off, either-or, efficient choice. The computer's memories are clean, crisp, clear, linear arrays of efficient choices. The hologramic continuum is not linear; it is not either-or; it is not efficient. Hologramic mind acts flat and Euclidean and imitates the computer only when the items of discrete, discontinuous data are few. We're swamped when we try to remember or manipulate an array of twenty-six individual digits, a simple task for the computer. Yet ask the digital computer to distinguish your face from a dozen randomly sampled other faces — with and without eyeglasses, lipstick, and mustaches, and from various distances and angles — and it fails. Brains and computers operate on fundamentally different principles, and they mimic each other only when the task is trivial.

Consider also the problem of perceptions of time and space, as opposed to physical time and space. People, the author included, have dreamed ten-year scenes within the span of a ten-minute dream. The reverse also can happen: a horror lived during a second of physical time can protract to many minutes, during a nightmare. To the scuba diver out of air, a minute seems very long. But time seems to compress during a race to the airport, when we are a few minutes behind schedule. Space may do strange things, too. A character in a recent Neil Simon play tells how, during a bout of depression, he couldn't cross the street because the other side was too far away.[9]

---

[9] The clinical literature abounds with reports of this sort, some related to obvious brain damage, others not. For instance, N. J. David (1964, p. 150) presents the

What do we do about subjective phenomena? Discount them from Nature because they are subjective?

In Fourier (and kindred) transforms, the time-dependent features of relative phase become space-dependent. But the relationships in transform space obey what time-dependent ones do in perceptual space: the axes don't contract and expand. Tensors, on the other hand, aren't constrained by presumptions about coordinate axes. In the curved continuum, time-dependent ratios may turn up on an elastic axis. And because the hologramic universe is a continuum, we lose the distinction between perceptual space and other kinds of space; or we may have the conscious impression that time is expanding or that distances will not close. Yes, it's ideal, subjective, illusory. Subjective time and space are *informational* transforms of what the clock gauges and the meter stick measures. The constraints on the clock and meter stick are physical. Constraints on the transformations of the mind are ideal. But both belong to Nature.

Nonetheless, hologramic theory suffers from a major deficit, and we will have to correct it. Our construct is too perfect, too ball-bearing smooth, too devoid of the chance for error, for the twig missing from a nest, or the freckles on a face. We can't see ourselves in such a picture. We must add to the theory what *doesn't* transform, what *won't* remain invariant in all other coordinates. Our picture needs precisely what the mathematician often goes to great pains to get out of his way — parochial conditions, particular features, local constants. Physiologist E. Roy John identified some local constants (see chapter 2) in the form of noise. I believe we must also place amplitude changes among

---

case history of a young man whom the police arrested for being drunk when he asked them why they were only two feet tall. The young man was not drunk. He was suffering an attack of psychomotor epilepsy.

the local constants, and, in addition, allow for the possibility of many other sources yet to be discovered.

Local constants make perception distinct from the recollection of the original percept. They make a kiss different from a reminiscence about it. They put that subtle but critical shade of difference into the spoken, as opposed to the written, word. Local constants represent how the general becomes the particular; how the ideal, abstract, informational hologramic mind transduces into experience; where theory stops and experiments take over. Because they are strictly parochial, the local constants necessarily vary with each individual. And the more dimensions a mind uses, the greater the impact of local constants on the collective behavior of the species. Hologramic theory, therefore, is a self-limiting theory.

We should not underestimate a theory's implications merely because it limits itself. A little humility sometimes goes a long way in logic. And this is true of hologramic theory. Let me illustrate what I'm driving at with the checkerboard metaphor we used earlier. Let's assign relative phase tensors, and everything else we may use explicitly in hologramic theory, to the red squares. Let's use the black squares to house local constants, which we cannot directly treat from hologramic theory. To ensure that the theory continues to restrict itself, let's maintain the rule that we cannot enter a black square from a red square (or vice versa). If the square contains black, it is off limits to our explicit use of hologramic theory. With this rule in mind, let's subdivide squares again and again, as we did earlier, and let's ask the same basic question: Is the infinitely small square red or black? Just as before, the answer is both: it is red *and* black. This time, however, we cannot reach the infinite square, not because of the way the textbook defines infinity, but because of our own rule. We have black (and red) in the infinite square. And black makes the square off limits to hologramic theory.

But consider this. Suppose we are on the red square that

lies just one step away from the off-limits infinite square. Aside from our rule, what guarantees that we can't make the next step? A corresponding black square just one step from the infinite square. Ironically, the very self-limiting nature of the theory establishes the existence — the *Existenz* — of a domain with local constants.[10]

In formal terms, the incompleteness of hologramic theory makes local constants an existential necessity. The term *existential* refers to existence.

Major philosophical implications emerge from what we've just deduced about hologramic theory's self-limiting character. The very incompleteness of the theory allows us to use it to resolve the mind-brain conundrum. Hologramic theory deals explicitly with mind. Yet the theory can do so only because it implicates local constants. And local constants exist in the brain. In other words, hologramic theory must work within a mind-brain system. The source of the mind-brain conundrum was the fallacy, inherent in holism and structuralism alike, that a unipolar view can let us comprehend the mind-brain cosmos. And once we remove this fallacy, and allow mind and brain to get back together again, the conundrum vanishes. Mind endows brain with the abstract universe in which to contain the realm of thought. But brain, in turn, gives life to mind.

We must reach outside of hologramic theory to give perspective to our conclusions. And I know of no system of thought more perfectly suited to our needs than Hegelian dialectics, in which theses merge with their antitheses to create syntheses.

What is the mind-brain synthesis? It is you or I, he or she. It is also we and they. It is general and ideal, as we are. And it is particular and real, as we are, too.

---

[10]*Existenz* refers to an entity that exists by force of implication. The existential philosophers (see summary in Flew, 1979) use the term more comprehensively than I do. But their usage and mine connote more than existence in the sense of being present (*Dasein*, in German). Infinity is a good example of *Existenz*.

10

Microminds and Macrominds

WE RETURN AGAIN to the imperfect but comfortable realm of experience. In chapters 5 and 6, we sought predictions. Now we will shift emphasis to explanations, to the use of hologramic theory in making rational sense of certain equivocal observations. And we will start with the behavior of bacteria.

Rod-shaped bacteria, bacilli, propel themselves through fluid by means of whiplike appendages called flagella. The flagella execute wave motion. Locomotion of a bacillus is a function of phase and amplitude spectra among its waving flagella. Flagellar motion depends on a contractile protein hooked to the base of the microbial appentdage. The overt behavior of a bacillus is a function of periodic activity — phase and amplitude spectra — in the rhythm of its contractile proteins. Thus if a hologramic mind exists in the bacillus, it shows up literally and figuratively right at the surface of the cell.

But is there a mind in a creature so primitive? We can describe a recoiling spring as a tensor transformation. But our intuitions would balk, and rightfully, if we tried to put hologramic mind into the spring. Thus before we apply hologramic theory to the bacillus, we need evidence only experiments and observations can supply.

Single cells of many sorts may be attracted or repelled by various chemicals. The reaction is called chemotaxis. In the 1880s, when bacteriology was a very young science, the German botanist Wilhelm Pfeffer made an interesting observation about chemotaxis in the common intestinal bacillus, *Escherichia coli (E. coli)*. Others had found that meat extract entices these organisms and alcohol repels them: *E. coli* will swim up into a capillary tube containing meat extract, but will avoid a tube that contains alcohol. What would happen, Pfeffer wondered, if he presented *E. coli* with a mixture of alcohol and meat extract? He found that a concentrated meat extract attracted *E. coli* even though the alcohol in the mixture would otherwise have chased them away.

Did Pfeffer's observations mean that bacteria actively make decisions? Naturally, the critics laughed at the suggestion. But during the past few years, biochemists have begun reinvestigating Pfeffer's question. In rigorously quantified experiments, working with chemically pure stimulants in very precise amounts, two University of Wisconsin researchers, J. Adler and W.-W. Tso, came to the conclusion that "apparently, bacteria have a 'data processing' system." Bold words, these. For even with quotation marks, "data processing" translates into what we ordinarily call thinking.

Adler and Tso established two important points. First, the relative, not absolute, concentration of attractant versus repellent determines whether *E. coli* move toward or away from a mixture. Second, the organisms do not respond to the mere presence of stimulants but instead follow, or flee, a concentration gradient. And it was the presence of this concentration gradient that led the California biochemist D. E. Koshland to discover bacterial memory.

Koshland became intrigued by the fact that an organism only 2 micrometers long (.000039 inches) could follow a concentration gradient at all. The cell would have to analyze changes on the order of about one part in ten thousand — the rough equivalent of distinguishing a teaspoon of Beaujolais in a bathtub of gin, a "formidable analytical problem," as Koshland wrote in 1977.

Was the cell analyzing concentration changes along its length? To Koshland's quantitative instincts, 2 micrometers seemed much too short for this. Suppose, instead, the bacterium analyzed over a period of time. What if the cell could *remember* the past concentration long enough to compare it with the present concentration? Koshland and his associates knew just the experiment for testing the two alternatives.

When a bacillus is not responding to a chemical stimulus, it tumbles randomly through the medium. But in the presence of the stimulus, the bacterium checks the tumbling action and swims in an orderly manner. What would happen, Koshland asked, if he tricked the bacteria? What if he placed organisms into a chemical stimulus and then quickly diluted the medium? If the bacteria indeed analyzed head-to-tail, they should continue tumbling, because there would be no spatial gradient, no change in concentration from one location to another. But if the bacteria remembered a *past* concentration, diluting the medium should fool them into thinking they were in a gradient and cause them to check the tumble.

"The latter was precisely what occurred," Koshland wrote.[1] The bacteria relied on memory of the past concentration to program their behavior in the present.

And there's more. Koshland called attention to another feature of bacterial behavior. He pointed out that in responding to a chemical stimulus, in checking the tumbling action, "the bacterium has thus reduced a complex problem in three-dimensional migration to a very simple on-off device."[2]

When a human being simplifies a complicated task, we identify the behavior as an example of intelligence. Thus bacteria show evidence of rudimentary minds. And we can use holo-gramic theory to account for this.

---

[1] Koshland, 1977, p. 1056.
[2] Koshland, 1977, p. 1057.

◇   ◇   ◇

Adler and Tso found that attractants induce counterclockwise rotation in *E. coli*'s flagella, whereas repellents make the appendages crank clockwise. In terms of hologramic theory in its simplest form, the two opposite reactions are 180 degrees, or π, out of phase. By shifting from random locomotion to movement relative to a stimulus, the organism would be shifting from random phase variations in its flagella to the equivalence of harmonic motion, as if from cacophony to melody.

Adler and Tso also identified the bacterium's sensory apparatus as a protein. Mutant strains of *E. coli* that lack this particular protein do not respond to the specific chemical stimulus.

The carriers of the bacterium's memory have not been found, experimentally. But we can use the hologramic continuum to explain the information: phase spectra must be transformed from the coordinates of the sensory proteins through the contractile proteins to the flagella and into the locomotion of the organism. (Amplitudes may be handled as constants.) The chemical stimulant in principle acts on the bacterium's perceptual mechanisms as the reconstruction beam does in the decoding of an optical hologram. As tensors in a continuum, the phase values encoded in the sensory proteins must be transformed to the coordinate system representing locomotion. The same message passes from sensory to motor mechanisms, and through whatever associates the two. Recall that tensors define the coordinates, not the other way around. Thus, in terms of information, the locomotion of the organism is a transformation of the reaction between the sensory protein and the chemical stimulus, plus the effects of local constants. Absolute amplitudes and noise, products of local constants, would come from such things as the viscosity of the fluid, the nutritional quality of the medium, the age and health of the organism, or whatever else the phase spectrum could not control. With respect to the storage of codes in such small physical areas, phase has no prescribed size, in the absolute sense. A single molecule may contain a whole message.

Evidence of memory in single-celled animals dates back at least to 1911, to the observations the protozoologists L. M. Day and M. Bentley made concerning paramecia.[3] They placed a paramecium in a capillary tube of a diameter less than the animal's length. The paramecium swam down to the opposite end of the tube, where it attempted to turn. But in the cramped lumen it twisted, curled, ducked, bobbed, and only managed to get faced the other way quite by accident. What did it do? It immediately swam to the other end, only to get stuck again. And again it twisted, curled, and ducked, finally making the turn after much trial and error. This continued for a while — back and forth, back and forth, the animal getting stuck, struggling, and only managing the turn by chance. Then Day and Bentley began to notice something. The animal was taking less and less time to complete the course. It was becoming more and more efficient at the maneuver. Eventually, it learned the moves necessary to make the turn.

Day and Bentley's observations don't fit the traditional criteria of learning. Their paramecia taught themselves the trick, which somehow doesn't seem to count. But in the 1950s the behaviorist B. Gelber conditioned paramecia by the same basic approach Pavlov had taken in using the smell of meat to make a dog drool at the ring of a bell.

Gelber prepared a pâté of her animals' favorite bacteria (a single paramecium may devour as many as 5 million bacteria a day[4]), and smeared some of it on the tip of a platinum wire. She dipped the wire into the paramecia culture. Immediately her

[3] See also discussion in Eisenstein, 1967.
[4] See 1964 edition of *Encyclopedia Britannica,* vol. 18, p. 624.

animals swarmed after the bacteria. In a few seconds, she with-
drew the wire, paused briefly, and then dipped it in again, with
the same results. On the third trial, though, she presented her
animals with a bare, sterilized wire, instead of bacteria. There
was no response, not at first anyway. But after thirty such trials,
Gelber's paramecia were swarming around the tip of the platinum wire whether it had bacteria on it or not.

Naturally Gelber had her critics, those who dismissed the
idea that a single cell could behave at all, let alone remember
anything. And I must admit that it isn't easy to fathom memory
in life at such a reduced scale. Yet I've sat entranced for hours
on end watching protozoa in the water with my salamanders.
Long before the development of hologramic theory, I wondered
if Gelber's critics had ever set aside their dogmas and doctrines
long enough to observe for themselves the behavioral capabilities of protozoa. Let me recount something I saw one Saturday
afternoon some years ago.

On occasion, a fungal growth infects a salamander larva's
gills. To save the animal, I must remove the growth. On the Saturday in question, I discovered one such fungus teeming with
an assortment of protozoa. I transferred the entire miniature
biosphere and its inhabitants to a glass slide, for inspection
under the much greater magnification of the compound phase
microscope.[5]

At least five different species of protozoa were working on
the vinelike hyphae of the fungus, but I was soon captivated by
the behavior of a species I couldn't specifically identify. They
were moving up and down the hyphae at a brisk pace. As an
animal reached the distal end of a strand, its momentum would
carry it out into the surrounding fluid. It would then turn and

---

[5] The phase microscope allows examination of cells without the use of stains.
The theory of the phase microscope is a special version of much we have discussed in this book.

go back to its "own" hypha, even when another lay closer. Something spatial, or chemical, or both, must be attracting these little critters, I thought almost out loud. Just as I was thinking this, one animal caught my attention. It had just taken a wide elliptical course into the fluid; but another hypha lay directly in its path along the return arc of the excursion. And my little hero landed on it.

After a few pokes at the foreign strand, the animal paused, as though something didn't seem quite right — although others of its species were busily working the territory. After a few tentative pokes, the animal moved away. It landed on a third hypha, moved on after a brief inspection, and landed on still another hypha. Soon it was hopelessly lost on the far side of the microscopic jungle.

But then something happened. As I was anticipating its departure, it hesitated, gave the new hypha a few sniffs, and began working very slowly up and down. After perhaps five or six trips along the strand, its speed began to increase. Within about a minute, it was working the new hypha as it had previously worked the old one. It seemed that the protozoan had forgotten its old home and learned the cues provided by the new one.

Had I conducted carefully controlled experiments, I might have discovered a purely instinctive basis for all I saw that Saturday. Perhaps Gelber's or Day and Bentley's observations can be explained by something other than learning per se. But instinctive or learned, the behaviors of protozoa — or bacteria — do not fit into the same class of phenomena as the reactions of rubber bands. Information exists in the interval between what they sense and how they respond. We employ identical criteria in linking behavior to the human mind.

But higher organisms require a "real" brain in order to learn, don't they? If such a question seems ridiculous, consider an observation a physiologist named G. A. Horridge made some years ago concerning decapitated roaches and locusts.

In some classes of invertebrates, including insects, collections of neurons — ganglia — provide the body's direct innervation, as do the spinal cord and brainstem among vertebrates. Horridge wondered if ganglion cells could learn without the benefit of the animal's brain. To test the question, he devised an experiment that has come to be known as the Horridge preparation: The body of a beheaded insect is skewered into an electrical circuit. A wire is attached to a foot. Then the preparation is suspended directly above a salt solution. When the leg relaxes and gravity pulls the foot down, the wire makes contact with the solution, closes the circuit, and delivers a jolt to the ganglion cells inside the headless body. In time, the cells of the ganglion learn to keep the leg raised in order to avoid the shock.

The electrophysiologist Graham Hoyle has perfected and refined the Horridge preparation during more recent years. By using computers to control the stimuli, and by making direct recordings from the specific nerves, he has been able to teach the ganglion cells to alter their frequency of firing — a very sophisticated trick. How does such learning compare with that of the intact animal? Hoyle raised this question in regard to pithed crabs, and he found that "debrained animals learned better than intact ones."[6]

I'm not suggesting that we replace the university with the guillotine. Indeed, later in this chapter the brain will return to our story. But the fact is that evidence of mind exists in some very strange places. Brain (in the sense of what we house inside our crania) is not a sine qua non condition of mind.

But does the behavior of beheaded bugs really have any counterpart in mammals?

---

[6] Hoyle, 1976, p. 147.

◇ ◇ ◇

In London, in 1881, the leading holist of the day, F. L. Goltz, arrived from Strasbourg for a public confrontation with his arch-rival, David Ferrier, at the International Medical Congress. Ferrier had very carefully and precisely mapped the motor cortex of the monkey. With specifically localized lesions he created very specific paralyses in his animals. Ferrier's experiments were so dramatic that they won him the confrontation — but not before Goltz had succeeded in demonstrating that a dog can stand up even after amputation of its cerebrum.[7] The decerebrated mammal has been a laboratory exercise in physiology courses ever since. Only a few years ago, three physiologists used the blink reflex to demonstrate convincingly that "decerebrate cats could learn the conditioned response."[8]

Hologramic theory does not predict that microbes, beheaded bugs, or decerebrated animals necessarily perceive, remember, and behave. Experiments furnish the underlying evidence; and some of it, particularly in the case of bacteria, has been far more rigorously gathered than any evidence we might cite in support of memory in rats or monkeys or human beings. But the relative nature of the phase code explains how an organism 2 micrometers long — or a thousand times smaller than that, if need be — can house complete sets of instructions; and transformations within the continuum give us a theory of how biochemical and physiological mechanisms quite different from those in the intact brains and bodies of vertebrates may nevertheless perform the same overall informational activities.

Yet hologramic theory does not force us to abandon everything else we know. As we will see from the theory's own internal logic, we do not dispense with the brain. The theory does not explode the foundations of our reality. Instead, hologramic

[7] See references in Clarke and Dewhurst, 1972, p. 115.
[8] See Norman et al., 1976, p. 551.

theory gives new meaning to old evidence; it allows us to reassemble the original facts, come back to where our quest began, and, in the words of T. S. Eliot, "know the place for the first time."

In the last chapter, I pointed out that two universes developed according to Riemann's general plan would obey a single unifying principle, curvature, and yet differ from each other totally if they varied with respect to dimension. Thus the hologramic continuum of both a salamander and a human being would depend on the phase code, and tensor transformations therein; but our worlds are far different from theirs by virtue of dimension. Now I would like to take this statement out of the abstract.

Given the capabilities of single cells, it is not surprising that a monkey will sit in front of a display panel and win peanuts by choosing a triangle instead of a square. By doing essentially the same thing, rats and pigeons follow a trend Edward Thorndike first called attention to during the late 1890s. Even a goldfish, when presented with an apparatus much like a gum machine, quickly learns that bumping its snout against a green button will earn it a juicy tubifex worm, whereas the red button brings forth nothing. It is not surprising that those who were aware of such choice-learning experiments began to think about the evolution of intelligence in terms of arithmetic: thus if we added enough bacteria, we'd get a fish or a man. In the late 1950s, the behavioral psychologist M. E. Bitterman began wondering if it was all this simple. Something about the choice method of assessing learning didn't smell quite right to him. Bitterman decided to add a new dimension to the experiment. His results showed that behaviors cannot be explained by simple linear addition and subtraction.

Bitterman began by training various species in the traditional choice method: his animals had to discriminate *A* from *B* in order to win a prize. Then after his goldfish, turtles, pigeons, rats, and monkeys associated *A* with reward and *B* with no reward, Bitterman played a dirty trick. He switched the reward button. Chaos broke out in the laboratory. Even the monkey became confused. But as time went by, the monkey began making fewer and fewer mistakes. Then the rat and pigeon began to get the idea. They were reversing the habit. The longer they played the game, the fewer mistakes they made and the more conspicuous the habit reversal became.

Meanwhile, over in the aquarium, the goldfish was still hammering away hopelessly, trying to win a tubifex worm by playing the same old choice. The fish could not kick the old habit and learn the new one.

What about Bitterman's turtle? It was the most interesting of all his subjects. Confronted with a choice involving spatial discrimination, the turtle easily reversed the habit. But when the task involved visual discrimination, the turtle was no better off than the goldfish. In other words, it was as though the turtle's behavior lay somewhere between that of the fish and the bird. Turtles are reptiles, remember. And during vertebrate evolution, reptiles appeared after fishes and amphibians but before birds and mammals.

Now an interesting event takes place in the evolution of the vertebrate brain. In reptiles, the cerebrum begins to acquire a cortex. Was the cerebral cortex at the basis of his results? Bitterman decided to test this hypothesis by partially damaging the rat's cerebral cortex. What did he observe? He found that a rat with a damaged cerebral cortex made the habit reversal when given a spatial problem, but failed to do so when the choice involved visual discrimination. Bitterman's rats acted like the turtle.

Bitterman's experiments tell us that with the evolution of a cerebral cortex something *different* began to emerge in the vertebrate character. Simple arithmetic won't take us from a bacterium to a human being.

As embryos, each of us once reenacted evolution, in appearance as well as behavior. Up to about the fourth intrauterine month, a human embryo is quite salamanderlike. We evolve a primate cerebrum between the fourth and sixth months. When the process fails, we see in a tragic way how essential the human cerebral cortex is to us.

Mesencephalia is one term applied to an infant whose cerebrum fails to differentiate a cortex.[9] A mesencephalic infant sometimes lives for several months. Like its more fortunate brothers and sisters — any of whom could have suffered the same fate — the mesencephalic child will cry when jabbed by a diaper pin; it will suckle a proffered breast; it may sit up; it can see, hear, yawn, and coo. It is a living organism. But human though its genes and chromosomes may be, it never develops a human personality, no matter how long it lives. It remains in the evolutionary bedrock out of which the dimensions of the human mind emerge. It stays at the stage where the human embryo looked and acted like the creature who crawls out of the pond.

Yet there is no particular moment in development when we can delineate human from nonhuman: no specific minute, hour, or even day through which we can draw a draftsman's line. Development is a continuous process. The embryo doesn't arrive at the reptilian stage, disassemble itself, and construct a mammal de novo. Embryonic development is a continuum: what's new integrates harmoniously with what's already there. The embryo's summation demands Riemann's nonlinear rule: curvature!

---

[9] See Wolff, 1969.

What do we mean by addition and subtraction? Minimally, we must have discrete sets. The sets must equal each other or be reducible to equality by means of constants; and their relationships must be linear. The correct adjective for describing a consecutive array of linear sets is *contiguous,* meaning that successive members touch without merging into, and becoming a part of, each other — just the opposite of Riemann's test of continuity. This may seem ridiculous, at first, but if the sets in $1 + 1 + 1$ surrendered parts of themselves during addition, their sum would be something less than 3. We literally perform addition and subtraction using our fingers, abacus beads, nursery blocks, and digital computers because they literally represent discrete, or discontinuous, magnitudes.

Continuity is an essential principle in the theory of evolution. We can understand why if we try to envisage a tree whose branches are not, and never were, continuous back to the main trunk. Continuity *in fact* during embryonic development is prima facie evidence for continuity *in theory* among the species. Evolution is inconceivable by way of a simple — discontinuous — arithmetic theory. In light of Bitterman's turtle, a straight-line theory of the natural history of intelligence would predict discontinuity among the species and render the theory of evolution itself no more defensible on formal logical grounds than are the events depicted in Genesis. Bitterman's ingenious investigations deny a simple, linear progression from fish to human and provide experimental evidence for the evolution of intelligence.

We have not constructed the hologramic continuum along linear lines. If we had, we would not be able to reconcile what we find. As is the case with many scientists even today, we would be forced to ignore some facts in order to believe others. Then our dogmas would take precedence over Nature. Without the continuum, we would be unable to explain not only the differences and similarities among the species, but also those in ourselves at various stages of development.

The hologramic continuum by nature allows new dimensions to integrate harmoniously with those already present. It permits us to explain how our biological yesterday remains a part of today, within a totally changed informational universe. Even though we share the same elemental rule, the phase code, with other life forms, we are not reducible to what we once were, or to bacteria or beheaded bugs. We are neither a linear sum of what we were nor a linear fraction of what we used to be. And our inner world begins to unfold with the advent of the cerebral cortex.

The physiology of the cerebral cortex was a near-total enigma until rather recently. But two physiologists, David Hubel and Torsten Wiesel, spent the better part of two decades exploring pattern recognition by the visual cortex, first in cats and eventually in monkeys. They identified three basic types of neurons there, cells that would respond to visual targets of different degrees of complexity. Hubel and Wiesel called these neurons *simple, complex,* and *hypercomplex* cells. Simple cells were those that fired in response to a barlike image of a target in a fixed position, with a particular orientation. Some simple cells would begin discharging if the target was a horizontal bar, say, and would cut off if it was vertical or oblique. Complex cells were those that continued to fire, in response to basically two-dimensional targets. But if Hubel and Wiesel used more complicated targets, the complex cells would not fire. And that's where hypercomplex cells came in: they continued to fire even when the complex cells stopped.

Now the visual system must handle a great deal of information in addition to patterns: color, motion, distance — a variety of independent abstract dimensions that have to be compiled into a single, composite picture. Hubel and Wiesel analogized the problem to a jigsaw puzzle, where the shape of the pieces is independent of the picture they form. We recognize a checkerboard as a checkerboard whether it's red and black or blue and yellow. We still recognize the colors, and they don't have to be on checkerboards. Yet we assemble the informational dimensions into a single composite scene. If we went to a three-dimensional object, or if the object were moving, or if we attached some emotional significance to it, those dimensions, too, would have to be integrated into the percept. And the dimensions must be handled simultaneously. Vary its capability for handling dimensions, and we change the organism's perceptions in a nonlinear way, as Bitterman did when he injured the cerebral cortex of the rat. It was not until Hubel and Wiesel began studying the monkey instead of the cat that they discovered hypercomplex cells in sufficient numbers to analyze their physiological features.

Nor should we ignore the other sensory perceptions. For the cortex also handles them. What we hear, touch, taste, and smell may also be multidimensional. For instance, we may recognize a melody from *Carmen*. But our understanding of the lyrics will depend on our knowledge of French, if the aria is sung in that language. And whether we're enraptured or kick off our shoes and go to sleep will depend on factors other than the words and the music.

We also harmoniously integrate diverse sensory data. Thus silent movies disappeared the moment talkies came along. We not only have the capacity to combine sight and sound, but we *like* to do it, which is a whole constellation of dimensions in itself.

I don't mean to suggest that the cerebral cortex is the only dimensional processor in the brains of organisms (although it may be the most elegant one). The frog, for instance, has a very well-developed roof on its midbrain — the tectum I mentioned in chapter 3 that helps process visual information among nonmammalian vertebrates. While it comes nowhere near the

capabilities of the mammalian visual cortex, the tectum nevertheless integrates different dimensions of the frog's visual
perception.[10]

Another structure I mentioned in chapter 3 was the zuc-
chini-shaped hippocampus. Lesions in it, remember, produce
short-term memory deficits and make it difficult to repeat
sequences of numbers or newly presented phrases. In rats,
however, the organ appears to aid in navigation.

The function of the rat's hippocampus became evident in
studies involving what is called the radial maze.[11] This is an apparatus consisting of a series of a dozen or so alleys that lead off
a central station like the spokes radiating from the hub of a
wheel. To win a reward, the rat must go through the alleys in a
predetermined sequence. And to carry out the task, the animal
must remember which alley he's in and how far it is to the next
one. He must compile at least two sets of memories: position
and distance. Lesions in the hippocampus erode the animal's efficiency.

Now think of what happens when a person first remembers
the lines of an unfamiliar poem. He or she must remember not
only the individual words but also their location in the
sequence. Although this task assumes verbal form in human
beings, its informational aspects are not unlike those a rat uses
to organize memories of geographic place and sequence.

But clinical and laboratory evidence does not prove that
the hippocampus is the exclusive seat of such short-term memory processing. Lesions do not totally nullify the rats' ability to
run the radial maze: performances dropped from 7 correct runs
out of 8 to 5½ to 6 correct runs out of 8, a significant decline
but far from a total loss of ability.[12] I recall a record film of a

---

[10] See Gordon, 1972.
[11] See Olton, 1977.
[12] See Olton, 1977, p. 91.

man with a damaged hippocampus. He made errors when repeating phrases; but he wasn't always wrong. In addition, he often employed subtle tricks to remember items. When he was allowed to count on his fingers, he could often repeat phrases correctly. The point is that other parts of the brain may compile memories of position and distance, but they do so much less efficiently than the hippocampus. The success or failure of a particular behavior may depend on how fast an organism can assemble different memories.

Out in the wild, the navigational problems the rat must solve are much more difficult — and perilous — than those in the laboratory. The ethologists Richard Lore and Kevin Flannery dug up a garbage dump in New Jersey to find out how rats live there. To their surprise, they found that wild rats live in family groups, each family with its own burrow. The garbage dump wasn't honeycombed with one communal rat labyrinth. Rats don't randomly infest a territory and eat, sleep, and mate wherever the opportunity presents itself. The wild rat is vicious. A strange rat who ends up in the wrong nest isn't welcomed as a dinner guest but may very well become the *pièce de résistance*. Thus when the rat ventures out into the night, and turns around to go home, it must choose one burrow out of hundreds in a multidimensional array. It would quickly succumb to its own social psychology if not for the superb navigational system its hippocampus provides.

The use to which a rat puts its hippocampus is at least as complicated as our own. I bring up this point to illustrate and solve the problem where the qualitative features of a behavior differ in homologous brain structures of two species, but the quantitative variations are similar.

We can construct two continua that have an identical number of dimensions and yet produce different universes. How? The shape of a universe depends not only on how many dimensions it has, but also on how they connect up. Recall that

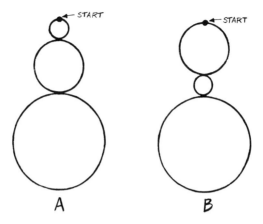

A   B

in the last chapter we envisaged adding a dimension by converting a figure 8 into a snowman. But we could have chosen to grow our third dimension as a sort of ear or handle off the side of, say, the upper cycle. Now, as I emphasized in the last chapter, we do not want to take these figures literally. Nonetheless, with such figures we can construct two ideal systems that have much in common, quantitatively, but yet have their own unique qualitative features. Thus to illustrate the theoretical point of the discussion, imagine a snowman versus a universe, with a handle emerging from the 90-degree position on the upper cycle of the 8. Imagine that the three parts add up to the same radius of curvature. Running at the same rate, we would complete a round-trip excursion through either universe in an equal amount of time. Yet during an excursion, we would recross the branch points at different times in the two universes; we would "calculate" dissimilar coordinate systems even though the two universes have equal dimensions. And if we have dissimilar coordinates, we have different sets of local constants. Thus the differences between a rat's hippocampus and that of a person would not obscure the similarities, at least not in hologramic theory.

As I mentioned earlier, some psychologists conceptualize short-term or working memory by means of an idealized compartment.[13] The hippocampus, as I suggested, may be a location of a portion of that compartment, at least in higher animals. Of course, as evidence from decerebrated cats and many other sources indicates, we can't consider the hippocampus the exclusive repository of short-term memory. But hippocampal functions may yet reveal critical details about the dynamics of perception and reminiscence in higher animals. Circumstantial evidence from observations and experiments on rats as well as humans indicates that an active memory in the hippocampus is short term. Short-term memory in general is extremely vulnerable to electroconvulsive shock. And relatively mild electrical stimulation of the hippocampus and the surrounding region of the brain can provoke violent convulsive seizures.[14]

Temporary memory would be valuable to us as well as to rats. When we no longer need a telephone number, for example, we simply erase it. Yet we wouldn't want to forget all telephone numbers. After a journey back from the garbage pile, the neural map in the rat's hippocampus could become a liability. But the rat wouldn't want to relearn all its maps. What could control the shift of information from short-term to long-term storage?

I'm not implying that there are final answers to the latter question. And I raise the question because speculation based on a few facts about our own hippocampus will allow me to illustrate how we can use hologramic theory to furnish interim explanations of empirical data. In addition, application of hologramic theory to the facts suggests the validity of something Norbert Wiener predicted many years ago about short-term memory. But first let's consider the facts.

The human hippocampus connects with vast regions, directly and indirectly. Its most conspicuous pathways lead to and

---

[13] See Atkinson and Shiffrin, 1971.
[14] See Carpenter, 1976.

from subdivisions of what is collectively called the limbic system. The limbic system is actively involved in emotions. One circuit, in particular, connects the hippocampus to a massive convolution in the cerebrum known as the cingulate gyrus. The cingulate gyrus was the first part of the limbic system ever identified, and it is the location of most psychosurgery operations performed today.

The hippocampal-cingulate circuit has three interesting features. First, a number of relay stations intervene between the hippocampus and the cingulate gyrus. These relay stations are locations where the signal can be modified and where messages can move to and from other areas of the brain and spinal cord. Second, the overall circuit makes a giant feedback loop. Feedback is fundamental to Wiener's theoretical prediction, which I will discuss in a moment. Third, the circuit consists of parallel pathways, all the way around. The significance of this is that, when activated, the circuit preserves phase information in principle in the same way Young and Fresnel did when making interference patterns. The circuit looks as though it was designed to handle phase information.

Now back to Norbert Wiener. Wiener was a mathematician, and he joked about his lack of knowledge of the brain. He knew that one existed somewhere in the head. Nevertheless, in 1947, on the basis of pure cybernetic theory, he theorized that short-term memories are carried in feedback loops and remain active until something turns them off. The hippocampus seems designed for just such activity.[15]

But what could turn the hippocampus off and on? The specific kinds of memories stored in the human hippocampus are highly susceptible to emotions. If you tell a class of students that a certain fact will appear on the final examination, it's as

[15] See Wiener, 1961.

though their limbic systems open the gates to permanent storage. Yet if you become frightened or angered before you can dial a telephone number, you may have to consult the directory again.

I bring up the hippocampus for an additional reason. Karl Pribram suggests that neural holograms exist in microcircuits within neurons. I think an argument could be made for this hypothesis, but not for the hippocampus. The evidence suggests that in the hippocampus, a short-term memory depends on vast numbers of neurons, indeed perhaps an entire feedback loop. Remember, the same feature of phase that allows the code to be very small also permits it to be very large.

Hologramic theory does not predict the biochemical or physiological mechanisms of memory. The absolute size of a whole phase code is arbitrary, however, meaning that it may be very tiny, as in a microcircuit or in oscillations within molecules; or gigantic, as in a firing order within an entire organ such as the hippocampus, or even within the whole nervous system. Indeed the same code may exist simultaneously in many different sizes and on many specific mechanisms, as I pointed out before. To make the memory of a telephone number permanent, what has to transform is not a protein or a voltage but a set of variational relationships — the tensors in our hologramic continuum.

In 1922, Albert Einstein wrote *The Meaning of Relativity.* In it he demonstrated that his special relativity theory $(E = mc^2)$ can be derived from the tensors of the four-dimensional space-time continuum. While the hologramic continuum is not the same as Einstein's theory, we do use Riemann's ideas, as Einstein did. The logic is similar. Einstein demonstrated the same relative principle in both the very small atom and in the universe at large. Hologramic theory, too, tells us that the same elemental rules operate in mind at small or large levels. If we find a memory in, say, the resonance of two chemical bonds within a hormone molecule, we should not abandon science for magic simply because someone else discovers the same code in the entire feedback loop of the hippocampus.

The frontal lobes also function in short-term memory. But whereas the back of the brain seems to synthesize a universe from independent dimensions, the frontal cortex appears to do just the reverse: given a composite sequence of information, the frontal lobes seem to sort out the independent parts.

Much of our knowledge about the frontal lobe comes from the research of Karl Pribram. Let me describe one of his interesting experiments.[16] Humans who have undergone prefrontal lobotomy often cannot solve problems consisting of many parts. Many messages sent from the frontal lobes have an inhibitory effect on other parts of the brain. Pribram began wondering if such inhibitory activities might resemble the parsing of a message. Perhaps lobotomy made it impossible for the person to recognize the dimensions of a complex message. The problem is analogous to what we might see if we randomized the spaces and punctuation marks on this page. Then "hologramic theory" might read "ho log ram icthe ory." Pribram tested his hypothesis on monkeys by using what he called the "alternating test," a modified version of the "shell game," as he describes it.

In the alternating test, the monkey sits in front of two inverted cups, one with a peanut under it. To win that peanut, the monkey must turn up the correct cup. And the correct cup in each trial is the one opposite the winning choice of the last trial. At the end of one trial, a screen descends between the monkey and the cups and remains down anywhere from a few seconds

---

[16] See especially Pribram, 1969.

to several hours. Monkeys find the game very easy, and they readily win the peanut, even after the screen has been down all day. But after frontal lobotomy, the monkey "will fail at this simple task even when the interval between trials is reduced to three seconds."[17]

It occurred to Pribram that "perhaps the task appears to these monkeys much as an unparsed passage does to us." What would happen, Pribram wondered, if he parsed the message for the lobotomized monkey? He realized that he could do this by alternating short and long pauses between trials. The animal would sit in front of the cups, as before, and win a peanut by selecting the cup opposite the correct choice on the previous trial. Again the screen would come down after the trial, but it would now remain down for either 5 or 15 seconds. The net effect of alternating the short and long pauses was to parse an amorphous sequence, as, for example, $LRLRLR$, into an orderly series of sets, such as $(L+R)(L+R)(L+R)$, with the 5-second pauses representing the plus signs and the 15-second pauses representing the parentheses.

How would a lobotomized monkey handle the sequence? In Pribram's words, "immediately the monkeys with frontal cortex damage performed as successfully as the control animals whose brains were intact."

Pribram's findings could have practical implications. It may be possible to develop strategies to assist a damaged brain in carrying out functions it has only apparently lost. Pribram, remember, is the person most responsible for bringing the possibilities of the hologram to the attention of biologists and psychologists. If he had regarded the frontal lobes as *the* seat of biological intelligence, he would never have thought of the alternating test.

Let's now return to the subject of dimension. The frontal

---

[17] See Pribram, 1969, p. 84.

lobes give us an example of differences in analytical capabilities among species, and perhaps even among individuals. Primates parse rather well, compared to other highly intelligent organisms; and the forward growth of the cerebrum, a primate characteristic, would seem to coincide with that parsing ability. But potential pitfalls await us if we oversimplify any particular brain function. Ponder this anecdote that Alexander Luria relates about the English neurologist Sir William Gower. Gower had a patient with a speech aphasia that occurred when the person tried to repeat certain words, "no" being one of them. After several failed attempts to follow Gower's instructions and repeat the word, the patient became exasperated and declared, "No, doctor, I can't say no."[18]

It was as though Gower's patient had more than one mental universe, and one universe was unaware of the other. The psychologist Julian Jaynes has assembled diverse evidence of this general sort in a book I've listed in the bibliography. Jaynes employed this evidence to construct a theory of human consciousness. He then used the theory to reinterpret human evolution and history. The potential implications of his theory are profound. Jaynes believes that human consciousness — in the sense of our active recognition of our thoughts as our own — evolved not when the species first appeared on earth, but when civilization began. According to Jaynes's view, when a prehistoric person reported, for instance, hearing the voice of the gods, he or she probably heard himself or herself without recognizing the actual source. Jaynes's theory maintains that the human mind was "bicameral" — divided into two parts, as, for example, the House and Senate in the U.S. Congress. And civilization didn't actually begin until the bicameral mind broke down and unified.

I don't know whether Jaynes is right or wrong. But the har-

---

[18] Luria, 1970, p. 73.

monious blending of mentalities is similar in many ways to Buster and the animals in the looking-up experiments. It's like the principle of independence on a cosmic scale. And the smooth, continuous blending of one universe with another is something the hologramic continuum does very easily, in theory.

In chapter 8, when we were simulating calculations optically, I demonstrated that identical phase-dependent memories can be produced both a priori and a posteriori. Thus one principle we can deduce directly from hologramic theory is that the ancient argument between rationalists and empiricists — whether ideas are innate or learned — has no meaning in the quest of mind-brain. On the one hand, we can rate but cannot define or reduce memory to learning and experience, as empirical schools of thought do. On the other hand, the question of whether learning, embryonic development, or combinations of both, create memory is something that we can only determine from empirical evidence, and not a priori. And the empirical evidence contains a great many surprises. Let's consider two examples: language and monkey group behavior.

What could seem less innate and more dependent upon experience than grammar? Yet one fundamental tenet of contemporary theoretical linguistics is that all human languages develop from common, universal, a priori rules of syntax. And the theoretical linguist makes a very convincing case.[19] Since many specific languages and cultures emerged and developed in total isolation from each other, those a priori rules of syntax must be present at birth, the reasoning goes. And the argument is hard to dispute.

At the same time, a great deal of evidence has emerged in

---

[19] See Chomsky, 1975; for a nontechnical reference see Bolles, 1972.

recent years to suggest that chimpanzees and gorillas can learn sign language and primitive forms of reading and writing.[20] The issue is still open and highly controversial at the present time,[21] and I won't contribute to the confusion by arguing either side of the case. But it is clear that apes do not spontaneously learn our language. Does this mean that to accept language in apes, we have to deny the foundations of theoretical linguistics? Or, on the other hand, if we believe the linguist, must we dismiss the findings of the Premacks, Gardners, Rumbaughs, and many others? Perhaps. But not from the point of view of hologramic theory. If a gorilla and a man encode and transform the same phase spectra, they hold a similar thought, whether it's the sensation of an itchy back or the statement, "I'm hungry." Yet demonstrating that the gorilla had to learn its syntax would show us nothing about the source of the man's grammar. Furthermore, if we invoke the principles of dimension and local constants, we would not reduce the man's and ape's behaviors to the "same thing," even if we could demonstrate identical phase spectra in both. Although hologramic theory cannot tell us whether or not apes can talk, it can explain the ape's behavior without forcing us to abandon the valuable teachings of the linguist.

What would be the basis for human language if it is inborn? The genes? Possibly. But in terms of constructing a phase code, there is at least one other possibility: imprintation during intrauterine life. If this sounds preposterous, consider the fact that the subsequent behavior of ducklings can be influenced by sounds they hear while still in the egg.[22]

A human fetus receives vibrations set up by its mother's voice and her heartbeats. The rhythm of the heart and the resonance of the human vocal apparatus share things in common

---

[20] Hahn, 1978; Rumbaugh et al., 1973; Gardner and Gardner, 1971; Premack and Premack, 1972; Savage-Rumbaugh et al., 1978.

[21] See Terrace, 1979.

[22] See Hess, 1972; Lorenz, 1966.

independent of culture; and the filtering of such waves by any human body would be similar.

I don't *know* that the latter hypothesis is correct. My hunch as I write is that it is not. Hologramic theory certainly does not supply the answer. But there may be practical as well as theoretical value in knowing whether intrauterine experiences set the stage for language. The resulting poetry alone would justify the study. Imagine what T. S. Eliot might have done with the idea that this most precious of our talents, language, has its genesis not in our embryonic heads but in the hearts of our hosts.

Concerning instincts, nothing seemed less learned to the experts of a generation ago than social behaviors of nonhuman organisms. Herds, covies, packs, bands, prides, schools, and the like generally do have a rigid, stereotypic order, the same today as it was when the particular strain of the species first evolved. But evidence of social ambiance within animal groups has come to the fore especially since the advent of ethology, the study of animals in their natural habitats. Jane van Lawick-Goodall's work on chimpanzees and George Schaller's studies of mountain gorillas are well known. Troops of Japanese monkeys seem to be held together as much by social learning as by physiological imperative.

An ethologist named Gray Eaton described the behavior of a troop of monkeys that had been relocated, in 1965, from southern Japan to a large fenced-in field in Oregon. Their social organization is highly structured, with a dominance order among males as well as females. At the very top is the so-called "alpha" male monkey, which a colleague of mine, Carl Schneider, used to call "the Boss." What makes for the Boss? Is he the monkey with the sharpest fangs, stoutest arms, quickest fists, meanest temperament, most male sex hormones?

In Eaton's troop, the Boss, whom he called Arrowhead, was

a fangless, one-eyed, puny little male who would have had a difficult time in a fight with most females, let alone the other alphas. Eaton even found significantly higher blood testosterone (male sex hormone) levels in subordinate males. Nor was Arrowhead aggressive. He didn't strut around displaying his penis, didn't beat up other monkeys to show everybody else who was in charge. The troop didn't respect Arrowhead's primacy because of a machismo he actually didn't have, but because of a highly complex interplay of social behaviors — and group learning.

Eaton discovered that female dominance plays a crucial role in establishing the male hierarchy among Japanese monkeys. The play of young monkeys often turns into combat. Mother monkeys are very protective. Howls for help from two small disputants usually bring two angry females head-to-head. Of course, the weaker of the two mothers usually runs away along with her infant. The little male monkey learns early which males to run away from. Meanwhile, the monkey with the dominant mother grows up expecting others to yield to his wishes.

Nor does maternalism end as the male monkey matures. Eaton described one mother, Red Witch, as he called her, who helped establish her son as the second-ranking member of the troop even after he was fully grown. Alone, her son was no match for the rank-two monkey. But after Red Witch jumped into her son's fight with the rank-two monkey, Boss Arrowhead soon found himself with a new second in command.

Why didn't Red Witch make her son the Boss? She could have run scrawny little Arrowhead off the field by herself. The study didn't bring out the reasons. Thus there are subtle complexities that even female dominance doesn't explain. Yet challenging Arrowhead seemed like one of those critical taboos that, when violated by a human society, often leads to its utter downfall. The job of the Boss is to lead the troop away from imminent peril. He must know the direction from which a hungry leopard may suddenly appear, and the quickest possible escape routes. And should a threat come, the Boss must direct an orderly, efficient, and hasty retreat: mothers and infants first, he and his strapping lieutenants last, to put up a fight and, if necessary, die to save the troop. Somewhere in the intricate behavior of the group, even Red Witch had *learned* who the Boss of her troop was.

June Goodfield is a historian of science who in a recent essay raised some important questions about scientists and scientific ideas. "Why," she asked, "with very few exceptions, have these themes or these people never stimulated great works of literature or art?"[23] And she went on to observe, "somehow science manages to extract the warmth and beauty from the world."[24]

I wish I could deny Professor Goodfield's words. But I can't. And I used to wonder if hologramic theory would so perfect our understanding of mind-brain as to leave no place for art. Has science finally claimed the last major source of mystery in Nature? Is mind now doomed to become perfected — and boring and dehumanized, too?

I'm really not sure. But I began to phrase the question in terms of what hologramic theory suggests about intelligence. The result was the final two chapters of this book.

---

[23] Goodfield, 1977, p. 581.
[24] Ibid., p. 583.

11

Intelligent Holograms

"CIVILIZATION, like life," wrote Will Durant, "is perpetual struggle with death."[1] The powerful urge to survive against the worst possible odds is the birthmark of intelligence, even in the most primitive form. A chunk of granite is in a far better position to survive than the mightiest among us. Yet when the shadow of a sledge hammer cuts across its surface, the stone is utterly helpless in the face of the impending blow. The stone plays no active role in its own destiny. But even a micro-intelligence can perceive danger while the peril is still in the abstract. Even a lowly mind cares about its fate and can amalgamate its past memories with its present percepts, before the abstract future becomes the perilous reality.

What do we mean by intelligence? I think we could defend the notion that civilization is one manifestation of it. And we might point to poetry and pinochle as other examples. In defining a subject, we draw a line around it and stake out not only what goes into the discourse but what stays out as well. Rendering an explicit definition implies that we already know the particular universe, the coordinate system, that contains the subject. The moment we define our universe, we virtually guarantee in advance the presence or absence of certain fea-

---

[1] Durant, 1954, p. 218.

tures in our subject. Indeed, if you get good enough at the definition business, you can prove or disprove just about anything you please. Definitions can remove so much from the subject that it's really no longer a subject anymore, but just words.

In ordinary mathematics, remember, we define relationships between X and Y (and W and Z) with reference to some prescribed coordinate system. Even when we are not conscious of it, we actually assume the nature of the coordinate system in advance. Our descriptions of X or Y, then, must always fit within boundaries imposed by our definition. Should we want to transfer X and Y (or Z) to some other coordinate system, we must obey the rules we imposed upon ourselves. Thus, by definition, we can't begin on a Cartesian graph and make a transformation to any and all conceivable kinds of universes. Yet with tensors in Riemann's kind of universe, we're able to make any transformations we wish. Why? The answer, very simply, is that with tensors the coordinate system doesn't come in advance. The process reverses the conventional wisdom. With tensors, the definition of the coordinate system *follows* rather than leads the description. We must calculate the universe. It doesn't come to us by divine revelation. To reach for the tensor is to admit that we are creatures too tiny to survey all that is, and too dumb to know in advance where the edge of the universe lies before the journey begins. We need a description of intelligence before we can even ask for a sharp, crisp, unambiguous definition of the word.

There's more to intelligence than dimension. Yet if I correctly judge the reader by my own feelings, there's too much π in the abstract sky for us to move directly from hologramic theory to a description that will ring true to our intuitions. Thus instead of proceeding logically, let's conduct an imaginary experiment.

Let's reach into the distant technological future and invent a new holography. Let's invent a hologram of a play, but one whose reconstructed characters are life-sized, full-color, warm, moving, and endowed with "holophonic" sound. Let's even give our characters breath and body odor. In short, let's invent the wherewithal for an imaginary experience even more eerie than my very real one with the dissected brain that wasn't there.

Now let's enter the theater while the play is in progress, with the mission of finding out whether the actors are at work or whether they've taken the night off and are letting their holograms carry the show. What test can we use? We might try touching them. But wait! If we were at a séance, touching wouldn't be a reliable test, would it? If we pass a hand through a ghost, so what? Ghosts aren't supposed to be material anyway. Just real. Thus, for want of adequate controls, we'd better think up a more imaginative experimental test. Suppose we sent a 515-pound alpha male gorilla up to the stage. What would live actors do? We could never specifically predict. But there would be a change in their behavior.

What about the holographic images? We can accurately predict their responses with a single word: nothing! If the holographer stays on the job, the show will go on as though our gorilla isn't there at all. Indeed, as far as the holographic scene is concerned, the gorilla isn't there at all. He is of the present; they are of the past.

What's the theoretical difference between our live players and their holograms? Both depend upon the same basic abstract principle — relative phase. And holography can be done with tensors. Yet the holographic players cannot let our gorilla into their universe. Our poor live actors don't have any choice.

The informational universe in our physical hologram is like a cake that has already been baked. If we want it continuously round (no cutting) instead of square, if we want the gorilla in the scene, we must make up our minds about that during construction — before the abstract dough congeals in the theoretical oven. The tensor calculations have already been made. The hologram's coordinate system has already been defined; it is what the philosopher would call *determinate*. We cannot add the new dimensions of information our gorilla brings upon the stage.

Our live players? Their informational universe is still being calculated; it is still fluid. Their coordinates are not yet defined, and won't be while they're still alive. Our live actors' minds are continuously *indeterminate*. And it is this feature of intelligence — continuous indeterminacy — that accounts for the addition of new dimensions, as well as for our uncertainty about the outcome of the experiment with live players.

Let me review this argument from a different perspective. Remember that any segment of a curve (and our continuum is curves) is an infinite continuum between any limits. In a determinate system, where the calculations have already occurred, we know which points along a curve connect with independent dimensions. In our indeterminate system, we never know just which points will suddenly sprout new axes or discard old ones. *Indeterminacy is the principle feature of intelligence!*

I'm not talking about vitalism, although, so far, only living minds let today continuously blend with yesterday. Maybe topologists will teach holographers of the future how to deal with infinitely continuous indeterminacy in an n-dimensional universe. One of my colleagues placed a cartoon about holograms in my mailbox not long ago. It depicts a receptionist standing with a visitor next to an open door marked "Holography" and "Dr. Zakheim." Dr. Zakheim is apparently standing in the room, looking out at the visitor. But the receptionist says, "Oh that's not Dr. Zakheim. That's a hologram." Should holographers and topologists team up and give holograms continuous indeterminacy, it won't make any difference whether Dr. Zakheim is actually there or not — except to Dr. Zakheim. For then holograms would be as unpredictable as we are — maybe even more so. Now my hunch on the subject (rather than what we can deduce from theory) is that it will always make a difference whether it's Dr. Zakheim or a holographic reconstruction of him. My hunch is that nobody will figure out just how to handle local constants. But this is pure hunch, not induction or deduction. And many a sophisticated savant said similar things about phase information, too, before Gabor.

Two useful concepts in our quest are ones Brillouin calls *tensor density* and *tensor capacity*. Density and capacity are two independent properties, conceptually. (How much hot air is in the balloon, and how much can it hold?) In a sense, density is the *what* and capacity the *where*. In Brillouin's words, *"the product of a density and a capacity gives a true tensor."* [2] And an incredible thing happens when density and capacity combine to produce a true tensor. The operators of their respective independence eliminate each other. When we have the true tensor, we have the *product* of density and capacity, yet the two independent properties themselves have vanished. Only in Brillouin's calculations can we conceptualize density and capacity as independent entities. The same is true with holographic intelligence: when we have the tensors of intelligence, we don't have independent capacity over here and independent density over there. Yet without capacity and density — what and where — there would be no intelligence at all. Can we conceptualize density and capacity of intelligence apart from each other? Science cannot. Even the philosophers don't give us much help. Nor can we pray or ride a magic carpet to the answer. But the artist can help us.

In *A Portrait of the Artist as a Young Man,* James Joyce gives us a look at the genesis of a genius. Joyce's hero is a mir-

---

[2] Brillouin, 1964, p. 58.

ror of Joyce's own limitless inner world. He does in words what Brillouin achieves with calculations. Joyce reinstates the operators and dissects the tensors of intelligence into capacity free of density. It is capacity that intrigues Joyce. And he sprinkles density like a few stingy grains of talc, just enough to bring out the invisible surfaces of capacity. If you want waxed, red-gray mustaches wet with warm ale, or cod-grease stains on brown derby hats, or the sight of spring heather, or the scent of the pubmaid's unshaven armpits, you'll have to put most of that there yourself. Reading Joyce is like looking at a universe of glass. How can you really see it at all? But there it is, anyway. Artistically, capacity comes to mean dimensions awaiting only densities to fill them up and give life to the intelligence we know.

The creative process itself shows us the meaning of expanding, contracting, and transforming the dimensions of the mind. Physical holograms don't create for the same basic reason they ignore our gorilla. The property that allows for expansions, contractions, and transformations at all, that lets the living mind enjoy an intelligence the physical hologram lacks, is continuous indeterminacy. Hologramic mind *is* a continuum of relative phase spectra. But we have to set the continuum into perpetual, complex, and unpredictable fluid motion in order for it to yield intelligence.

The artist is the transformationist of themes too large, too small, too remote, too abstract, too subjective, too personal for science — but too critical to culture to be ignored. The artist creates the telescope or the microscope and the perspective that enables a human mind to operate within a cosmos where it has no philosophical right to go, but where it goes anyway.

So where does our discussion take us? What does theory show us? First of all, it would be silly even to attempt a strict definition of intelligence. The calculation is always in progress, and we are always ignorant of the coordinate system. But a description is something else. And theory does deliver this.

Hologramic intelligence turns out to have three main features: *dimensions*, which we have dealt with already; *indeterminacy*, which we shall soon come to respect in the laboratory; and *rectification* — corrections of size or shape or complexity to fit the mind to the context and the context to the mind.

12

Smart Eyes

I MENTIONED my former colleague, Carl Schneider, in connection with the Boss monkey. Carl and I collaborated for several years, before I became a believer in hologramic theory. He carried out the behavioral studies, and I did the operations. One of our projects brought out hidden features of intelligence that I have only recently begun to appreciate, in the retrospect of hologramic theory. This chapter is about that research. But first, let's talk about Carl Schneider, who made it happen.

Carl's training was in physiological psychology, and vision was his formal field of research. Part of his laboratory was a forest of multiplex stimulators, stereotactic instruments, oscilloscopes, etc. — the sophisticated contraptions of the contemporary brain scientist. But the other half belonged to behavior, Carl's true and abiding love and his reason for being in science at all.

Carl knew very little about larval salamanders when we first teamed up. That changed fast. Did they prefer light to darkness? he asked on the very first day. He wanted to train them against their natural preferences, if they had any. I confidently misinformed him with the conventional wisdom that the larval salamander avoids light. I recall his looking down, hands clasped behind his back for a long pensive moment, watching a few larvae in the water. Would it be all right if he took some of them back to his lab? he turned and asked.

Carl invented a miniature Y-shaped maze so that he could let the animals have an unbiased choice between light and darkness. In the article he eventually published in *Animal Behavior*, the first definitive investigation of larval-salamander learning, he reported that salamander larvae "approached the illuminated arm in 92 percent . . . of the trials." The source of the conventional misinformation was not light, he found, but heat.

Carl had been profoundly influenced by the ethologists, and like them he spent hours, days, and even weeks just observing animals perform freely, before he designed an experiment. He always shaped the paradigm to the subject, not the other way around. "It's arrogant to do otherwise," he said once. And he could coax the most unexpected behaviors from the most unlikely creatures.

I remember an adult axolotl I'd given him as a birthday present, a greedy, aggressive monster that Carl named Julius. Julius had been a feeding problem in my lab. The tubifex worms we had flown in were actually more expensive than filet mignon, and in a single day the axolotl could consume two weeks' supply for my entire larva colony. I'd tried feeding him guppies, with which I was overrun, but the clever little fish were far too fast for the axolotl. Carl, too, had guppy-population problems, and he asked me if the axolotl could catch guppies. "Too stupid," I said. Carl didn't seem to like that remark; he frowned but said nothing. Several weeks went by, and then one afternoon Carl burst into my lab, took me by the arm, and dragged me back to his quarters. He wanted to show me something but wouldn't say what. I knew it had to be good.

Julius was in a large enamel pan, and I recoiled at the sight of him. He had almost doubled in size, and I was glad the pan was covered securely by a coarse mesh screen. Carl netted a guppy into a beaker of spring water and flicked off the overhead

lights. The room turned an eerie brownish color in the indi-
rect illumination. He turned on a spotlight and aimed it at
one corner of Julius's pan. The axolotl became alert, glided to
the spot, and parked at its edge. Carl poured the guppy through
the mesh, into the spot of light. Bam! It vanished.

"That's not fair!" I protested.

I thought I made out a grin on Carl's face. As he was net-
ting another guppy, he told me that Julius had learned *that*
trick the first day. Carl poured a second guppy into the pan, but
over on the opposite end from Julius. The axolotl's massive external gills seemed to tense ever so slightly, but he remained
parked at the spot of light. Light attracts guppies. What did the
one in the tank with Julius do? It swam to the spot of light,
right into Julius's jaws.

"Maybe," I conceded.

Carl removed the spotlight, flicked on the overheads, and
went for a third guppy. He was definitely grinning, I noticed. In
went a third guppy, again at the end of the pan opposite from
Julius; but this time there was no spotlight. Julius turned, and
he began to chase the little fish. But just as I was about to call
him stupid again, I realized that his behavior wasn't like what
he'd shown me before. He didn't seem to be trying to catch the
guppy, wasn't putting fury into the chase. But he didn't break
off, either, as he had previously done when his lunges gained
him nothing. Now his pursuit was almost casual: a lazy flick of
the gills here, a swush of the giant tail there, just enough to
keep the guppy moving frantically around the pan. The chase
continued for perhaps two minutes, the fish moving at high
speed almost constantly. Then the smoothness began to disappear from its movements; it was clearly becoming fatigued.
And as I became aware of this, Julius began to close in, steadily,
inexorably, boxing the tired little fish into a corner. Suddenly
the water churned as though a volcano was erupting beneath it.
Julius feinted to his left with his bushy gills. The guppy darted

to the right. Julius was already there, along the azimuth of the ill-fated path.

Carl had trained Julius to associate light with the imminent presence of food. But the beast had somehow managed to learn the rest of the hunt by himself. Conventional laboratory tests would not even hint at such capabilities. Carl had allowed Julius's behavior to determine the training. The man respected behavior in the large, which made him a master of it in the small.

Carl often came to my lab around ten in the morning for his coffee break. We'd sometimes spend hours or even the rest of the day talking about anything from chemical transfer of memory, on which we had worked, to Jane Goodall, whom we both revered, to politics, which was on everyone's mind at the time.

One morning, Carl arrived a little earlier than usual. Squatting, propping his coffee cup on his knee, and using the floor drain as an ashtray, he asked, "How hard is it to add an extra eye to a salamander?" He then went into a coughing spasm, but between paroxysms and drags on his cigarette he managed to phrase a very interesting idea.

There is an important principle in sensory physiology known as the psychophysical law. First suggested in the 1830s by Ernst Weber, it was perfected and verified in 1860 by the philosopher-biologist Gustav Fechner. Fechner found that a *change* in the strength of a stimulus accurately predicts the increase or decrease a person reports in the intensity of a sensation. If H is the sensation, k a constant for the particular sense, and S the strength of the stimulus, then H equals k times the logarithm of S ($H = k \log S$). Very close to threshold, or at extremely high intensities, the law may not hold true. But in the range where sensations generally occur, the law works remarkably well. And there is also a body of evidence that suggests —

again within limits — a one-to-one relationship of sensation to perception to learning.

Carl had reservations about the one-to-one principle, as I shall call it here. But to him it had seemed impossible to test the principle, until he began thinking about salamanders. If the one-to-one principle were valid, what would it mean? Would the sense organ impose the principal constraints on learning? If the answer to the last question was yes, then the addition of a functional eye should increase an animal's learning rate.

After much procrastination on my part, about which Carl chides me to this day, we launched the study the following spring. I conducted a fairly extensive pilot series, and concluded that the best approach was to mount the extra eye on top of the animal's head, just above the pineal body, the vestigial third eye. I would cut a window in the top of the skull, and aim the stump of the optic nerve right at the roof of the diencephalon. I called these animals, collectively, Triclops.

Our main controls were animals with an eye transplanted atop the head but with their two natural eyes removed. I tried calling them monoclops, then uniclops; but we eventually decided to use the name *Cyclops*. Cyclops would tell us not only *whether* but also *when* the transplanted eye worked: whether the experiment was worth carrying to conclusion, and, if so, when training should begin.

The one-to-one principle applies to increments of change, not static levels of perception or performance. We had no way of knowing a priori just what those increments would be. But if the sense organs control the rate of change, and if our experiments could demonstrate this, then a normal salamander with two eyes would learn faster than an animal with one eye removed; and the observed difference in the learning rate, if there was one, would define the increment. This increment, when added onto the two-eyed animals' scores, would predict the performance of Triclops, if one-to-one was a valid principle. This was the basic prediction of the study.[1] We called normal animals *Two-Eye*, collectively, and those with an eye removed, *One-Eye*.

Carl had already developed and perfected the training apparatus and testing routines we used. He called the paradigm the "light-shock avoidance test." The light, like the bell in Pavlov's experiments, provided the conditioned stimulus (CS, the behaviorists abbreviate it). The shock the animal had to learn to avoid, 10 volts of direct current, 10 Hz for 10 milliseconds, represented the unconditioned stimulus (US). The rig itself was a marvel of simplicity and ingenuity: two low cylindrical dishes, one larger than the other by a little more than the width of a salamander larva's body, the smaller inverted in the larger thus creating a circular alley. Platinum wires around the two walls served as the electrodes. The animal would not have to be dragged back to a starting point. Carl would merely reposition the light wherever the animal stopped. Yet the circular nature of the alley meant that, geometrically, every starting point was identical to every other starting point. In the training, a salamander had 10 seconds to escape from the light before receiving a shock. Carl performed 25 trials on an animal per session, 2 sessions a day for 4 days. He randomly varied the intervals between trials from 10 to 25 seconds, to make sure the animals did not cue on some tempo instead of associating the light with shock.

Over the years, behaviorists have learned to take great care to eliminate pseudoconditioning, a positive response by an animal when there is no actual association between the two stimuli. One control measure is known as the extinction test. After an animal has apparently made a specific association, its performance will drop, upon withdrawal of the reward or punishment (US), in direct relationship to the number of trials made with

---

[1] Let T be Triclops's score, and X the mean learning rate of two-eyed animals. Then $T = X + \Delta X$, where ΔX is the observed difference between the scores of two-eyed and one-eyed animals.

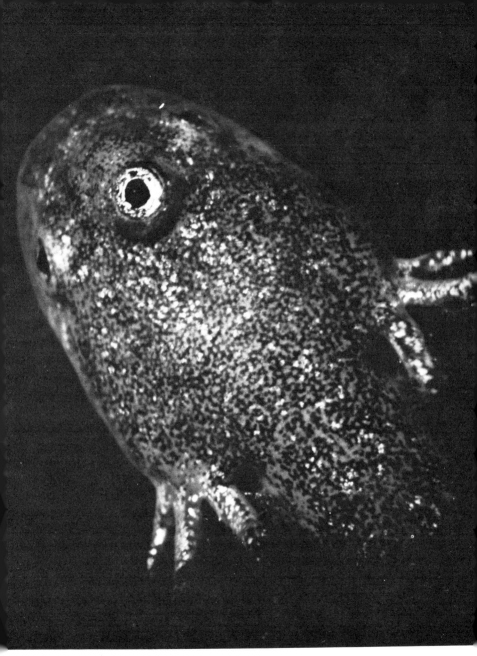

Triclops

only the conditioned stimulus. If the animal associates the conditioned stimulus with an extraneous variable in the paradigm, performance will not drop off simply because of the removal of the US.

Carl applied the extinction test to every subject. He also stimulated animals with light or shock alone, as additional controls against pseudoconditioning. In addition, he insisted on including eyeless animals in the study. "How is an animal without eyes going to see?" I teased him. "Do the eyeless animals control for telepathy?" Although eyeless salamanders never learned the task, I was glad a few years later that Carl had been adamant. Not long after our experiments, excellent evidence came along to show that animals have some nonvisual light perception.[2]

I had personally raised each animal from very early embryonic stages. The salamanders were *Amblystoma punctatum*, and I had taken the entire stock from two large clutches of eggs. I kept accurate records on individuals; later we ran comparisons of data from the two clutches, and eliminated egg clutch as a factor in our findings. I made sure that each animal in the study developed through the same stages at the same time. They were of identical length, and each displaced the same volume of water (this is how I weigh salamander larvae).

Given all the controls Carl had insisted upon, and the numbers necessary to make learning differences statistically significant, he could not train and test the entire colony together. Therefore, I organized the animals into working squads, each squad with at least one representative of each type of animal. All members of a squad went under anesthesia at the same time, and I likewise revived them all together. Squad members lived in individual dishes, but I kept the dishes in the

---

[2] See Menaker, 1972.

same stack. And where one dish went, the others went too. Their spring water came from the same carboy, and even their tubifex worms came from the same culture. I spaced operations for different squads over a period of days, to give Carl the latitude he needed. At the end of the study, we conducted analyses and found no difference attributable to the particular squad the animal was in.

As I pointed out earlier, we let Cyclopses dictate when to begin light-shock training. These animals began using their top-mounted eyes about two weeks after surgery. When one of us dangled a worm above the water, the denizens would ascend hungrily from the depths "like a submarine surfacing to salvage a free bargeload of beer," as a pharmacologist colleague of ours characterized it one day. Once the transplanted eye began to work, Cyclopses preferred sight to all other senses. They seemed compulsive about looking at a worm before making a strike. Often, inspection required acrobatics. If a worm fell below the plane of the salamander's surface-oriented visual field, the animal would duck, twist, and pirouette on its snout in an attempt to aim the eye. It would even poke and thrust at the wriggling red mass, using the eye as a prod and reminding our pharmacologist colleague of "a rhinoceros chasing one of the Three Stooges around a mimosa tree."

Carl's instincts told him to wait an extra couple of weeks before starting the training. So that he could control temperature and keep the animals in darkness, I turned my inner sanctum over to him.

Carl and I always observed an important rule: we never discussed data until they were retrieved, cleaned up, and run through statistics. It wasn't just a matter of introducing bias, which is hard enough to control. The ban also hedged against that potential hell experimentalists usually learn about early on: letting imagination run wild with a false lead. It is agony to retract such speculations. Thus when the big day finally came, I had no hint at all of what the returns would say about the one-to-one principle.

Carl entered my lab, arms loaded with sheaves of data. He spread out the rolls on a long high lab bench, then tried to talk but instead began to giggle. The giggle turned into a laugh and the laugh into a fit. I feared he might collapse against a tall stack of dirty dishes in the soapstone sink behind him. Finally he managed to tell me some of the findings.

One-Eye, the normal animal minus a natural eye, had learned more slowly than Two-Eye, which seemed just fine to me. And Triclops had learned faster than Two-Eye, which sounded marvelous.

"What's so funny?" I asked, puzzled. It's fine to be delighted, but that shouldn't send one into a hebephrenic attack. Carl supported himself against the gray steel fume hood beside my sink. "Heee . . ." Of course I was laughing myself now, although I still didn't know why. "Cyclops . . . (gasp) . . . Cyclops learned faster than all the rest . . . Heeeeeee . . ." Carl got out one last clause just before his eyes closed tight and he became incoherent: the Cyclops data had been statistically significant. And then I broke down too.

Why? Why was this all so hilarious? One-Eye, Two-Eye, and Triclops had behaved according to our expectations. But Cyclops, with the one transplanted eye, should have learned at about the same rate as One-Eye — not far faster than Triclops, as he had done. Our results looked flukey. Mother Nature had played a practical joke on us, it seemed. And she was rubbing it in with statistics — at a very high level of significance, at that.

This was what made Carl, and eventually me, come apart. The Cyclops data simply looked preposterous. And statistics seemed to turn them into absurdity.

I'm not saying that it's funny when ridiculous results become statistically significant. This happens all the time, really. Indeed, it's tragic when statistics prevent a scientist from recognizing absurdity. This too happens frequently. Absurd was how our results appeared, statistics or not.

Statistics furnish a rational test for determining whether or not differences within populations can be predicted simply from random individual variations. They don't *guarantee* the test. Also, statistics let an observer decide, formally rather than intuitively, what the random chances are that two sets of events will occur together, given normal fluctuations among the samples. And statistics let us compare results against, say, the honest roulette wheel: they give us the odds against winning when we bet on an alleged difference or correlation. But statistics aren't the same thing as truth. They're not the same thing as being right or wrong. And the term *significant* only refers to how many times in a hundred, thousand, million, etc., you may obtain the same results at an unrigged dice table. People have been known to roll eight or nine sevens in a row, which is not very likely, statistically.

A statistical test may violate unknown mathematical conditions. Cross the wrong abstract boundary and you may quickly generate absurdity, without knowing it and without being able to control the sources of error. (I've often wondered how many people who swear by statistics have actually looked at the theorems underlying their tests.) Then, too, there's the matter of criteria. Much IQ gospel and parapsychology data, for instance, depend on levels of statistical significance that would be useless in, say, quantum physics or statistical mechanics. At the other extreme, some of the most important discoveries in the history of science are *statistically* insignificant. Few of Pasteur's experiments were replicated sufficiently or sampled properly for statistical analysis. None of Koch's were. Nor were Galileo's or Newton's.

The use of statistics does add a dimension to quantitative analysis that wasn't there before the subject came along. Nobody denies this. But, like any data, statistical results must be considered within the context of all the facts. If statistics tell you that a rat learned a maze after it died, something obviously has gone haywire. And if your results are clearly absurd, you're best off laughing at yourself and going on to the next project, which is what Carl and I thought we were doing.

Carl pitched the data to me. I tossed them up on a dusty shelf above a computer terminal, where they moldered for many months, and where they might still be, but for chance.

That computer terminal, a teletype machine, connected my lab with a communal computer a block away. I'd had the terminal installed to handle data from an assay involving growth of bacteria. The analysis depended on an operation of calculus known as numerical integration. A brilliant young woman from the comp lab had tailored an excellent program to my system, and my work in regeneration depended on it. But the people in the comp lab bought a bigger, fancier computer, to the chagrin of us poor users. The change meant that we had to repeat the tedium of learning new access routines; and then we had to recheck the reliability of our libraries of programs. The changeover cost me two laborious weeks.

One day, while sitting in front of the terminal, after having finally convinced myself that I was in business again, I decided, on impulse, to feed the integration program a little absurdity. Carl's data sheets had just caught my attention. I'd previously discovered a built-in safety feature in the integration program: if you fed in an alleged data curve that really wasn't a curve, the computer would either balk outright or send back utterly preposterous results. In went some of Cyclops's avoidance data. I sat waiting, smiling, wondering if the machine would simply say nix or if it would tell me that Cyclops had learned to avoid light forty-eight years before Carl began the training.

It did neither. Back over the teletype came very realistic values. In went more data. Same thing. And this went on for every animal in the entire study.

I called up a different program that would integrate by an alternate method. Same thing again. Now the method for back-checking integration is called differentiation. It's like checking subtraction with addition in arithmetic, but with calculus. The results survived differentiation. I even rechecked Carl's statistical analyses, and they held up too.

We were in a genuine jam, I realized. It's one thing to set aside data because they tell you a dog has a twenty-foot tail, but quite another to dismiss facts when there's a very good reason to believe them. And the little dancing ball on the teletype machine had just hammered out very excellent reasons for belief. This was mathematics talking now, the mathematics that builds bridges, sends spaceships into orbit, transmits television shows, and runs chemical reactions. It was Peirce's mathematics, forcing necessary conclusions. I didn't say anything to Carl, not right away. I didn't know what to say, actually. This wasn't funny anymore. And I went into seclusion to think.

One thing the calculations did yield, besides a bad headache, was a splendid body of data to work with. Differentiation permits a close estimate of the instantaneous rate of change. At any point along the curve, I could tell just how fast an animal was learning its task. By carrying out a second differentiation, it's also possible to make a close estimate of acceleration. Acceleration in avoidance gave a precise measure of how an animal's previous learning affected its learning in progress — something raw empirical data did not reveal. Integration (the sum of minute changes) enabled me to look at total learning, both as a whole and between any given time periods.[3] But when polished up, the evidence was more baffling than before.

Triclops didn't just learn faster than the normal salamander, Two-Eye. Triclops's IQ was precisely on the mathematical mark, as predicted by the one-to-one principle. Let me convert the values to the scale used for determining IQ, to show you exactly what I mean.

Let Two-Eye's normal IQ be 100. One-Eye's IQ turned out to be 80; in other words, 20 points less than normal. Now, take this 20, the increment of change, and add it back to the normal 100, thereby predicting Triclops's IQ at 120. What did we actually find? The tricloptic animals had a mean IQ of 117, plus or minus enough standard deviation to make the score the same thing as 120! By themselves, these data seemingly made a perfect case for the one-to-one principle. Triclops had clearly obeyed the principle to the letter.

Light-Shock Avoidance in Salamander Larvae			
	AVOIDANCES		IQ
	RATE PER TRIAL	ACCELERATION PER TRIAL	
One-Eye	0.085	0.2364	80
Two-Eye (normal)	0.112	0.3044	100
Triclops	0.126	0.3504	117
Cyclops	0.188	0.5228	173

Data from Schneider, C. W., and P. Pietsch, *Brain Research,* volume 8, pages 271–280, 1968.

---

[3] Incidentally, it was Riemann who devised the method of integrating between specific limits.

But the case doesn't rest with Triclops alone. There's still Cyclops, remember! And what is Cyclops but Triclops minus two natural eyes? The mean cycloptic IQ turned out to be 173. And it wasn't just that Cyclops's IQ was much higher than Triclops's. What was so utterly baffling was this. To predict Triclops's IQ, we should have been able to take the normal 100 and add to it the 173 score generated by Cyclops. Triclops's IQ should have been 273 points, not the measly 117 we actually observed.

I began to put an explanation together over a big bottle of cheap Chianti late one night at the kitchen table, while musing over a picture of a Riemann surface, no less, in a book I'd borrowed from a colleague.

Just consider what 273 visual IQ points might mean. For the sake of simplicity, let's round off the value to 300, which would make it three times the average. Now consider the IQ to be dependent upon only one form of perception, as was the case with Triclops and Cyclops. And let's shift from the visual system to the auditory system. Then ask yourself what it would mean to have your mind's ear made three times more efficient. Suppose, suddenly, the crackle of corn flakes took away your appetite. And what if the cat's meow summoned like the lion's roar? I recall a sad line of graffiti on a wall in an Ann Arbor john: "Every blip a blop/And me a flop!"

No, we wouldn't survive if we woke up one morning with a single mode of perception tuned up anywhere near the level of Triclops's calculated IQ. Nor would the salamander make it, out in the woods with 273 visual IQ points. Not where too fast a response to a glint from the belly of a hungry trout might draw the egg-heavy female away from her partner before she has ensured next season's crop of new salamanders. Maybe even 173 points would be too much to bear in a world where reward and punishment come in the form of life and death. Some amphibians once had a functional third eye atop their heads. They've mostly vanished. Maybe they weren't gifted with Triclops's talent for making perception fit the one-to-one principle. Maybe they had failed Nature's test of intelligence, the price of which is not a mild shock with electricity but the demise of the species.

Triclops wasn't dumber than Cyclops, I concluded. His normal eyes let him do with extra visual perception what the knife had taken away from Cyclops: he could impose minus signs in calculating final behavioral outcome. Cyclops's 173 IQ points represented a more primitive response than Triclops's 117. Higher IQ wasn't smarter. It was just higher. To borrow a metaphor from Hemingway, Cyclops's higher IQ was "fat on the soul."

I tried making a quick interpolation from 273 to 117 to see just what kind of math Triclops's mind would have to mimic to perform as he had. I couldn't get the answer with pencil and paper. Triclops had toned down his response, we eventually wrote, "with integrative precision." His IQ had algebra in it — complex algebra. Poor old Cyclops had only performed arithmetic.

I reasoned that there must be an active-negative component in the salamander's intelligence. What Triclops *didn't do* was as important as what he *did*. But manifested as nonresponse, indistinguishable from no reaction at all, hidden on a completely invisible hyperplane, the active-negative mode would, of course, go undetected in the conventional paradigm, which is what light-shock was. Trying to determine intelligence from IQ is like fighting an opponent who has an invisible arm. You never know when a thunderbolt will come flying out of Kant's realm of noumena and lay you flat on your back. No, I concluded, the conventional paradigm doesn't measure intelligence. It measures IQ.

I also concluded that one-to-one was a valid principle. And the active-negative mode meant that the one-to-one principle, like balancing a checkbook, was not simple arithmetic but rather an algebraic sum. One-to-one is not a governing law of perception and learning. It is a by-product of intelligence. The one-to-one principle is something the mind imposes on the incoming information, not something the incoming information imposes upon the mind. The one-to-one principle is an effect, not a cause.

I translated the main argument into scientese, drafted a manuscript, and gave it to Carl. He made a few minor changes. We shipped it off to *Brain Research*. They published it in 1968. And Carl and I went on to other things.

◇   ◇   ◇

What did Triclops's two normal eyes do for him? The question remained unanswered for several years. The main obstacle was the conventional paradigm itself, which, after Triclops and Cyclops, looked to me like a sure route to misinformation. But a few years ago, I found an eye-dependent response that has reopened the issue. Oddly enough, the discovery was another outcome of making do.

We had a large number of *Amblystoma punctatum* larvae in the lab, and I'd bought polystyrene dixie cups, to have something cheap but inert in which to keep them individually. The cups were a brilliant bride's white. Against this background, normal animals took on a dramatically bright coloration, which they maintained even when the illumination was drastically curtailed. In sharp contrast, eyeless animals assumed dark coloration in the cups when the lights were on but brightened within about an hour with the lights off. Now I had seen some of this over the years, and there is scientific literature that links eyes to coloration. But the dramatic response of the eyeless larvae raised several questions in my mind. And I decided to look further, to find out what was going on.

Was coloration an index of visual perception, but at the

level of automatic (autonomic) physiological responses?[4] Was the animal able to "remember" the coloration of its immediate background? (I use quotation marks because the processing would go on at the same neurological level as, say, blood-pressure changes or peristalsis, and presumably would not involve cognitive behaviors, such as feeding or looking up or learning the light-shock avoidance test.) If the answer to either question was yes, I could use coloration as an independent test for determining whether Cyclops had "normal" visual perception; and also I could use the response to explain Triclops's active-negative behavior.

Changes in coloration depend directly on certain pigment cells beneath the animal's skin. The cells contain the brown pigment, melanin. When the cells contract into dense but tiny puncta, the animal's coloration becomes bright. In the process of darkening, the cells expand, and spread their melanin-laden cytoplasm over a broad area. An ordinary eyeless animal brightens up in the dark in less than two hours. Turn the lights on, and the eyeless larva begins darkening almost immediately. Rate of change depends on the intensity of illumination, is virtually independent of the specific background, and levels off in about ninety minutes. It's as much an action-reaction response as the change of a person's pupils in response to light.

But in animals with at least one natural eye, the response is very complex. Their coloration changes depend on the reflections from the immediate background.[5] I found this out by keeping animals against backgrounds of various colors and absorbancies — clear glass finger bowls, black plastic photographer's pans, polystyrene cups, and a range of differently colored plastic oleo containers my wife brought home from the supermarket.

---

[4] See Miller, 1967.
[5] "Immediate background" depends on the animal's size. In my experiments, the term meant roughly the zone within ten body lengths of the animal.

But that is only part of the story. When I shifted animals from one background to another, I found that for some days they maintained their former colorations, gradually shifting during a week or two to conform to the new reflections. And the changeover time depended on how long the animal had lived in the former environment, with one interesting exception: animals raised in clear finger bowls assumed the new coloration within a few hours. Were they my naive animals? I wondered. Had the other animals showed me evidence of both perception and memory?

I was pretty sure about the perception part already. But the question of memory became very tricky, as I thought about it more and more. Then, while watching Christmas-tree lights blink, the critical experiment flashed into my mind.

If an animal remembers its background for some days, removal of its eyes won't make the creature act like an eyeless animal right away. And I had a colony of *Amblystoma opacum* on hand, the perfect animals to run the experiment. I jumped into the car, raced to the lab, and began the experiments right then and there. My study used animals from clear finger bowls; groups that had been in white plastic cups for varying periods of time, from several hours to many weeks; and a group of eyeless animals. I put all the animals to sleep, removed both eyes from some, one eye from others, and kept some as normal controls. The newly created eyeless animals from the clear dishes began darkening almost immediately, just as the control eyeless animals did. The eyeless salamanders from the white cups? Those that had been in the cups for less than a day acted like typical eyeless animals. The others maintained their bright coloration in direct proportion to the length of time they had been in the white cups — more than a week, in some cases. Coloration did depend on memory.

What about Triclops and Cyclops? First of all, let me mention again that a single natural eye is enough to enable the animal to assume a coloration consistent with its background. (There may be some quantitative rate variations in One-Eye versus Two-Eye, but both reach the same plateau.) Triclops acts like One-Eye or Two-Eye. Cyclops doesn't act like a typical eyeless salamander. But Cyclops becomes noticeably darker in the light, and, like eyeless animals, his changes are approximately the same against any background. Thus if eyeless animals are one step back in the evolution of visual perception, Cyclops is a half-step back.

But what in the name of heck, I wondered, is the nature of the stimulus? How can the animal learn about its background? I applied a little hologramic theory to the problem, and came up with a testable hypothesis.

Imagine a normal animal in a plastic cup. It's receiving light from above, but it's also receiving reflections from the sides. The reflected light and incident light are from the same source. Although these two sets of waves won't make an interference pattern, they do have some consistent phase differences. These phase differences would, I reasoned, inform the animal about the absorptive properties of its environment. An eyeless animal, of course, wouldn't be able to make the necessary discrimination, because it doesn't have vision. What about Cyclops? With his eye aimed straight up, he'd receive too little reflection from the sides of the cup to create the posited phase difference. His visual field wouldn't let him learn about his environment. I developed a very simple test for this hypothesis by creating animals I called, collectively, Cyclops of the Second Kind. I removed both eyes, and, as in a regular Cyclops, I transplanted an eye to top of the head. But instead of directing the eye upward, I tilted it about 45 degrees off the vertical axis. Whereas regular Cyclopses went on behaving a half-step back in visual evolution, Second Kind could assume and maintain the coloration of his background. The hypothesis worked.

Even Cyclops wasn't as dumb as I'd originally concluded. His problem was geometric optics, not lack of intelligence. He just didn't have a correct visual angle on the world. He wasn't stupid, any more than you or I would be if we couldn't hold a page in front of our faces and were given an IQ test based on the page's contents. The evolutionary back-step in progress in his behavior wasn't immutable. Given half a fair chance, Cyclops could learn and remember the coloration he ought to assume.

How does all this relate to human intelligence? If the connection were obvious and straightforward, I wouldn't have to raise the question. But let's take a look at some active-negative events at work in human beings.

Take so-called "functional" amblyopia, the condition in which an eye can go blind because of double vision. The loss of acuity, or even outright blindness, is independent of the eye's physical health. The opthalmologist L. J. Girard and his colleagues convincingly demonstrated in 1962 that certain optical procedures can have dramatic effects on this condition. Let me present some samples from their data tables. One little girl entered treatment with a 20/80 eye; in four weeks the eye was up to 20/20. A forty-seven-year-old man with 20/200 vision — legally blind in some states — had the vision in his amblyopic eye improved to 20/20. A teenager who entered treatment with a 20/400 eye improved it to 20/50. Just as with Triclops, our perceptual processes impose minus signs and cancel information that doesn't work out to a one-to-one result. When the eye sends confusion to the brain, the mind may decide to compute that eye out of action, which seems to be what happened in many of Girard's patients.

Optical illusions show the active-negative component at work at an even more complex level. R. L. Gregory has a delightful treatment of the subject in *Eye and Brain,* as does Martin Gardner in *Mathematical Circus.*

Even with motivation, we find the active-negative mode

among the evidence. Let me illustrate with studies the child psychologist Leon Festinger made on the theory of motivation called cognitive dissonance. The theory of cognitive dissonance explains what often occurs when we must choose between conflicting opinions, or must select among competing objects of our desire. Festinger suggested the following little experiment as an illustration of cognitive dissonance. Buy two similar but not identical presents for your wife, husband, or sweetheart, things he or she will like about equally well. Let him or her examine the two items, rate both, and keep only one. Then take the reject back to the store (or at least hide it in the garage or in the glove compartment of the car). When you get back, ask the person to reevaluate the two items. Festinger predicted that the chosen item's new rating would be even higher than it was during the selection, while that of the reject would go down. Of course, there are going to be exceptions. We're complicated beings (remember our live actors in the gorilla experiment). But extensive research shows that we do, indeed, remold opinions and beliefs, after the fact, to bring them into harmony with the choices reality imposes upon us.

But I'm sure the reader knows that we're not all *that* wishy-washy. Cognitive-dissonance principles take this into account. Consider studies where volunteers were forced to tell lies about their initially held beliefs. When the issue wasn't serious, the subjects would often come to believe their lies — reduce the dissonance by changing their opinions. But when the issue seemed serious, when subjects told lies about what they believed were important matters, they didn't change their opinions. The dissonance remained.

Carl and I certainly didn't discover the active-negative mode. Inhibition is as much a part of brain physiology as is excitation. Repression was a critical element in Sigmund Freud's psychoanalysis. Konrad Lorenz talked about inhibition in aggressive behavior. But Triclops and Cyclops show us, first of all, that the active-negative mode lies at the basis of the one-to-one principle. Second, the one-to-one principle depends on an adequately informed mind. One-to-one, when it operates, is intelligence at work.

Is amblyopia an expression of the one-to-one principle? How do illusions fit into the one-to-one picture? Where's the one-to-one feature in the reduction of dissonance? If the connection were obvious, conventional experts would long since have belabored the subject into extinction.

But let's look at amblyopia. Each eye focuses on an object. Yet there's only one target. If the eyes don't aim to fuse the two images into a single view, the mind will cancel the signals from one eye. Fusion of the two images is an attempt to make targets correspond one-to-one with percepts. The same is true of illusions, except on a much more complex scale. To handle depth, we must synthesize several complex informational dimensions into a composite scene — one whole scene to one whole perception of the scene. And we must add as well as subtract in order to work out the complicated algebra. If not, we'd fall down. We have auditory illusions, too, according to R. M. and R. P. Warren. If somebody snaps bubble gum while you are listening to a lecture, you'll miss a few phonemes in the audible message. Yet your mind is able to cut out the gum snaps and insert the phonemes most likely to be there. If we didn't have auditory illusions, we wouldn't be able to match a whole message with a whole memory and understand what we've heard.

Cognitive dissonance is our way of matching one opinion with one set of apparent realities. Even in conscious reasoning, with mind working at the peak of intellect, the one-to-one principle shows up. Proceeding from standard axioms of logic (there are nonstandard logics), the logician tells us that a valid proposition cannot be both true and false at the same time. If it can, we're in one heck of a philosophical fix. Standard logic is linear: one logical relationship between valid premises has to yield one valid conclusion. And if it weren't this way, if we really did invoke nonstandard forms, reason would falter.

Yet the one-to-one principle doesn't always hold up, not even in carefully controlled psychophysical experiments. At the very lowest limits of detectability, the relationship is nonlinear. Near the point of intolerable agony, there's no simple one-to-one relationship between the change in the stimulus and the change in the way it feels to us. When we are at our upper limits, a little extra "boo!" can come across with the import of the growl of a famished werewolf. Dissonance reduction won't work at extremes either. If we become abstract enough, formal logic will fail us too.

Viewed as an effect rather than a cause, though, what happens at the limits makes sense. For the one-to-one principle is an attempt by the mind to make our reality linear. One-to-one is the mind's attempt to flatten out the world — even though the world is not flat, even though the universe is not linear, even though mind-brain is a curved, nonlinear continuum. One-to-one is error!

To envisage the one-to-one principle, imagine that you're on an invisible but gently curved surface. You don't know you're on it, and below your invisible surface there's a flat but visible map. And you can take your cues only from this flat map. Where your surface curves close to the map, your world and everything about it seems nice and flat and linear — one-to-one! And the one-to-one zone is where you spend most of your time. Thus most of your experiences reinforce what the flat map indicates, namely, the one-to-one principle. But as you move in the direction of the map's boundaries, as you travel out of the zone where your surface approximates the map, your linear rules begin to fail. Then when you try to gauge distances with the T-square or the straight ruler, things begin to seem screwy. At the limits, error really counts. And if you move far enough out, everything goes haywire. For you haven't been on a one-to-one surface after all. You just didn't know it.

What are we living creatures, then? Are we a bunch of stupidos let loose to contaminate this grand, logical universe? Is intelligence some form of transcendental stupidity? Are we an insult to Nature? Maybe. But let's consider this argument before you make up your mind and I make up mine.

The curvature of our Earth is very gentle over the short distances even the largest living creature walks. A charging elephant runs across a perceptually flat surface. If he didn't treat the savannah top as linear, he'd fall on his tusks. And how would we deal with time, if we fused it into a four-dimensional continuum with space? We can't sit down and perform tensor calculus to tell us when to warm the baby's bottle. For us to deal with seconds, minutes, and years, time has to seem constant. *Our* time must seem constant in order for us to live in it. If one tick were not the same as the next, it wouldn't be *our* time anymore. Our time must be immutable. Our space must be Euclidean. Our coordinates must be Cartesian — or linear transformations thereof. Our information must be in the form of linear bits. Our logic must be standard. Our world must be flat and straight. Our reality must be one-to-one, or we could not survive it.

No, I, at least, cannot pronounce the one-to-one principle dumb, in spite of the error. One-to-one is the automatic artist in each of us, the transformationist from our theory, the telescope and microscope that fits us to the world and the world to us. One-to-one is a by-product of a continuous, indeterminate — and living, and delicate — intelligence, striving to exist. In the end, the perpetuation of the species may be the only true measure of intelligence.

From my office early one morning I watched a winter day arrive while trying to fathom what we humans are capable of doing. How would an Einstein or a Riemann clutch the one-to-one principle with his left hand while using the right to untie the imagination and the intellect from their innate constraints? What glory happens in Nature when we consider hologramic mind! And how often, how very often, our kind has done such things during seven thousand short years of civilization! I could feel the answer but couldn't articulate it. Snow covered the trees, the ground, and the rooftops and announced the sun a little ahead of schedule. Soon students would be crossing the white fields. Cars would be rolling tentatively along the slippery streets. Human intelligence would begin another day. I turned and winked at Triclops's picture on the wall. He had fooled us, he had. And he always would. But his eye had enabled us to take a quick peek into noumena. Carl and I hadn't known where we were at the time. Hologramic theory wasn't there to guide us. I sat down at my desk. *Respect* was the word I wanted. Punky and Buster and Triclops, and Carl, had taught me what that word should mean. Without it, there's no hope of using hologramic theory to ask the most human of human questions: Who are we?

I closed my eyes and pictured Carl Schneider at work in the inner sanctum.

The illumination is just enough safe-light to cast red-black shadowy hints of the work area. Salamanders wait unseen in solitary plastic dishes. In rows and columns, the dishes form the tiers of a cell block, with the lonely occupants awaiting training as a convict awaits a tour in the yard — the only break in an otherwise amorphous daily routine. A dot of amber indicator light shows where the punishment switch may be pressed. The oversized air conditioner hums a monotonic baritone background din. Carl's breathing is deep, slow, controlled, regular. The stopwatch is set for ten seconds and cocked at zero.

Starch in Carl's lab coat crackles the signal that he is about to begin a twenty-five-round bout for an inmate of the plastic tiers. Soundless transfer of dish to work area. Isometric wavelets wash the animal aboard a body scoop miniaturized to the scale of things here. The animal enters the training alley on an invisible cascade. Carl pauses while the salamander adjusts.

Suddenly, without warning, like an unexpected slap in the face, on comes the spotlight. A lonely narrow shaft of white moves through our tiny universe, catching, in transit, random eddies of moonlike dust, and ending in a gold-fringed halo around the little salamander's head.

The sweepsecond hand of the stopwatch is already fast at work, sprinting around the track toward the finish line as though driven by a will against all that goes on in places such as this. How can a goddamn dumb salamander really learn anything, anyway? the anatomist wonders to himself.

Carl's steady fingers now partially shade the amber indicator light and poise at the punishment switch. But the salamander swims forward and out of the light only a millifraction of a tick within the allotted ten seconds. He has avoided the light and escaped the shock.

The spotlight goes off. Carl's fingers withdraw into the black of our space. There's a silent, indeterminate pause. Again without warning another trial begins. Again, light. Again micromoons in a minicosmos. Again, halo. Again, torture inflicted on a shaky faith by the relentless race of the stopwatch. But again, escape just before the sweepsecond hand devours the last precious measure of short-rationed time.

It's like this through almost all the remaining trials. Only during the seventeenth round does the stopwatch win. At the end of the bout, the animal safely back in the tier, the steel springs in Carl's armless swivel chair squeal out under the full welter of his suddenly relaxed weight. He laughs a loud high bar of F-sharp, and, with the universal pride of proud coaches everywhere, proclaims, "The little shitasses! They really make you sweat out those last few seconds!" Then it's silent again. And the miracle repeats itself, full cycle.

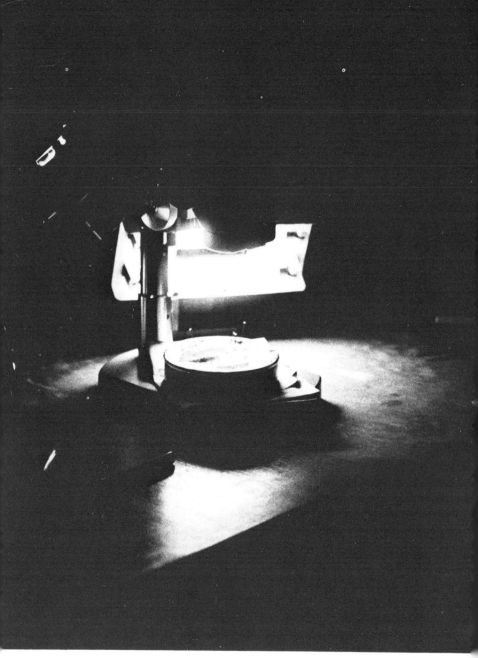

Bibliography

Index

Bibliography

Adler, J., and W.-W. Tso. " 'Decision'-Making in Bacteria: Chemotactic Response of *Escherichia coli* to Conflicting Stimuli." *Science,* vol. 184, pp. 1292–1294, 1974.

Atkinson, R. C., and R. M. Shiffrin. "The Control of Short-term Memory." *Scientific American,* August 1971.

Bartlett, F., and E. R. John. "Equipotentiality Quantified: The Anatomical Distribution of the Engram." *Science,* vol. 181, pp. 764–767, 1973.

Bitterman, M. E. "The Evolution of Intelligence." *Scientific American,* January 1965.

Blakemore, C., and J. F. Cooper. "Development of the Brain Depends on Visual Environment." *Nature,* vol. 228, pp. 477–478, 1970.

Bogen, J. E., and H. W. Gordon. "Musical Tests for Functional Lateralization with Intracarotid Amobarbital." *Nature,* vol. 230, pp. 524–525, 1971.

Bogen, J. E., and P. J. Vogel. "Treatment of Generalized Seizures by Cerebral Commissurotomy." *Surgery Forum,* vol. 14, p. 431, 1963.

Bolles, E. B. "The Innate Grammar of Baby Talk." *Saturday Review,* March 18, 1972.

Brillouin, L. *Tensors in Mechanics and Elasticity.* Translated by R. O. Brennan, S. J. Academic Press, New York, 1964.

Brinley, D. "Excitation and Conduction in Nerve Fibers." In *Medical Physiology,* vol. 1, edited by V. B. Mountcastle. C. V. Mosby, St. Louis, 1974.

Carpenter, M. B. *Human Neuroanatomy.* 6th ed. Williams & Wilkins, Baltimore, 1976.

Chomsky, N. *Reflections on Language.* Pantheon, New York, 1976.

Clarke, E., and K. Dewhurst. *An Illustrated History of Brain Function.* University of California Press, Berkeley, 1972.

Cohen, P. J., and R. Hersh. "Non-Cantorian Set Theory." *Scientific American,* December 1967.

Collier, J., C. B. Burckhardt, and L. H. Lin. *Optical Holography.* Academic Press, New York, 1971.

David, N. J. "Cerebral Syndromes of Ophthalmological Interest." In *Neuro-Ophthalmology,* vol. 1, edited by J. L. Smith. Charles C Thomas, Springfield, Ill., 1964.

Day, L. M., and M. Bentley. "A Note on Learning in *Paramecium.*" *Animal Behavior,* vol. 1, pp. 67–73, 1911.

Detwiler, S. R. "Further Quantitative Studies on Locomotor Capacity of Larval *Amblystoma* Following Surgical Procedures upon the Embryonic Brain." *Journal of Experimental Zoology,* vol. 108, pp. 45–74, 1948.

De Valois, K. K., R. L. De Valois, and W. W. Yund. "Responses of Striate Cortex Cells to Grating and Checkerboard Patterns." *Journal of Physiology,* vol. 291, pp. 483–505, 1979.

Dewey, J. *Human Nature and Conduct.* Holt, New York, 1922.

Durant, W. *The Story of Civilization.* Vol. 1. Simon & Schuster, New York, 1954.

Eaton, G. G. "The Social Order of Japanese Macaques." *Scientific American,* October 1976.

Einstein, A. *The Meaning of Relativity.* Princeton University Press, Princeton, N.J., 1956.

Eisenstein, E. M. "The Use of Invertebrate Systems for Studies on the Bases of Learning and Memory." In *The Neurosciences,* edited by G. C. Quarton, T. H. Melnechuk, and F. O. Schmitt, pp. 653–665. Rockefeller University Press, New York, 1967.

Festinger, L. "Cognitive Dissonance." *Scientific American,* October 1962.

Finlay, D., and T. Caelli. "Frequency, Phase and Colour Coding in Apparent Motion: 2." *Perception,* vol. 8, pp. 595–602, 1979.

Flew, A. *A Dictionary of Philosophy.* Pan Books, London, 1979.

Gabor, D. "Holography, 1948–1971." *Science,* vol. 177, pp. 299–313, 1972.

Galaburda, A. M., M. LeMay, T. L. Kemper, and N. Geschwind. "Right-Left Asymmetries in the Brain." *Science,* vol. 199, pp. 852–856, 1978.

Gardner, B. T., and R. A. Gardner. "Two-Way Communication with an Infant Chimpanzee." In *Behavior of Nonhuman Primates*, vol. 4, edited by A. M. Schrier and F. Stollnitz, pp. 117–184. Academic Press, New York, 1971.

Gardner, M. *Mathematical Circus*. Alfred A. Knopf, New York, 1979.

Gazzaniga, M. S. "The Split Brain in Man." In *Altered States of Awareness*, edited by T. J. Teyler. W. H. Freeman, San Francisco, 1972.

Gelber, B. "Studies of the Behavior of *Paramecium Aurelia*." *Animal Behavior*, supplement 1, vol. 13, pp. 21–29, 1965.

Girard, L. J., et al. "Results of Pleoptic Treatment of Suppression Amblyopia." *American Orthoptics Journal*, vol. 12, pp. 12–31, 1966.

Goodfield, J. "Humanity in Science: A Perspective and a Plea." *Science*, vol. 198, pp. 580–585, 1977.

Gordon, B. "The Superior Colliculus of the Brain." *Scientific American*, December 1972.

Gregory, R. L. *Eye and Brain*. 3rd ed. McGraw-Hill, New York, 1978.

Hahn, E. *Look Who's Talking*. Thomas Y. Crowell, New York, 1978.

Halstead, W. C., et al. "Sparing and Nonsparing of 'Macular' Vision Associated with Occipital Lobectomy in Man." *Archives of Ophthalmology*, vol. 24, pp. 948–966, 1940.

Harrington, D. O. *The Visual Fields*. C. V. Mosby, St. Louis, 1976.

Herrick, C. J. *The Brain of the Tiger Salamander*. University of Chicago Press, Chicago, 1948.

Hershkowitz, M., M. Segal, and D. Samuel. "The Acquisition of Dark Avoidance by Transplantation of the Forebrain of Trained Newts (*Pleurodeles waltl*)." *Brain Research*, vol. 48, pp. 366–369, 1972.

Hess, E. H. " 'Imprinting' in a Natural Laboratory." *Scientific American*, August 1972.

Holmes, K. C., and D. M. Blow. "The Use of X-ray Diffraction in the Study of Protein and Nucleic Acid Structure." In *Methods of Biochemical Analysis*, vol. 13, edited by D. Glick, pp. 113–239. John Wiley and Sons, New York, 1966.

Horridge, G. A. "The Electrophysiological Approach to Learning in Isolated Ganglia." *Animal Behavior*, supplement 1, vol. 13, pp. 163–182, 1965.

Hoyle, G. "Neurophysiological Studies on 'Learning' in Headless Insects." In *12th International Congress of Entomology*, edited by J. E. Treherne and J. W. L. Beament. Academic Press, New York, 1965.

Hoyle, G. "Learning of Leg Position by the Ghost Crab *Ocypode ceratophthalma*." *Behavioral Biology*, vol. 18, pp. 147–163, 1976.

Hubel, D. H. "The Visual Cortex of the Brain." In *Perception: Mechanisms and Models,* edited by R. Held and W. Richards. W. H. Freeman, San Francisco, 1972.

Hubel, D. H., and T. N. Wiesel. "Receptive Fields and Functional Architecture of Monkey Striate Cortex." *Journal of Physiology* (London), vol. 195, pp. 215–243, 1968.

Huygens, C. *Treatise on Light.* Dover Publications, New York, 1962.

The International Dictionary of Applied Mathematics. Van Nostrand, Princeton, N.J., 1967.

James, R. C., and G. James. *Mathematical Dictionary.* 3rd edition. Van Nostrand, Princeton, N.J., 1968.

Jaynes, J. J. *The Origin of Consciousness in the Breakdown of the Bicameral Mind.* Houghton Mifflin, Boston, 1976.

John, E. R. "How the Brain Works." *Psychology Today,* May 1976.

Julesz, B., and K. S. Pennington. "Equidistributional Information Mapping: An Analogy to Holograms and Memory." *Journal of the Optical Society of America,* vol. 55, p. 604, 1965.

Kimura, D. "The Asymmetry of the Human Brain." *Scientific American,* March 1973.

Koshland, D. E. "A Response Regulator Model in a Simple Sensory System." *Science,* vol. 196, pp. 1055–1063, 1977.

Kraut, E. A. *Fundamentals of Mathematical Physics.* McGraw-Hill, New York, 1967.

Kromer, L. F., A. Björklund, and U. Stenevi. "Intracephalic Implants: A Technique for Studying Neuronal Interactions." *Science,* vol. 204, pp. 1117–1119, 1979.

Lashley, K. S. "Nervous Mechanisms in Learning." In *The Foundations of Experimental Psychology,* edited by C. Murchison. Clark University Press, Worcester, Mass., 1929.

Lashley, K. S. *Brain Mechanisms and Intelligence.* Dover Publications, New York, 1963.

Lashley, K. S. "The Problem of Cerebral Organization in Vision." In *Perceptual Processing: Stimulus Equivalence and Pattern Recognition,* edited by P. C. Dodwell, pp. 12–27. Appleton-Century-Crofts, New York, 1971.

Leith, E. N., and J. Upatnieks. "Wavefront Reconstruction with Diffused Illumination and Three-Dimensional Objects." *Journal of the Optical Society of America,* vol. 54, pp. 1295–1301, 1964.

Leith, E. N., and J. Upatnieks. "Photography by Laser." *Scientific American,* June 1965.

Leith, E. N., and J. Upatnieks. "Progress in Holography." *Physics Today,* March 1972.

Leith, E. N., et al. "Holographic Data Storage in Three-Dimensional Media." *Applied Optics,* vol. 5, pp. 1303–1311, 1966.

Lore, R., and K. Flannelly. "Rat Societies." *Scientific American,* May 1977.

Lorenz, K. *On Aggression.* Harcourt Brace Jovanovich, New York, 1966.

Lund, R. D., and S. D. Hauschka. "Transplanted Neural Tissue Develops Connection with Host Rat Brain." *Science,* vol. 193, pp. 582–584, 1976.

Luria, A. R. "The Functional Organization of the Brain." *Scientific American,* March 1970.

Mandelbrot, B. B. *Fractals.* W. H. Freeman, San Francisco, 1977.

Mellor, J. W. *Higher Mathematics.* Dover Publications, New York, 1955.

Menaker, M. "Non-Visual Light Perception." *Scientific American,* March 1972.

Metherell, A. F. "The Relative Importance of Phase and Amplitude in Acoustical Holography." In *Acoustical Holography,* edited by A. F. Metherell, H. M. A. El-Sum, and L. Larmore. Plenum Press, New York, 1969*a*.

Metherell, A. F. "Acoustical Holography." *Scientific American,* October 1969*b*.

Miller, N. E. "Certain Facts of Learning Relevant to the Search for Its Physical Basis." In *The Neurosciences,* edited by G. C. Quarton et al. Rockefeller University Press, New York, 1967.

Moses, R. A. *Adler's Physiology of the Eye.* 6th ed. C. V. Mosby, St. Louis, 1975.

Norman, R. J., J. S. Buchwald, and J. R. Villablanca. "Classical Conditioning with Auditory Discrimination of the Eye Blink in Decerebrate Cats." *Science,* vol. 196, pp. 551–553, 1976.

Olton, D. S. "Spatial Memory." *Scientific American,* June 1977.

Peirce, C. S. *Essays on the Philosophy of Science.* Bobbs-Merrill, New York, 1957.

Penfield, W. *The Excitable Cortex in Conscious Man.* Charles C Thomas, Springfield, Ill., 1958.

Penfield, W. *The Mystery of the Mind.* Princeton University Press, Princeton, N. J., 1975.

Perlow, M. J., et al. "Brain Grafts Reduce Abnormalities Produced by

Destruction of Nigrostriatal Dopamine System." *Science*, vol. 204, pp. 643–647, 1979.

Pettigrew, J. D., and M. Konishi. "Neurons Selective for Orientation and Binocular Disparity in the Visual Wulst of the Barn Owl." *Science*, vol. 193, pp. 675–677, 1976.

Pietsch, P. "Independence of Chondrogenesis from Myogenesis During Limb Regeneration in *Amblystoma* Larvae." *Journal of Experimental Zoology*, vol. 150, pp. 119–128, 1962.

Pietsch, P. "Shuffle Brain." In *Human Connection and the New Media*, edited by B. N. Schwartz. Prentice-Hall, Englewood Cliffs, N.J., 1973.

Pietsch, P., and C. W. Schneider. "Brain Transplantation in Salamanders: An Approach to Memory Transfer." *Brain Research*, vol. 14, pp. 707–715, 1969.

Pollen, D. A., B. W. Andrews, and S. E. Feldon. "Spatial Frequency Selectivity of Periodic Complex Cells in the Visual Cortex of the Cat." *Vision Research*, vol. 18, pp. 665–682, 1979.

Pollen, D. A., J. R. Lee, and J. Taylor. "How Does the Striate Cortex Begin Reconstruction of the Visual World?" *Science*, vol. 173, pp. 74–77, 1971.

Polyak, S. L. *The Vertebrate Visual System*. University of Chicago Press, Chicago, 1968.

Premack, A. J., and D. Premack. "Teaching Language to an Ape." *Scientific American*, October 1972.

Pribram, K. H. "The Neurophysiology of Remembering." *Scientific American*, January 1969.

Pribram, K. H. "The Brain." *Psychology Today*, September 1971a.

Pribram, K. H. *Languages of the Brain*, Prentice-Hall, Englewood Cliffs, N.J., 1971b.

Riemann, G. [Excerpts on surfaces.] In *Source Book in Mathematics*, edited by D. E. Smith, pp. 404–410. McGraw-Hill, New York, 1929a.

Riemann, G. "On the Hypotheses Which Lie at the Foundations of Geometry." Translated by H. S. White. In *Source Book in Mathematics*, edited by D. E. Smith, pp. 411–425. McGraw-Hill, New York, 1929b.

Rose, S. M. "A Hierarchy of Self-Limiting Reactions as the Basis of Cellular Differentiation and Growth Control." *The American Naturalist*, vol. 86, pp. 337–354, 1952.

Rumbaugh, D. M., T. Gill, and E. C. von Glasserfeld. "Reading and

Sentence Completion by a Chimpanzee (Pan)." *Science,* vol. 182, pp. 731–733, 1973.

Russell, B. *The Principles of Mathematics.* W. W. Norton, New York, 1902.

Russell, B. *The Problems of Philosophy.* Oxford University Press, London, 1959.

Saul, R., and R. W. Sperry. "Absence of Commissurotomy Symptoms with Agenesis of the Corpus Callosum." *Neurology,* vol. 18, p. 307, 1968.

Savage, G. E. "Function of the Forebrain in the Memory System of the Fish." In *The Central Nervous System in Fish Behavior,* edited by D. Ingle, pp. 127–138. University of Chicago Press, Chicago, 1969.

Savage-Rumbaugh, E. S., D. M. Rumbaugh, and S. Boyen. "Symbolic Communication Between Two Chimpanzees *(Pan troglodytes)."* *Science,* vol. 201, pp. 641–644, 1978.

Schaller, G. B. *The Mountain Gorilla.* University of Chicago Press, Chicago, 1963.

Schneider, C. W. "Avoidance Learning and the Response Tendencies of the Larval Salamander *Amblystoma punctatum* to Photic Stimulation." *Animal Behavior,* vol. 16, pp. 492–495, 1968.

Schneider, C. W., and P. Pietsch. "The Effects of Addition and Subtraction of Eyes on Learning in Salamander Larvae *(Amblystoma punctatum)."* *Brain Research,* vol. 8, pp. 271–280, 1968.

Shinbrot, M. "Fixed-Point Theorems." *Scientific American,* January 1966.

Smith, H. M. *Principles of Holography.* Wiley-Interscience, New York, 1969.

Sperry, R. W. "Restoration of Vision After Crossing of Optic Nerves and After Contralateral Transposition of the Eye." *Journal of Neurophysiology,* vol. 8, pp. 15–28, 1945.

Sperry, R. W. "Split-Brain Approach to Learning." In *The Neurosciences,* edited by G. C. Quarton et al. Rockefeller University Press, New York, 1967.

Sperry, R. W. "Lateral Specialization in the Surgically Separated Hemispheres." In *The Neurosciences Third Study Program,* edited by F. O. Schmitt and F. G. Worden, pp. 5–20. MIT Press, Cambridge, 1974.

Terrace, H. W. "How Nim Chimpsky Changed My Mind." *Psychology Today,* November 1979, pp. 65–76.

Torpin, R. "Fetal Amputations, Constrictions and Clubfoot Associated with First Trimester of the Amnion." *Anatomical Record,* vol. 157, p. 404, 1967.

van Heerden, P. H. "Theory of Optical Information Storage in Solids." *Applied Optics,* vol. 2, pp. 393–400, 1963.

van Lawick-Goodall, J. *In the Shadow of Man.* Houghton Mifflin, Boston, 1971.

Warren, R. M., and R. P. Warren. "Auditory Illusions and Confusions." *Scientific American,* December 1970.

Westlake, P. R. "The Possibilities of Neural Holographic Processes Within the Brain." *Kybernetik,* vol. 7, pp. 129–153, 1970.

Wiener, N. *Cybernetics.* John Wiley and Sons, New York, 1961.

Wolff, P. H. "Motor Development and Holotelencephaly." In *Brain in Early Development,* edited by R. J. Robinson. Academic Press, New York, 1969.

Young, T. *Miscellaneous Works.* Vol. 1, edited by G. Peacock, pp. 131–215. Johnson Reprint Corp., New York, 1972.

Index

Abstractions, 65. *See also* Code
Additive primaries, 73. *See also* Color
Adler, J., 192, 193
Alexia, 23
All-or-none law, 79
Alternating test, 212–13
Amblyopia, functional, 29, 247, 249
Amblystoma opacum, 116
American Sign Language, 76
Amobarbital test, 27, 28
Amplitude: in diffuse hologram, 62; and Fourier transform, 143; in optical holograms, 47; in photographs, 47; of sine and cosine waves, 134, 135; in wave theory, 44, 45, 139
Analogue, defined, 49
Analogy, 65
Anatomy: brain in, 16–17; language and, 23; scope of, 13–14; of vision, 18. *See also* Brain
Aphasia: Broca's motor-speech, 22; Wernicke's, 22–23
Arago, François, 53
Arcuate bundle, 23
Associating, in hologramic theory, 158
Axolotl, 114, 228. *See also* Salamanders

Bacteria: data-processing system of, 192–95; memory in, 192–95
Behavior: of embryo, 111–13; and human mind, 197; learned vs. instinctive, 118
Bentley, M., 195, 197
Bitterman, M. E., 200, 202, 203
Black light, 73
Blanking, in brainless salamander, 92
Blow, D. M., 145
Bogen, Joseph, 25, 27, 28
Braille, 76
Brain: anatomical view of, 16–17; arcuate bundle in, 23; coronal section of, 24; and diffuse hologram, 63; early research in, 15; evolution of, 201; hippocampus, 32–33, 206–8, 210–11; physiology of, 79. *See also* Split-brain research, 26
Brain damage, and hologramic theory, 81
Brain-transplant experiments, 90; cerebral hemispheres in, 93; diencephalon in, 93; guppy-to-salamander, 110; histology of, 98–102; learning response in, 117; and looking-up response, 121; medulla in, 94; rejection in, 96–102; results of, 91–102, 104.

Meaning: vs. organization, 81; verbal, 49

Mellor, J. W., 127, 128

Memory: activated, 152; in bacteria, 193, 194; in brain transplant experiments, 110–11, 120–23; and coloration, 245–47; defined, 151; equipotential distribution of, 38; in hippocampus, 209; hologramic, 59–60, 64; and mind-brain conundrum, 12; molecular property of, 30; optical theory of, 60; in perceptual space, 159; phase codes, 159; research on, 30; in Riemannian context, 178; short-term, 209, 210, 212; short-term vs. longterm, 31–32; in shufflebrain experiments, 91–98; in singlecelled animals, 195; and splitbrain research, 27; survival of, 2; usages of, 11

Mental activity: abstraction, 65; analogy, 65–66; color manipulations in, 74; of embryo, 111–13; encoded in sound, 67; innate vs. learned, 215; language in, 76; theory, 65

Mercator projection, 144, 148

Mesencephalia, 202

Metaphor, and wave, 49

Metherell, Alexander, 3n, 47, 75, 76, 153

Meyers, Ronald, 25

Midbrain tectum, 34

Milstein, Victor, 26

Mind: and behavior, 197; vs. computer, 187; evidence of, 198; in Fourier theorem, 164; geometry of, 125; hologramic, 64, 184, 186, 189; intelligence of, 225; as phase information, 163; "piece of," 183; and split-brain research, 27

Mind-brain conundrum: and classes of memory, 31; and hologramic theory, 40; and role of hippocampus, 33; source of, 190; Wilder Penfield on, 35–36

Molecular biology, structuralism in, 14

Montagu, Ashley, 14

Morse code, 76

Multiplication, and convolution, 147

Music memory: and lateralization, 29; in split-brain research, 27

Naperian logarithms, 169n

Nervous system, phase spectrum in, 152

"Neural noise," 69

Neural signals, and frequency modulation, 78

Neuroanatomy, 15

Neurons, and Fourier transforms, 153

Neuroscience, 15

Newton, Isaac, 166–68

Objective waves, 61 (fig.)

Occipital-lobe damage, and macular sparing, 21

Oganesoff, Igor, 119, 120

One-to-one principle, 230–31, 240, 243, 249, 250, 251

Opacum, 116

Optic chiasm, 18

Optic tracts, 19

Organization, vs. meaning, 81

Organs, regeneration of, 3. *See also* Salamanders

Paramecium, memory in, 195

Particles, 50

Pavlov, I., 195, 232

Peacock, George, 53